SOCIAL POLICY REVIEW 29

Analysis and debate in social policy, 2017

Edited by John Hudson, Catherine Needham and Elke Heins

First published in Great Britain in 2017 by

Policy Press
University of Bristol
1-9 Old Park Hill
Bristol BS2 8BB
UK
t: +44 (0)117 954 5940
e: pp-info@bristol.ac.uk
www.policypress.co.uk

North American office:
Policy Press
c/o The University of Chicago Press
1427 East 60th Street
Chicago, IL 60637, USA
t: +1 773 702 7700
f: +1 773-702-9756
e:sales@press.uchicago.edu
www.press.uchicago.edu

© Policy Press/Social Policy Association 2017

British Library Cataloguing in Publication Data
A catalogue record for this book is available from the British Library.

Library of Congress Cataloging-in-Publication Data
A catalog record for this book has been requested.

ISBN 978-1-4473-3621-1 hardback
ISBN 978-1-4473-3731-7 paperback SPA members' edition (not on general release)
ISBN 978-1-4473-3622-8 ePdf

The right of John Hudson, Catherine Needham and Elke Heins to be identified as
editors of this work has been asserted by them in accordance with the Copyright,
Designs and Patents Act 1988.

Cover design by Policy Press
Front cover: photograph kindly supplied by istock
Printed and bound in Great Britain by CPI Group (UK)
Ltd, Croydon, CR0 4YY
Policy Press uses environmentally responsible print partners

Contents

List of tables and figures

Tables

Figures

Notes on contributors

Sigrid Betzelt is Professor for Sociology of Work and Organisations at the Berlin School for Economics and Law in the Institute for International Institutional Economics and the Harriet-Taylor-Mill Institute for Economics and Gender Research (since April 2009). Her work focuses on labour markets and social policy and their impact on social inequality. She was involved in two large European research networks (FESSUD – Financialisation, Economy, Society and Sustainable Development, 2011-16, EU-FP7; and RECWOWE – Reconciling Work and Welfare in Europe, 2006-11, EU-FP6).

Ingo Bode is Professor for Social Policy, Organisation and Society at the University of Kassel in the Institute for Social Work and Social Welfare (since April 2009). Working as a German sociologist on institutional and organisational dynamics of welfare sectors and systems, he has been involved in various international and national research activities, also in combination with longer academic stays or appointments abroad (in Canada, the UK, France and Mexico).

Natalie Booth is an Early Career Academic Fellow at De Montfort University, Leicester. Her recent doctoral research, conducted at the University of Bath, critically explored maternal imprisonment in England and Wales. She is interested in penal policy and processes in women's prisons, and specifically how these are experienced from a family-centred perspective.

Philip Brown is Professor of Social Change and Director of the Sustainable Housing and Urban Studies Unit (SHUSU) at the University of Salford. Philip has a long-standing interest and involvement in the area of Gypsy, Roma and Traveller research, including undertaking studies funded by the Equality and Human Rights Commission, Joseph Rowntree Charitable Trust, various local authorities and the EU Fundamental Rights and Citizenship Programme. He recently received funding from the Joseph Rowntree Charitable Trust and the Metropolitan Migration Foundation to undertake a project called Supporting Roma Voice (2015-2017).

Rebecca Ehata is a research associate at the Institute of Social Policy, University of Oxford. She gained her PhD in Politics from the University of Manchester. After a decade spent working with refugees and migrants in Northwest England, her research interests focus on the politics of migration and belonging, and the intersection between domestic policy discourses and state bordering practices.

Nick Ellison is Professor of Social Policy and Head of the Department of Social Policy and Social Work at the University of York. Nick's research interests include UK welfare politics, comparative social policy and citizenship in theory and practice.

Kayleigh Garthwaite is a Post-Doctoral Research Associate at Newcastle University. Kayleigh explores issues of health inequalities, welfare reform and austerity through ethnographic research. She is author of *Hunger Pains: Life inside foodbank Britain* (Policy Press, 2016) and co-author of *Poverty and insecurity: Life in 'low-pay, no-pay' Britain* (Policy Press, 2012), winner of the 2013 British Academy Peter Townsend Award.

Lee Gregory is Lecturer in Social Policy at the University of Birmingham. Lee's research interests lie in the connections between community, poverty and welfare ideology, specifically the role of welfare provision in perpetuating and challenging current levels of poverty and the search for alternative approaches. He has written extensively on the subjects of poverty, inequality and welfare, including *Trading time: Can exchange lead to social change?* (Policy Press, 2015).

Elke Heins is Lecturer in Social Policy at the School of Social and Political Science, University of Edinburgh. Her research interests mainly focus on comparative and European social policy as well as the politics of welfare in Britain. Recently she has co-edited (with C. de la Porte) the book *The sovereign debt crisis, the EU and welfare state reform* (Palgrave Macmillan, 2016).

Chris Holden is Reader in International Social Policy at the University of York, UK. He has published widely on the relationships between the global economy, transnational corporations and health and social policy. He has been a member of the Editorial Board of the *Journal of Social Policy* and of the International Advisory Board of the journal *Global*

Social Policy. He co-edited *The global social policy reader* (Policy Press, 2009) and *Social policy review* (Policy Press, 2009-2011).

Daniel Horsfall is Lecturer in Comparative Social Policy at the University of York. He has two main research interests: the political economy of welfare states; and issues around patient mobility and health service exports. Dan recently co-edited the *Handbook on Medical Tourism and Patient Mobility* (Edward Elgar, 2015) and is often invited to speak on the issue of medical tourism at industry, clinical and academic events.

John Hudson is Professor of Social Policy at the University of York. His research and teaching are focused primarily on comparative analyses of social policy and on the politics of social policy. Recent projects include analyses of: inequalities of child well-being in rich countries; the historical evolution of public attitudes to 'welfare' in the UK; and of the linkages between societal values and welfare regimes in the OECD.

Philip Martin is a Research Assistant at the Sustainable Housing and Urban Studies Unit (SHUSU) at the University of Salford. His principal research interests lie in Gypsy, Roma and Traveller communities and migrants, the structural inequalities experienced by such communities and the implications for ideas of citizenship, participation and identity. He also conducts qualitative research with a range of individuals and groups on topics including energy efficiency, business start-ups, homelessness, and welfare support.

Catherine Needham is Professor of Public Policy and Management at the Health Services Management Centre, University of Birmingham. She has written extensively on themes related to personalisation and co-production in public services, including an edited collection entitled *Debates in personalisation* with Professor Jon Glasby (Policy Press, 2014).

Ricardo Pagan is a Professor at the Department of Economía Aplicada (Hacienda Pública) at the University of Malaga. Ricardo specialises in microeconomics, health economics and labour economics. Recent publications have focused on disability and how this interacts with both work and life satisfaction. Ricardo is Chair of the Tourism, Health and Wellbeing Centre at the University of Malaga.

Lisa Scullion is Reader in Social Policy and Associate Director of the Sustainable Housing and Urban Studies Unit (SHUSU) at the

University of Salford, UK. She currently leads the University of Salford's involvement in a five year ESRC funded project Welfare Conditionality: Sanctions, Support and Behaviour Change and a linked two-year project funded by the Forces in Mind Trust (FiMT) focusing on the impact of welfare conditionality on Armed Forces Service leavers. She sits on the Editorial Board for the journal *Social Policy & Society* and is also a member of the Greater Manchester Poverty Action Group and the Salford Sanctions and Conditionality Task Force.

Martin Seeleib-Kaiser is Professor of Comparative and Applied Public Policy at the Institute of Political Science, Eberhard Karls Universität Tübingen (Germany). His research currently focuses on the social rights of EU migrant citizens. He has published widely in English and German, among others in: *American Sociological Review, Comparative Political Studies, Journal of Common Market Studies, Journal of European Social Policy, Politics and Society, Politische Vierteljahresschrift, Social Policy and Administration, Social Politics, West European Politics* and *Zeitschrift für Soziologie*.

Isabel Shutes is an Assistant Professor in the Department of Social Policy at the London School of Economics and Political Science. Her research interests focus on citizenship, migration and social policy, and the mixed economy of care, work and welfare.

Katherine E. Smith is a Reader in the Global Public Health Unit at the University of Edinburgh, where she analyses efforts to influence and change policies impacting on public health (especially health inequalities). This includes studying processes of advocacy, lobbying and knowledge translation. She is currently Co-Director of SKAPE (the Centre for Science, Knowledge and Policy at Edinburgh) and Series Co-Editor of Palgrave Studies in Science, Knowledge and Policy.

Emma Wincup is Senior Lecturer in Criminology and Criminal Justice and Director of Student Support in the School of Law at the University of Leeds. Her research focuses primarily on drug use and its control, particularly on drug treatment, the interconnections between welfare and drug policy, and the impact of drug policy on women. She is also interested in the interconnections between crime and social policy and the policy-making process.

Part One
Developments in social policy

John Hudson

The twelve months since the publication of the previous volume of *Social Policy Review* have been politically momentous, presenting great challenges for us as editors of review. At the time that the previous volume was going to press it appeared that many of the big political questions had been settled – domestically at least – following the victory of David Cameron's Conservative Party at the 2015 general election. From a social policy perspective, a lengthy further period of public sector austerity was anticipated and, indeed, this was firmly signalled in George Osborne's eighth budget as Chancellor in March 2016, when an additional £3.5 billion of spending cuts by 2020 were announced, despite relatively positive projections for the economy (BBC News, 2016a).

Not many would have anticipated that, a few months later, neither Cameron or Osborne would be members of the government. However, the narrow victory for the 'leave' campaign in the June 2016 EU referendum turned much of UK political life on its head. As well as leading to a change in prime minster, with as yet largely unknown consequences for the Conservative Party's social policy agenda, the 'Brexit' vote has also resulted in deep debate about the UK's social and economic divisions. At the 2016 Social Policy Association (SPA) annual conference, which took place shortly after the referendum, an emergency plenary session was called to debate the issue; the then SPA Chair, Nick Ellison, convened this session and, in Chapter One, he explores the 'whys and wherefores of Brexit', examining not just the political roots of the referendum result but also its complex social and economic roots.

Upon becoming the UK's prime minister in July 2016, Theresa May acknowledged that economic and social policy was working inadequately for many in the UK, vowing to do more for the JAMs (the 'just about managing') and to govern as a 'One Nation' leader rather than for the 'privileged few' (BBC News, 2016b). In part this seemed to be an acknowledgement that some of the changes to the labour market and the tax and benefit system facilitated by the Cameron governments needed to be reassessed, though at the time of writing there were few concrete signs of what policy changes might be forthcoming. The agenda here is huge, including changing working patterns arising from greater use of zero-hours contracts, rising self-employment and the impact of disruptive technologies. Social security policy, including the ongoing roll-out of Universal Credit and seemingly fluctuating approaches to conditionality, is also fundamentally important here. In Chapter Two, Lee Gregory explores these issues, focusing in particular on the rise of the so-called 'gig economy'.

While the economic implications of Brexit remain the focus of ongoing debate, claim and counter-claim, it seems likely that the already lengthy period of public sector austerity will now extend some way into the future in the UK. In Chapter Three, Emma Wincup looks at how this extended period of fiscal readjustment has changed the landscape of the prisons system, with new providers, new governance mechanisms and promises of radical reform. But, as she makes clear, no policy sphere operates in isolation, and reforms and cutbacks to important provision in other areas of social policy, particularly housing and social security, have affected the progress of criminal justice reform agendas.

The finger of blame for the UK's current economic woes has been pointed in many directions and the Brexit debate brought many of these arguments to the fore. It goes without saying that this debate was often tense and raw, with some groups being demonised and scapegoated, and the legitimacy of many political actors and institutions called into question. The strongly populist tone of some of the debate was mirrored in other countries in 2016, most notably in the United States, where Donald Trump's presidential campaign echoed many of the themes around migration, the economy and elites found in parts of the Brexit campaign. Indeed, connections between the two campaigns appeared to become increasingly direct in the latter half of the year, with Nigel Farage joining Trump and his team on more than one occasion. In Chapter Four, Chris Holden reflects on the connections between Trump and Brexit, and particularly the role (and nature) of globalisation and related economic changes, asking how a socially progressive form of globalisation might respond to the challenges laid down by these two seismic political victories.

References

BBC News (2016a) 'Budget 2016 summary: key points at-a-glance', 16 March. www.bbc.co.uk/news/uk-politics-35819797

BBC News (2016b) 'Theresa May vows to be "one nation" prime minister', 13 July. www.bbc.co.uk/news/uk-politics-36788782

ONE

The whys and wherefores of Brexit

Nick Ellison

In the myriad arguments and counter-arguments about the virtues, or otherwise, of Brexit, it is hard to discern what role, if any, was played by social policy in the referendum result. Following an account of the key factors that contributed to the decision to call a referendum, this chapter examines the pattern of voting across the UK before moving on to consider how the particular configuration of the referendum vote relates to wider issues that concern the conduct of economic and social policy in the UK. The analysis suggests that although voters were largely influenced by a narrow range of core issues – notably the impact of rising net migration, anxieties about sovereignty and fears about the trajectory of the UK economy – these concerns may in turn have been provoked by two factors. First, labour markets became increasingly 'flexible' and less secure as a result of globalisation, and, second, this insecurity was compounded by the significant tilt towards 'austerity' in the period after 2010. This latter factor, in particular, had an immediate negative impact on the living standards of the most deprived groups in the UK and on the public services upon which they depend.

Although it is not possible, in any simple manner, to equate the effects of globalisation and the rise of austerity, on the one hand, with, on the other, a decision to leave the European Union (EU), one general observation can be made. Many of those who voted to leave expressed a sense of being 'left behind' – 'left out' might be a better phrase – by economic growth and the political elites that design and implement key economic and social policies (Wright and Case, 2016). This understandable sense of marginalisation led large numbers of people to protest against their treatment by voting to leave an institution that, however unfairly, had in their view come to embody a toxic combination of democratic deficit and elite 'remote control'. The irony here is that this revolt against a hostile economic environment and policies that appeared to be intentionally designed to reduce living standards in the interests of preserving that environment, may well result in the further deterioration of those standards as the UK struggles with the economic and social implications of Brexit.

Towards the referendum

Some of the key structural factors that contributed to the referendum result will be considered below, but before examining these, it is important to appreciate the 'contingency' of the decision to hold an in/out referendum in the first place – something that concerns the fluctuating fortunes of 'Europe' in UK high politics. The decision itself had much – though not everything – to do with the increasing dissatisfaction with the EU that developed in the Conservative Party in the period immediately following the political demise of Mrs Thatcher in 1990. The party had been largely united behind the original desire to join the European Economic Community (EEC) in 1973 – a unity that extended into the 1975 referendum called by the Labour Prime Minister Harold Wilson. However, ambitions for greater political and monetary union, championed in the later 1980s by the President of the European Commission Jacques Delors, were not universally welcomed, and certainly not by Thatcher, who was more than content to see the EEC as, at most, a single economic market. Thatcher's abrupt removal from office, following a Cabinet coup partly provoked by arguments about Europe, provided the growing number of 'Eurosceptic' MPs with a formidable figurehead during the 1990s – a decade that saw a marked hardening of pro- and anti-European positions in Conservative ranks. This internal argument, which included a dramatic leadership election designed to resolve the issue while the party was actually in office, was principally about UK sovereignty. Although Thatcher's successor, John Major, had succeeded in keeping the UK out of key elements of the European Union Treaty signed at Maastricht in 1992 – notably the 'Social Chapter' and the single currency, in addition to the preservation of member state vetoes in foreign and home affairs – Eurosceptics were hostile to what they saw as persistent threats to parliamentary authority, not only in the form of direct treaty legislation but also from the twin sources of regulatory 'interference' and the cumulative effects of 'soft law' (Majone, 1994).

Whether or not these fears of the loss of sovereignty were justified (see Hay and Wincott, 2012), the Eurosceptics' refusal to accept the Maastricht logic of ever-closer union and the state of near-civil war to which the Tory party was consequently reduced, were key factors in the Tory defeat at the hands of New Labour at the 1997 general election.

As Bale's (2010) account of the Tories' opposition years makes clear, the party continued in a state of unrest about Europe through three periods of weak leadership before the election of David Cameron as party leader in the autumn of 2005. At the time, there was some reason to believe that the unexpected victory of a Tory moderniser committed to party renewal and the capturing of the centre ground of UK politics from New Labour might heal the rifts of the 1990s and produce a version of One Nation Conservatism fit for the 21st century (Evans, 2008). However, at least four factors confounded such hopes.

First, Euroscepticism did not evaporate with Cameron's election to the leadership, and indeed the Eurosceptic wing of the party became increasingly hard to control as time went on. Ironically, Cameron himself contributed to continuing Eurosceptic influence during the leadership election campaign by promising to pull the Conservatives out of the centre-right, but federalist, European People's Party (EPP) grouping in the EU Parliament. Although the promise was made largely to neutralise the short-term threat posed by Cameron's right-wing competitors, Liam Fox and David Davis, both of whom had made a similar promise, Cameron nevertheless 'set himself on the path of tactical retreat' from this moment (Shipman, 2016: 14). Other 'moments' abounded as time went on. As Prime Minister of the Coalition government, Cameron faced no less than 22 backbench rebellions on Europe within 17 months. Significant among these ongoing indications of dissent was the October 2011 Commons motion for an EU referendum, proposed by David Nuttall, that attracted the support of no less than 81 Conservative MPs (Shipman, 2016: 7). This vote was particularly significant because it came only three months after the passing of the European Union Act, which introduced a 'referendum lock', designed to ensure that any future EU treaties would have to be endorsed by the British people (Wellings and Vines, 2016). Seemingly, even this clear signal of the UK's intention to preserve parliamentary sovereignty did not go far enough for convinced sceptics.

Second, during the early 2000s, Euroscepticism – indeed outright anti-Europeanism – emerged as an issue capable of galvanising support outside the confines of the Tory party. The establishment of the United Kingdom Independence Party (UKIP) in 1993 was not regarded as any great threat at the time, but UKIP's increasing success in European parliamentary elections – rising from fourth to first place in successive campaigns between 1997 and 2014 – acted as an electoral warning to a Conservative Party that had failed to win an outright majority in 2010 and, judging from pre-election polling, was not necessarily expecting to do better in May 2015. This pattern of success in European elections was complemented by significant improvements in the UKIP vote at local council elections in 2013 and 2015. Emboldened by this mounting evidence of anti-Europeanism in the country, so ably supported by a vociferous right-wing press, Conservative Eurosceptics adopted a progressively harder line on Europe in the face of leadership dithering over how best to position the party in relation to UKIP.

'Immigration' constitutes a third factor that militated against Cameron's initial One Nation strategy – and one that also contributed to UKIP's success as a political force. According to figures from the Oxford Migration Observatory (2016), net migration was 333,000 in 2015 (i.e. 333,000 more people entered the UK than left it). Net migration stood at 177,000 in 2012 – 156,000 lower than 2015. EU citizens counted for 43% of the total 2015 inflow (630,000), with roughly 22% coming from the A8 Accession states that covered much of Eastern Europe. Despite the fact that the majority of people who come to the UK intend to study or work and stay less than four years (Oxford Migration Observatory, 2016) – and that the apparent rise in net migration was a result of falling emigration – the headline figures need to be set in the context of a Coalition government commitment to reduce net migration to the 'tens of thousands'. The failure to keep this promise contributed to growing fears about the impact of migration – fears that were fully exploited by much of the press, UKIP and the Conservative right.

Finally, mention needs to be made of the Eurozone crisis. The very fact of the financial difficulties that swept through EU countries in the wake of the 2007/08 banking crisis meant that Europe remained a significant presence in Coalition politics, irrespective of the desires of Cameron, Clegg, Osborne and others to focus on other, equally pressing, matters. At issue was the EU's attempt to deal with the sovereign debt crises in southern European member states, notably Greece. Despite efforts to enlist Angela Merkel's support for the UK's position against a formal fiscal compact, the prime minister, having absented the Tories from the EPP grouping, and therefore not having been party to informal EPP discussions (and with the European Union Act anyway demanding a referendum on any future EU treaty), found himself effectively isolated (Smith, 2015). Although Cameron's ensuing 'veto' of the proposed compact was greeted with jubilation by Eurosceptics, the UK was left visibly isolated while 25 of its European neighbours signed a new Treaty on Stability, Coordination and Governance in the Economic and Monetary Union in March 2012.

Taken together, these factors created considerable and mounting pressure, within and outside Parliament, on Cameron and his allies to accede to demands for an in/out referendum on the UK's EU membership. On this matter, the Conservatives' coalition partners, the Liberal Democrats, were of little help. Although an avowedly pro-EU party, the Liberal Democrats accepted the European Union Act without significant opposition and, in so doing, endorsed not only the referendum lock but, in effect, the principle that major decisions about EU matters should be put to the British people. Of course, Cameron pronounced himself agnostic about whether or not the UK remained in Europe – much depending, in his view, on the concessions that needed to be won from the EU as the price of the UK's continuing membership. In the event, the EU conceded remarkably little ground during the 'negotiations' with Cameron in the early winter of 2015/16. In particular, there was no compromise on the key matter of freedom of movement, with the result that the prime minister was unable to guarantee the significant reductions in EU migration that many in his own party and the wider electorate were demanding (Shipman, 2016).

The referendum: public opinion

The 'high politics' involved in Cameron's eventual commitment to an in/out referendum are important because the precedents set and the fractious tone of the parliamentary debates capture, in microcosm, the main issues and sentiments that also came to dominate UK public opinion in the decade or so leading up to the vote. Ipsos MORI polling data, used by the Oxford Migration Observatory, show how public attitudes to what became the key issues during the referendum campaign – the economy and immigration – have changed over time. Although the NHS was consistently regarded by the public as the most important issue in the 1990s and early 2000s, immigration grew in salience, particularly after 2000. By the time of the financial crisis this issue was vying with the economy as that which was of most concern to the public. In the immediate run-up to the referendum, survey data indicate that immigration and the economy continued to be the issues most likely to influence voting behaviour, with the former edging ahead in the later stages of the campaign. According to Ipsos MORI polls carried out in May and June 2016 – ones that predicted the final referendum outcome with great accuracy – immigration rose by 5% over this four-week period, becoming the clear majority concern in the final weeks (Ipsos MORI, 2016). These figures are supported by other research. For example, a British Election Study Internet Panel sampled just before the beginning of the formal referendum campaign found that those intending to vote Leave cited 'immigration', followed by 'sovereignty' and 'control', as the most important issues for them, while those intending to vote Remain cited the 'economy' and 'rights'. A word cloud constructed by Prosser et al (2016), which represented the views of undecided voters – 33% of the electorate at the beginning of the campaign – indicated that 'immigration' and the 'economy' outstripped sovereignty issues for this important group.

Voting patterns in the referendum

If these key concerns were the two most significant pre-referendum issues for voters, how did people actually cast their votes in the referendum itself? The basic facts are well known: on a clear one-question, 'in–out' voting model, with no provision made for a reinforced majority or other measures designed to mitigate the social, economic and constitutional aftershocks of a small majority verdict, the impact of the overall result was a narrow victory for the Leave campaign, with 52.1% of the vote. However, voting patterns displayed a range of significant divisions, which suggested that perceptions of Europe fractured, if not apparently around gender, then certainly according to geography, age, class, income, education and ethnicity. These divisions were most marked in England and Wales, whereas in Scotland (62% to 38%) and Northern Ireland (55.8% to 44.2%), which voted by substantial majorities for Remain (albeit for different reasons), they were rather less evident.

Taking the UK as a whole, Goodwin and Heath (2016), in their research for the Joseph Rowntree Foundation, found that households with incomes of less than £20,000 per year (58%) favoured Brexit, as did people in the 66+ age group (59%). Routine manual workers were much more likely to favour Leave than their professional counterparts and, in like manner, those with no educational qualifications also voted Leave in large numbers (75%), while more highly qualified individuals preferred Remain.

The figures in Table 1.1 provide a snapshot of the overall pattern of the vote – however they mask a geographical dimension that is particularly significant in the *English* context. There is a clear spatial element in the relationship between voting intention and income, for example. According to ONS (2015a) figures, the median incomes of people living in London vary between £575 and £890 per week, depending on the particular borough. Conversely, many English district councils,

Table 1.1: Vote Leave demographics

Category	% Vote Leave
Household income > £60,000	35
Household income < £20,000	58
Routine manual employment	71
Higher professional employment	41
Not in paid work	59
Working full time	45
Postgraduate degree	27
No qualifications	75
Age 66+	59
Age 18–25	28
Women	50
Men	52
BAME	36
White British	52

Source: Adapted from Goodwin and Heath (2016).

especially those that cover coastal areas (Lincolnshire district councils were among the very few areas where over 50% of the *electorate* voted Leave) see median weekly earnings of between £280 and £400. Age distribution follows a similar pattern. Many coastal districts – specifically those in Lincolnshire, East Anglia and along much of the south coast – have higher proportions of people aged 66 and above (BBC, 2010). Where education is concerned, Kirk and Dunford, writing in the *Daily Telegraph* (2016), commented that 'only three of 35 areas where more than half of residents had a degree voted to leave the EU – South Bucks, West Devon, and Malvern Hills in the West Midlands'. As Kirk and Dunford (2016) have demonstrated, those areas where the population lacks a university education correspond closely to areas that contain higher proportions of older people – and also lower median incomes. It is likely, of course, that these spatial divisions produced 'area effects', meaning that different localities became 'more like themselves'. Taking educational qualifications as an example, Heath and Goodwin show that the overall skills composition of local communities influenced voting behaviour. Despite the generally positive relationship between people with higher qualifications and the desire to remain, those with such qualifications were less likely to vote against Brexit if they lived in low-skill communities. Goodwin and Heath (2016: 2) estimate that, 'in low-skilled communities the difference in support for Leave between graduates and those with GCSEs was 20 points. In high-skilled communities it was over 40 points'.

Voting patterns in relation to immigration – specifically in England – are interesting. On the face of it, and acknowledging the salience of this issue for Leave (and initially undecided) voters, it appears that the areas that favoured Brexit were not necessarily those with particularly high levels of inward migration, whether from the EU or elsewhere (see Figure 1.1). Indeed, as Figure 1.2 demonstrates, the areas with the highest levels of migration were virtually all in London (with the exception of Oxford), which unequivocally voted Remain. To be sure, voting in localities that had experienced high net migration did not consistently reflect the London pattern. However, there does appear to be a relationship between the desire to leave the EU and the rapidity of the increase in net migration, where this was from an initially low base (Goodwin and Heath, 2016). Leeds, for example, which voted Remain, experienced an 80% increase in its non-UK population between 2001 and 2011, but this increase built upon firmly established migrant communities. Conversely, Hull, which voted Leave by a substantial margin, experienced a 195% rise in migration over the same period. While overall numbers of migrants, at approximately 30,000 (Buck, 2016), were proportionately much lower, these new arrivals did not join an existing community.

Figure 1.1: Local authority areas with highest Leave vote/% non-UK-born populations

Area	Leave vote (%)	% non-UK-born
Boston	75.6	15.2
South Holland	73.6	9.5
Castle Point	72.7	3.6
Thurrock UA*	72.3	11.9
Great Yarmouth	71.5	6.6
Fenland	71.4	8.6
Mansfield	70.9	5.6
Bolsover	70.8	2.9
East Lindsey	70.7	3.6
North east Lincolnshire UA	96.9	4.3

*unitary authority

Source: Compiled from *Financial Times* (2016).

Figure 1.2: Local authority areas with lowest Leave vote/% non-UK-born populations

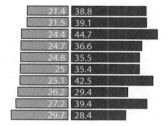

Lambeth	21.4	38.8
Hackney	21.5	39.1
Haringey	24.4	44.7
City of London	24.7	36.6
Islington	24.8	35.5
Wandsworth	25	35.4
Camden	25.1	42.5
Cambridge	26.2	29.4
Southwark	27.2	39.4
Oxford	29.7	28.4

Source: Compiled from *Financial Times* (2016).

It is not surprising that areas containing large numbers of people who had themselves migrated to the UK and become UK citizens, or whose families had migrated in the past, voted to remain. A total of 64% of black, Asian and minority ethnic (BAME) voters were remainers and this fact, combined with others such as the relative affluence and youth of Londoners and other urban populations, and the wider acceptance of cultural diversity that these attributes can bring to urban life, goes some way towards explaining the greater levels of toleration towards, and acceptance of, migrant populations. As to the areas with high Leave votes but smaller populations of non-UK residents, the speed of increase in numbers of migrants is likely to be accompanied by the proportionately greater impact of rising net migration on both public services such as schools, GP surgeries and hospitals, and established cultural norms and assumptions. Taking Lincolnshire as an example, there was a marked rise in the non-UK population in many districts immediately following the entrance of the A8 Accession countries in 2004 (see Table 1.2). Although net migration fluctuates thereafter, it nevertheless increases consistently over the period. A full analysis of the impact of rising net migration on public service provision would require a much more thorough exploration than can be provided here, but it is perhaps indicative that Lincolnshire reported a deficit of 75 GPs in 2016. This lack of medical cover may have added to local concerns about pressure on services from inward migration (see Table 1.3) (Pidluznyj, 2016). It is ironic in this regard that a Lincolnshire International Recruitment Pilot was designed specifically to attract GPs from EU countries – a fact that says something about the complex and contradictory character of so many of the issues that lay at the heart of the referendum.

Table 1.2: Inward/outward migration of non-UK population in Lincolnshire district councils

Lincolnshire: international migration 2004–15				
Year	In	Out	Net +/-	% annual gain/loss
2004–05	3,089	2,056	+1,033	
2005–06	6,898	2,804	+4,094	+296
2006–07	6,497	2,856	+3,641	-11
2007–08	6,221	2,610	+3,611	-0.82
2008–09	6,020	1,915	+4,105	13.6
2009–10	5,435	1,740	+3,695	-9.9
2010–11	3,901	2,149	+1,752	-52.5
2011–12	3,760	2,349	+1,411	-19.4
2012–13	4,342	1,697	+2,645	+94.5
2013–14	4,732	1,567	+3,165	+19.6
2014–15	5,161	1,751	+3,410	+7.7

Source: ONS (2015b), figures compiled by author.

Table 1.3: Lincolnshire GP registrations, 2004/05–2014/15

Year	New migrant GP registrations per year
2004–05	4,498
2005–06	5,442
2006–07	5,776
2007–08	6,192
2013–14	5,916
2014–15	6,160

Source: ONS (2016a), figures compiled by author.

The referendum vote: Scotland and Northern Ireland

A brief word about voting in other parts of the UK is important because of the clear differences between voting behaviour in England and Wales, on the one hand, and Scotland and Northern Ireland, on the other. Taking Scotland first, it is not too surprising that the decision was unanimously for Remain – although it is worth remembering that, although no Scottish constituency voted Leave, the margins of Remain victories varied considerably. Edinburgh recorded a 74.4% vote in favour, while Moray saw 49.9% of voters opting to leave the EU. The key reasons for rejecting Brexit no doubt concern the distrust of Westminster governments that, if anything, had increased in the wake of the 2014 referendum on Scottish independence. Just as importantly, however, Scotland has become quite used to multi-level governance over time with the result that the Scottish people do not appear to regard issues of sovereignty and control in the same way as many of their English counterparts. Indeed, continued membership of the EU is perceived as a counterweight to control from Westminster – albeit in the context of Scottish administrations continuing to demand more self-government.

As to other features of the Scottish vote, Curtice (2016) has shown that, although the key associations of age and education with Leave in England were also apparent in Scotland, the percentage differences between leavers and remainers in each category were lower. For Curtice then, 'while the social divisions exposed by the referendum were clearly in evidence north of the border, voters of all ages and of all educational backgrounds in Scotland were more likely than their counterparts elsewhere in Great Britain to want to stay in the EU'. On the key issue of immigration, an Oxford Migration Observatory study (2014) found that immigration was viewed somewhat more favourably in Scotland than in England, with fewer people – 58% – believing that immigration should be decreased either 'a lot' or 'a little', compared to the English figure of 75%. Significantly, immigration lagged well behind the economy as a key issue in Scotland, with EU membership being regarded as a positive benefit. Curtice (2016) notes, for example, that as many as 41% of people in Scotland felt that the 'general economic situation in the UK' would be worse if Scotland left the EU, compared with 34% in England and Wales. Finally, income levels do not appear to have played such a significant role in the Scottish vote. Low-income areas such as Dumfries and Galloway (<£344 pw) had a majority Remain vote of 53.1%, and Angus (<£338 pw) 55.3%. No area in England with similar income levels opted for Remain.

Voting in Northern Ireland differed in certain respects to patterns in both Scotland and England. Although the Remain majority at 55.8% of the vote looks substantial, it masks significant variations across the region. Mills and Colvin (2016) note that turnout patterns, as well as attitudes to Brexit, differed between the Catholic and Protestant communities – the former having lower overall turnout. They make the point, however, that Protestant communities also preferred Remain, albeit by rather narrower margins. Remain was also strongly associated with younger age groups, though not with the strength of educational qualifications, partly at least because graduates in Northern Ireland are both fewer and more thinly spread across urban and rural areas. A clear difference with the English vote, in particular, was the fact that rural areas in Northern Ireland strongly favoured Remain. According to interviews conducted by *The Guardian* (Fishwick, 2016) in the immediate aftermath of the referendum, this preference for the EU was less to do with the availability of agricultural subsidies than with the general perception that EU membership brought significant economic benefits overall – and this despite the undoubted importance of agriculture and the wider agri-food sector to the region's economy. European funding has helped to transform Northern Ireland's economy in recent years – and, of course, two related factors are of particular significance. First, the region shares the UK's only land border with the EU, thus making Northern Ireland an attractive proposition for inward investment; second, and of crucial importance, the 1998 Good Friday Agreement contained specific provision for a North/South Ministerial Council 'to develop consultation, co-operation and action within the island of Ireland including through implementation on an *all-island and cross-border basis* – on matters of mutual interest within the competence of the Administrations, North and South' (Northern Ireland Office, 1998: Strand Two, paragraph 1, emphasis added).

Why Brexit?

While the reasons why the referendum was called are clear enough, there is no doubt that the verdict itself came as a surprise to many people, politicians, commentators and ordinary voters alike. In some ways, the level of surprise is understandable. Although polling over the past twenty-five years or so indicates, at best, a rather lukewarm attachment to the EU, Ipsos MORI polling showed consistent support for Remain between the 2015 General election and May 2016 (Mortimore, 2016). There is also evidence to suggest that key figures in the Leave campaign were themselves unprepared for the result (see Moore, 2016). However, a different standpoint would argue that the referendum outcome is not quite so surprising once a number of important factors associated with medium-term economic and shorter-term social policy developments are taken into account. Taken together, these factors, while not necessarily *determining* the result, surely contributed to the effective 'alienation' of those English voters who most visibly turned against the EU – the worst off, those in routine manual occupations, the less well educated and those in older age cohorts. It is people in these groups who felt most exposed to what they perceive as uncontrollable economic and social pressures.

Taylor-Gooby's (2013) concept of 'double crisis' aptly describes how the post-war welfare state has declined in the face of two major forces. First, long-term structural changes associated with globalisation and technological change have altered labour markets, employment prospects and working conditions. Second, short-term phenomena associated with the impacts of particular social and economic policies, have damaged the prospects and life chances of those groups least able to defend their living standards. 'Globalisation', of course, can be defined in a range of different ways, but of the most importance here are its economic effects. Prime among these has been the trend towards ever-greater labour market flexibility, with the associated ills of downward pressure on wages and conditions. Although some groups – the better educated and the better 'connected' – have benefited significantly from an economic environment that has allowed them to maximise their social, cultural and economic capital on a global stage, many others have been abandoned in distinctly 'local' environments characterised by low wages, heightened insecurity, job losses resulting from labour-substituting technologies, and reduced welfare support. The financial crisis did not itself cause this state of affairs, but most certainly exacerbated it, ensuring, as recession deepened, that wage levels for those in poorly paid routine work either declined or remained static. Moreover, the crisis was the sole reason for the ensuing obsession with deficit reduction in the UK – and therefore for the short-term economic and social policies that compounded the already deleterious effects of globalisation.

The combination of these long-term labour market trends and shorter-term policy decisions has had two particular consequences. First, aided by government-led privatisation strategies and direct legislation that reduced the power of organised labour, increasing labour market flexibility has contributed to rising income inequalities in the UK and other liberal democracies over the past 35 years. Figure 1.3, taken from ONS's February 2016 Statistical Bulletin (ONS, 2016b), charts the ratio of total equivalised disposable income between the richest and poorest fifths of the population, clearly demonstrating the dramatic rise in income inequality in the 1980s, which has never subsequently been redressed. Second, the deep recession caused by the financial crisis and the austerity regime subsequently imposed by the UK Coalition government, while it did not lead to markedly high unemployment, nevertheless resulted in an extended period of no- or low-wage growth, compounded by severe cuts in public spending as the preferred strategy for deficit reduction. Hills and Stewart (2016: 247–48), estimate that mean wages fell by 5.6% between 2006–08 and 2013, with an accelerated decline after 2010. Although overall poverty rates remained relatively stable between 2006 and 2013, largely as a result of continuing welfare support, as Hills and Stewart point out, specific groups fared more or less well. For example, those in social housing experienced higher unemployment and greater falls in earnings than other groups (Hills and Stewart, 2016: 286), while people in their twenties, particularly men, experienced very high rates of unemployment in addition to more rapidly falling wages as the effects of the emerging 'gig economy' began to take hold. Pensioners, on the other hand, protected by the 'triple lock', saw their incomes rise over the period of the Coalition government. In general terms, the combination of the shift of the index-linking of benefits from the Retail Price Index to the less generous Consumer Prices Index, the abandonment of commitments to reduce child poverty, the imposition of a welfare cap, significant changes in housing benefit and a considerably tougher conditionality regime did much to reduce support for those in the poorest income groups, while static or falling wages eroded living standards for those in employment.

Figure 1.3: S80/20 ratio, UK 1977–2014/15

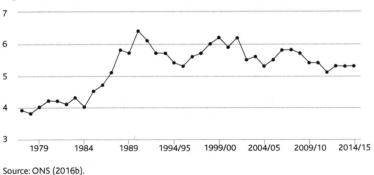

Source: ONS (2016b).

To this picture, it is important to add the onslaught on public services in the period after 2010/11. Figure 1.4 provides a snapshot of the changes made to departmental budgets between 2010/11 and 2015/16, the key point for present purposes being the size of reductions to the Department for Communities and Local Government (DCLG) and the Department for Work and Pensions (DWP). Where the DCLG is concerned, this department is largely responsible for the grants to local authorities that fund key public services such as social care, Sure Start and Children's Centres, and personal social services. The fact that many cuts fell disproportionately on the poorest local authorities (Hastings et al, 2012, 2015) meant that further damage was visited upon communities already experiencing the sharp end of unemployment, wage reductions and reductions in welfare spending. Elsewhere, budget cuts at the Ministry of Justice saw spending on public order and safety, and legal aid, reduced, while education, where spending reductions were less drastic, nevertheless saw funding for early years education reduced by 11%, and reductions in spending on sixth form and further education colleges (Ellison, 2016).

Figure 1.4: Real change in departmental budgets, 2010/11–2015/16

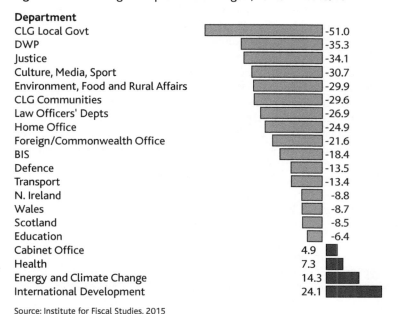

Department

Department	Value
CLG Local Govt	-51.0
DWP	-35.3
Justice	-34.1
Culture, Media, Sport	-30.7
Environment, Food and Rural Affairs	-29.9
CLG Communities	-29.6
Law Officers' Depts	-26.9
Home Office	-24.9
Foreign/Commonwealth Office	-21.6
BIS	-18.4
Defence	-13.5
Transport	-13.4
N. Ireland	-8.8
Wales	-8.7
Scotland	-8.5
Education	-6.4
Cabinet Office	4.9
Health	7.3
Energy and Climate Change	14.3
International Development	24.1

Source: Institute for Fiscal Studies, 2015

Some observations

It is important to be clear about the general 'dynamics' of Brexit. An extremely blunt instrument was chosen to resolve difficulties largely stemming from the slings and arrows of Tory high politics, exacerbated, to be sure, by increasingly negative perceptions of 'immigration' and fears about a putative loss of sovereignty. Although fears about the economic consequences of leaving the EU were also forcefully expressed, it appears that those most concerned about this issue were largely 'globalisation winners' and/or voters living in Scotland, Northern Ireland or Gibraltar, who, as discussed, had compelling reasons to vote remain. Once the referendum process was set in train, 'Europe' became a focal point of largely English protest on the part of those who felt that they had 'lost control'. Of course, a deceptively simple yes/no question that in reality contained a veritable cauldron of complex economic, political, social and cultural issues – further spiced by two dishonest and incompetent campaigns – provided the perfect fulcrum around which various forms of protest and disaffection could coalesce.

It is the abiding sense of a *loss of control*, bringing with it a deepened experience of marginalisation and abandonment, which is ultimately the most significant aspect of Brexit. This feature is brought out by panel data from the British Election Study (2016), which analyses voting in terms of 'locus of control'. Respondents who were classed as having an 'external' locus of control, because they believed that they had little influence over the course of events and 'the things that happen to me', were 'much more likely to vote Leave' than those with an 'internal locus' of control, who considered themselves 'largely responsible for the things that happen to them'. It is hardly surprising if the direct experience of labour market changes, with which successive governments willingly colluded, exacerbated feelings of alienation on the part of those who were most exposed to the effects of globalisation. That these same people also experienced the full weight of the Coalition government's assault on the welfare state makes the desire for protest – perhaps better characterised as a cry for help – understandable.

Where apparent paradoxes exist – notably the majority of young people in favour of Remain, despite their experience of higher unemployment, falling earnings and lack of access to housing markets, and the majority of older people in favour of Leave, despite rising pensions – perceptions of control offer an explanation. In the case of many in the 18–25 age cohort, continuing membership of the EU was understood as a means of *retaining* control. Why? Because the EU, with its large labour market, free movement and apparent variety of employment opportunities appeared to offer something 'better' around which life chances could be organised. Other, less tangible, factors associated with many young people's self-perception as 'European', point to a sense of cultural familiarity and belonging that also enhance feelings of identity and control. Conversely, the anti-European sentiments of older people can be readily explained by feelings of a loss of control – or *fears* of a loss of control – over their local communities and, more generally perhaps, fears about the changing demographic structure of the UK and their place in a more culturally diverse society.

Finally, looking ahead, the potential irony of the referendum result is that the very people who most favoured Leave are likely to be those who suffer most from the effects of the UK's withdrawal from Europe. As analyses by Dhingra et al (2016) and the Institute for Fiscal Studies (2016) suggest, Brexit is likely to exert downward pressure on incomes over the next five years largely as a result of higher inflation and the potential impact of declining trade with the EU. Accuracy is by no means assured, but Dhingra et al (2016: 3) calculate that the UK could experience a permanent change in average per capita income with a fall between 1.28% and 2.61%, or between £850 and £1700 per household, depending on a variety of assumptions including, inter alia, reductions in trade, potential tariff barriers and the extent of countervailing fiscal savings. More pessimistic assumptions about the UK's future trade with the EU would see these predicted reductions deepen further.

In retrospect, for a variety of reasons, many of which have been touched upon here, it seems that 'Europe' became a proxy for a range of dissatisfactions, some understandable, some less so. Undoubtedly the EU was a difficult institution to defend, although the Better in Europe campaign hardly defended it well. Indeed, as the 2000s progressed, Europe became increasingly associated with what Mark Lilla (2016: 225) has referred to more widely as 'an unreflective faith in the cost-free benefits of free trade, deregulation, and foreign investment', with 'next to nothing to say about collectivities and their enterprises, and the duties that come with them'. Even so, the attention paid to human rights and social justice, equal opportunities, working conditions and other important facets of a social democratic *Weltanschauung* – even if too frequently at a symbolic level – was 'not nothing'. With its economic fortunes very much in the balance and life outside the single market a 'known unknown', and with cultural, social and political connections to the EU either closed off, or much reduced, the UK is in a perilous position and those who voted to leave may yet come to regret their great moment of protest.

References

Bale, T. (2010) *The Conservative Party from Thatcher to Cameron*, Cambridge: Polity.

BBC (2010) 'Ageing Britain', BBC News website, 1 October, www.bbc.co.uk/blogs/thereporters/markeaston/2010/10/ageing_britain.html

BBC (2016) 'Five facts from Scottish EU referendum vote', BBC News website, 24 June, www.bbc.co.uk/news/uk-scotland-scotland-politics-36614284

British Election Study (2016) 'Brexit Britain: British Election Study insights from the post-EU referendum wave of the BES internet panel', 6 October, www.britishelectionstudy.com/bes-resources/brexit-britain-british-election-study-insights-from-the-post-eu-referendum-wave-of-the-bes-internet-panel/#.WHuzr2SLRlN

Buck, T. (2016) 'Immigration resonates on the streets for Brexit campaign', *Financial Times*, 8 June, www.ft.com/content/e7bfc9b4-2bcb-11e6-bf8d-26294ad519fc

Curtice, J. (2016) 'Why did Scotland vote to remain?', 24 October, http://ukandeu.ac.uk/why-did-scotland-vote-to-remain/

Dhingra, S., Ottaviano, G., Sampson, T. and Van Reenen, J. (2016) 'The consequences of Brexit for UK trade and living standards', PaperBrexit02, Centre for Economic Performance, London School of Economics and Political Science, http://cep.lse.ac.uk/pubs/download/brexit02.pdf

Ellison, N. (2016) 'The Coalition government, public spending and social policy', in H. Bochel and M. Powell (eds) *The Coalition government and social policy: Restructuring the welfare state*, Bristol: Policy Press, pp 27–51.

Evans, S. (2008) 'Consigning its past to history? David Cameron and the Conservative Party', *Parliamentary Affairs*, 61(2): 291–314.

Financial Times (2016) 'The EU referendum results', https://ig.ft.com/sites/elections/2016/uk/eu-referendum/

Fishwick, C. (2016) 'Why Northern Irish and Irish voters want to remain in the EU', *The Guardian*, 20 June, www.theguardian.com/politics/2016/jun/20/why-northern-irish-and-irish-voters-want-to-remain-in-the-eu

Goodwin, M. and Heath, O. (2016) *Brexit explained: Poverty, low skills and lack of opportunities*, York: Joseph Rowntree Foundation.

Hastings, A., Bailey, N., Gannon, M., Besemer, K. and Bramley, G. (2012) *Serving deprived communities in recession*, York: Joseph Rowntree Foundation.

Hastings, A., Bailey, N., Gannon, M., Besemer, K. and Bramley, G. (2015) 'Coping with the cuts: the management of the worst financial settlement in living memory', *Local Government Studies*, 41(4): 601–21.

Hay, C. and Wincott, D. (2012) *The political economy of European capitalism*, Basingstoke: Palgrave.

Hills, J. and Stewart, K. (2016) 'Socio-economic inequalities', in R. Lupton, T. Burchardt, J. Hills, K. Stewart and P. Vizard (eds) *Social policy in a cold climate: policies and their consequences since the crisis*, Bristol: Policy Press, pp 245–66.

Hood, A. (2016) 'The outlook for living standards', www.ifs.org.uk/uploads/publications/budgets/as2016/as2016_ah.pdf

Institute for Fiscal Studies (2015) 'Recent cuts to public spending', October 1, www.ifs.org.uk/tools_and_resources/fiscal_facts/public_spending_survey/cuts_to_public_spending

Ipsos MORI (2016) 'Voting intention', *Political Monitor*, July, www.slideshare.net/IpsosMORI/ipsos-mori-political-monitor-june-2016

Kirk, A. and Dunford, D. (2016) 'EU referendum: how the results compare to the UK's educated, old and immigrant populations', *The Telegraph*, 27 June, www.telegraph.co.uk/news/2016/06/24/eu-referendum-how-the-results-compare-to-the-uks-educated-old-an/

Lilla, M. (2016) *The reckless mind: Intellectuals in politics*, New York: New York Review of Books.

Majone, G. (1994) 'The rise of the regulatory state', *West European Politics*, 17(3): 77–101.

Mills, E. and Colvin, C. (2016) 'Why did Northern Ireland vote to remain?', http://qpol.qub.ac.uk/northern-ireland-vote-remain/

Moore, F. (2016) '"Surprised" Leave camp did not expect Brexit, top out campaigner admits', 1 August, www.express.co.uk/news/uk/695233/brexit-leave-camp-surprised-labour-gisela-stuart-immigration.

Mortimore, R. (2016) 'Polling history: 40 years of British views on "in or out" of Europe', 21 June, http://theconversation.com/polling-history-40-years-of-british-views-on-in-or-out-of-europe-61250

Northern Ireland Office (1998) The Belfast Agreement, www.gov.uk/government/uploads/system/uploads/attachment_data/file/136652/agreement.pdf

ONS (2015a) 'What are the average earnings where you work?', www.neighbourhood.statistics.gov.uk/HTMLDocs/dvc126/

ONS (2015b) 'Local area migration indicators', August, www.ons.gov.uk/ons/rel/migration1/migration-indicators-suite/2014/rft-lami-august-2015.xls

ONS (2016a) 'Local area migration indicators', www. ons.gov.uk/peoplepopulationandcommunity/ populationandmigration/migrationwithintheuk/datasets/ localareamigrationindicatorsunitedkingdom

ONS (2016b) 'Household disposable income and inequality: financial year ending 2015', *Statistical Bulletin*, February.

Oxford Migration Observatory (2014) 'Scottish public opinion', February 10, www.migrationobservatory.ox.ac.uk/resources/reports/ scottish-public-opinion/

Oxford Migration Observatory (2016) 'Long-term international migration flows to and from the UK', www.migrationobservatory. ox.ac.uk/resources/briefings/long-term-international-migration-flows-to-and-from-the-uk/

Pidluznyj, S. (2016) 'European doctors heading to Lincolnshire to plug gaps in GP services', July, http://thelincolnite.co.uk/2016/07/ european-doctors-heading-to-lincolnshire-to-plug-gaps-in-gp-services/

Prosser, C., Mellon, J. and Green, J. (2016) 'What mattered to you most when deciding how to vote in the EU referendum?', British Election Study, www.britishelectionstudy.com/bes-findings/what-mattered-most-to-you-when-deciding-how-to-vote-in-the-eu-referendum/#. WHuoFWSLRlM

Shipman, T. (2016) *All out war: The full story of how Brexit sank Britain's political class*, London: William Collins.

Smith, J. (2015) 'Europe: the Coalition's poisoned chalice', in A. Seldon and M. Finn (eds), *The Coalition effect, 2010–2015*, Cambridge: Cambridge University Press, pp 370–96.

Taylor-Gooby, P. (2013) *The double crisis of the welfare state*, Basingstoke: Palgrave.

Wellings, B. and Vines, E. (2016) 'Populism and sovereignty: the EU Act and the in–out referendum, 2010–15', *Parliamentary Affairs*, 69(1): 309–26.

Wheeler, B. (2015) 'Spending review: department by department cuts guide', www.bbc.co.uk/news/uk-politics-34790102

Wright, D. and Case, R. (2016) 'Leave voters felt ignored and left behind as post-Brexit poll reveals extent of economic division across UK', Joseph Rowntree Foundation, July, www.jrf.org.uk/press/leave-voters-felt-ignored-and-left-behind-brexit-poll

Workers on tap but income drying up? The potential implications for incomes and social protection of the 'gig economy'

Lee Gregory

Poverty and low income continue to be central to policy debates over the past year. While there are early signs that earnings may be returning to their pre-recession levels, the UK referendum to leave the European Union (EU) may hinder this change. Consequently 'austerity' has remained the driving focus of policy makers seeking to bring public spending 'under control' in the context of economic uncertainty following 'Brexit'. It is difficult to predict, so soon after the vote, exactly how this will impact on incomes and earnings. However, other trends that have received significant attention over the last year open up some wider concerns, not just about income but about how social protection itself is designed. Recently, the context of employment and work has come under increasing scrutiny, calling into question the stability and security of income and employment. With the emergence of the 'on-demand economy', a political awakening towards the implications of this form of employment seems to have occurred. This chapter explores a number of these themes, drawing out considerations it may have for earnings, affordable living and social security. It seeks to go further than this and explore similarities between the language of the 'on-demand' economy and the re-emergence of moralistic and pathological accounts of poverty. Together, these revitalise narratives which individualise social problems and the agency necessary to resolve them. This shift – not only in terms of the 'on-demand' economy, but how it is being positioned – offers a challenging context for the provision of social protection, and it remains unclear how to counter these narratives and developments.

Austerity and the cost of living

The global economic recession since 2007/08 has called into question the pursuit of economic growth as the sole means of improving welfare. Although some continue to argue in favour of unrestricted economic growth (Ben-Ami, 2012), others have sought to reawaken Tawney's concern with the problem of riches, suggesting that such vast inequalities underpin the persistence of poverty (Seabrook, 2015). Wider 'macro' debates regarding the nature of the contemporary economy occur alongside concern with the 'micro' level of welfare provision and its impact on human lives. As the politics of austerity (and its impact) has grown in prominence, policy debates are reframed, altering provision of public services in significant ways (Gough, 2011; Clarke and Newman, 2012). Although globally there is no single crisis, rather a variety of crises and responses (Farnsworth and Irving, 2011), the UK response has been to pursue welfare reform and cuts through an increasing focus on the need for individuals to take a greater role in managing the risks generated by a global economy. Debates in social policy, and in the social sciences more generally, have sought to draw attention to not only the consequences of austerity politics (Farnsworth, 2011) but also wider analysis about the concept itself and how it facilitates a shift in the mixed economy of welfare (Bochel, 2016). For some, this shift entrenches these changes, making it exceptionally difficult to reverse such developments in the future (Taylor-Gooby, 2013).

This occurs within a context of continued challenges for individuals and households in relation to the cost of living. In terms of the economic recovery and the impact not only on wages but on low- and middle-income households, Corlett et al (2016a) show that a recovery was starting to take place early in the year 2015, facilitating an improvement of the condition of households. Although real wages had been pushed back down to 2003 levels by mid-2014, Corlett et al predict an improvement in incomes from 2015 onwards; this is not the case for living standards and typical hourly pay, which is unlikely to return to its peak before the end of the decade. Alongside these developments there is diminishing access to the housing market, especially for Millennials, and, Corlett et al speculate, the proposed cuts to benefits and in-work support will be concentrated at the bottom of the income distribution, resulting in higher growth in incomes at the top. In fact they predict a 25% decline in incomes for the poorest households between 2015 and 2020.

However the November 2016 Autumn Statement potentially created barriers to these predictions coming to pass. Emmerson and Pope (2016) suggest that growth forecasts would need to be cut, resulting in an increase in the deficit, even if the planned spending cuts were successfully implemented. Thus austerity is predicted to continue after 2020. In fact, in their response to the Autumn Statement, Emmerson and Pope (2016) suggest that the government has not succeeded in keeping to its own fiscal targets, stating that it had failed to keep forecast spending on welfare within a cap, failed to reduce debt as a share of national income every year and would fail to keep its commitment to eliminate the deficit by 2019– 20. Inflation looks likely to rise as growth diminishes and, with greater uncertainty in the economy, Emmerson and Pope recommend hesitating before further tax and cut plans are devised. Similarly, Corlett et al (2016b) raise similar concerns regarding the impact of 'Brexit'. Drawing attention to family income rather than public finances, they suggest a rather grim picture. Revising the earlier forecast, they suggest that average earnings are likely to be £830 a year lower than expected in 2020, resulting in this decade being set to become the weakest one for wage growth since the 1900s.

They further suggest that the statement had removed some of the proposed welfare cuts that would impact on the 'just managing' families the new prime minister has highlighted as in need of support. But Corlett et al (2016b) suggest that, despite some positive announcements regarding letting agent fees and the benefits taper rate, there is limited overall improvement for family incomes. The taper rate is counterbalanced by the costs of higher inflation and there will be a three-year freeze on benefits. Consequently, their revised forecast predicts incomes growing by an average of 0.2% a year: lower-income families, and the entire bottom third of the income distribution, look set to see incomes fall in the coming years. It is within this context that it is possible to consider the current policy concern with the on-demand economy.

The on-demand economy

One emerging issue set to radically alter the context of employment has been the 'on-demand' or 'gig' economy. Encompassing the image of the 'gig' – a sought-after opportunity to perform and earn an income – the term seeks to capture a whole series of employment practices. From well-publicised activities such as those of Uber, the on-demand taxi app, to online marketplaces such as Etsy and accommodation platforms like Airbnb, there has been an increase in small-scale entrepreneurship. Such developments are described as 'exciting' by Department for Work and Pensions Secretary of State Damien Green (2016), while for US presidential candidate Hillary Clinton these new opportunities come with a warning regarding working conditions and stable employment. Tinson et al (2016) demonstrate how underemployment and in-work poverty have become consistent features of the UK context for a number of years. Developments such as the on-demand economy look set to continue these trends.

For the US, Intuit (2015) estimates that by 2020 7.6 million people will be employed through the gig economy. Although no similar predictions have been made for the UK, Corlett and Finch (2016) suggest that, of the 1.1 million people with multiple jobs, 590,000 had multiple employee roles, while 120,000 had multiple self-employment jobs, and 420,000 combined employment and self-employment. Further, their research indicates that the most common sectors for workers with multiple jobs are education, health and social care, arts and sports, hairdressing and bar work. This suggests that a more nuanced approach must be adopted when exploring the development of the on-demand economy. Rather than illustrating a new development in employment practices that provides the employee with greater control over their work practices, this shift may be showing, once again, how household income is insufficient to meet living costs and additional sources of income are pursued.

Thus the UK context seems to suggest that the on-demand economy has yet to reach a scale that matches the level of concern it seems to have attracted in the press, but its implications for stable employment and income should not be sidelined. In part this could reflect the implication drawn out in the Autumn Statement regarding the impact of the on-demand economy on budget revenues, with the Office for Budget Responsibility predicting that it will cost the Treasury £3.5 billion by 2020/21 (O'Connor and Holder, 2016). While this is important, considering the above discussion of continued austerity narratives, resulting in continuing (and probably deepening) cuts in public services, pay and income must still be at the forefront of our concern. Corlett and Finch (2016) suggest that workers in some sectors, notably education and health, are much more likely than those in others to have multiple jobs. Popular second jobs include working in a fitness centre and bar work, as well as in education.

Taking some of the headline working patterns in relation to pay, O'Connor and Holder (2016) highlight how UberEats initially offered to pay £20 an hour but began to reduce pay as customer demand increased. This resulted in a pay formula whereby the employee is paid £3.30 a delivery plus £1 a mile, minus a 25% 'Uber service fee', plus a £5 'trip reward'. Eventually, and without notification, employees found that the 'trip reward' had been cut to £4 for weekday lunch and weekend dinner times, and to £3 for weekday dinner and weekend lunch times. Outside those periods, it had been cut altogether. There is no comment in O'Connor and Holder's discussion as to whether employees were consulted on this, but the tone of the article suggests this is not the case.

Associated with the debates around the on-demand economy, Corlett and Finch (2016) added that there had been a broader shift towards self-employment. There are now more than 5 million people who are self-employed, including those with a second job that is in self-employment. D'Arcy (2016) suggests that the self-employed have seen a drop in their earnings by £100 a week between 2006/07 and 2013/14, a more drastic squeeze than employees experienced overall. This broadens the focus beyond the on-demand economy (as not all of the self-employed will work in this format) and draws attention to an area of employment which has, potentially, received less attention in discussions about low pay.

Consequently this may be challenging for efforts to tackle poverty in the coming years. First, as Broughton and Richards (2016) highlight, 49% of the UK's self-employed are on low pay, measured on an hourly basis, compared with 22% of employees. This figure is determined through hourly earnings. Furthermore, the former group continues to grow while the latter has remained relatively stable. In fact, as Broughton and Richards note, 1.7 million people will remain on low pay because the national living wage legislation does not include the self-employed, making this an invisible feature of the UK labour market. This, they suggest, is setting up a context in which the employer–employee relationship is shifting towards a firm–contractor model, attached to new technological developments, underpinning growth in the on-demand economy. Additionally, the self-employed are less likely to have access to other sources of income (their self-employment being their only source) and they are, consequently, more likely to live in low-income households compared to their employee counterparts.

Second, in 2014 the Social Security Advisory Committee (SSAC, 2014) highlighted concerns about the nature of support offered to the self-employed. Their report highlighted a disparity between both contributions and entitlements of the self-employed and employees.

Current media attention focused on the on-demand economy has resulted in the Office of Tax Simplification (OTS, 2016) suggesting a need to review National Insurance contributions of those employed in this way. Yet the OTS report appears to make no comment on entitlements to social security provision for those working within the on-demand economy. The government has instigated an independent review, led by Matthew Taylor (RSA, 2016), to consider the wider regulatory framework surrounding employment, and whether the support provided to businesses and workers, alongside job security and workplace rights, are suited to the changes being noted in the economy.

However, in relation to self-employment – the category that is closest to the on-demand economy – the SSAC has highlighted that the context of self-employment will impact on both National Insurance contributions (usually at a lower rate), which also, to an extent, reflects a lower entitlement to contributory benefits, especially pensions (prior to the introduction of the Single Tier Pension). Part of the challenge seems to be the historic legacy of the design of social security systems. Little attention has been given to the self-employed in relation to unemployment support. This may be challenging, considering the development of Universal Credit in relation to the diversity of the self-employed and, we can potentially add, the greater diversity of forms of on-demand employment.

Universal Credit has established a work allowance, indicating how much an individual may earn before the taper is applied. The rules guiding this vary depending on whether the individual is employed, self-employed or on a zero-hours contact. In essence, the taper will alter monthly, depending on earnings, and consequently seems to fit neatly with potential fluctuations in income the on-demand economy might generate. Thus variation in incomes on a month-to-month basis may impact significantly on Universal Credit entitlement, even though the government has agreed to consider some form of loss carry-forward from month to month. But how variation will be accounted for, and the impacts it may have on people's day-to-day lives, and the anxieties that insecure income will create, remain unknown. The exact interaction between Universal Credit and the on-demand economy needs consideration (and could be part of the Taylor review); greater flexibility in the *type* of employment activities and *when* this income is received may fit neatly with the taper design, but the administration of Universal Credit with regard to such employment patterns must be designed to provide support without being overly intrusive.

Additionally, the SSAC refers to the term of 'false self-employment', meaning the phenomenon whereby employers (re)define their employees as being self-employed. This could be a useful way for employers of encapsulating activities within the on-demand economy. The SSAC (2014: 31) states that this 'false self-employment is generally bad for low-paid workers who may be exploited by "employers" wishing to avoid employers' contributions as well as the employment law rights of "employees"'. The challenge at present is the uncertain position of those employed in the on-demand economy in terms of employee rights and protection. Future considerations of this trend may encompass auto-enrolment into pensions, and whether those working in the on-demand economy – where they operate within a wider corporate structure – are included in this provision. But what is the situation for those operating in ways more akin to self-employment, such as through Etsy? In such circumstances it is unlikely that auto-enrolment will apply and wider implications therefore arise for pension planning and efforts to tackle poverty and low income in the future. The on-demand economy seems set up to address income concerns today and not those of the future. Furthermore, entitlement for Contributory Jobseeker's Allowance, Statutory Maternity/Paternity/Adoption Pay, as well as Sick Pay, all become uncertain. The SSAC suggests that 'false self-employment' can be instituted as a means to circumvent rights and protections, and this is likely to be replicated in the on-demand economy. Additionally, while the Universal Credit taper may fit with those on formal, multiple employment contracts, it remains unclear if the administrative practices for self-employment will adequately encompass the potential variation of 'self-employment' in the on-demand economy.

There is a further element that should cause concern here. Consider the flexibility of income for those working within the on-demand economy, or for those on zero-hours contracts. Income streams start to adapt and change to these new patterns, but bills do not. Monthly payments, from rent to council tax to direct debits, will still need to be made at a set time. With regard to direct debits, this is potentially problematic as it is often cheaper to pay bills in this way rather than using quarterly payments. Rowlingson and McKay (2016) highlight that basic bank accounts are often made affordable to the banks by limiting account holders access to ATMs and charging them for failed direct debits, with only five major banks opting to remove fees on missed payments in 2015. This latter limitation is important; as Hill et al (2016) note, the suitability of direct debits depends on the security of having sufficient income in the account for regular monthly payments, whereas other payment methods, controlled by the individual, offer flexibility and 'peace of mind'.

For those employed within the on-demand economy or on zero-hours contracts, this potentially creates a new tension through which they must navigate. Do they move towards systems of payment which give them greater control, such as pre-payment meters for utilities, thus missing out on savings generated through direct debit payments as they cannot guarantee sufficient income when the direct debit payment is due? Or do they take the 'risk' of capitalising on the savings and seek to secure sufficient hours of work – which is potentially beyond their control? If low-income families were able to access direct debits, safe in the knowledge they could afford the monthly costs, they would save on average £250 a year (Save the Children, 2011). Yet for many this is not an option and reliance on pre-payment meters not only costs more but can also lead to self-disconnection (O'Sullivan et al, 2013). There is a need for an alternative solution. Here service providers could respond with new payment methods that give flexibility in when to pay (or even how much to pay) at times specified by the customer. Supplying a bill, and allowing customers to defer, pay in full or pay a portion of that bill, could match the flexibility of those working on zero-hours contracts or within the on-demand economy. But this would likely come with clauses and conditions which incentivise the providers to offer such payment systems but add costs for the consumer (for example through a deferment charge, or charging interest on deferred payments).

While the on-demand economy remains marginal at present, this is not to say that it will not grow. In addition, many of these potential challenges will apply equally to those on zero-hours contracts, if not more so. For those in the on-demand economy, as noted above, it may actually represent a second job for additional income, rather than the main source of their income. For those on zero-hours contracts, this fluctuation is likely to be embedded within their main source of income. Consequently, there may be shifts in employment patterns, which have come to the foreground of debates over the last year and which open up some important concerns and considerations for policy academics interested in poverty, low income and social protection.

Reinvigorating behavioural explanations?

Debate with regard to the on-demand economy must be viewed within the wider context of debates around social protection and poverty. Over recent years there has been a very clear steer towards pathological explanations of poverty which adopt moralistic undertones. Among the debates around incomes, wages and stable employment, this is illustrated in relation to the less than subtle shift towards redefining child poverty by the UK government. A number of these proposed changes, and the associated debates, were instigated under the Cameron government. The selection of Theresa May as the new leader of the Conservative Party, and therefore UK prime minister, seems to have resulted in a more overt, discursive critique of those reliant on social security provision, which emphasises the moral underclass discourse (MUD) noted by Levitas (1998). Having identified three discourses around social exclusion, one of which is MUD, Levitas explains that this draws attention to the imputed behavioural or moral deficiencies of specific 'problem' groups. This discursive framework offered both a means for criticising welfare provision by the state during the 1990s and a means by which causes of social problems are identified in relation to particular behavioural indicators.

The form of arguments perpetuated by MUD draw on the work of Charles Murray (1990), who argues that the welfare state acts in ways that make acceptable short-term behaviours which are damaging in the long term. In short, welfare encourages bad behaviour but does not stimulate good behaviour as it erodes responsibility, self-help and individuality. Social provisions also remove the fear of poverty and insecurity that are necessary to ensure good behaviour and acceptance of responsibility – thus the welfare state has weakened individual responsibility. Consequently, this fosters certain behaviours which create dependency and, in more contemporary language, 'risk-avoidance' (Seymour, 2012). The current relevance of this line of thought rests in reasserting that it is specific traits and actions which cause social problems, and these are located not at a societal or structural level, but in the individual.

The focus on risk-avoidance suggested by Lord Freud (Seymour, 2012) is important here, for it places the individual at the centre of social problems and their solutions. Such a view emanates from the rise of the 'Third Way' ideology and its acceptance of neoliberal economic theory as a replacement for the Keynesianism that had guided earlier Labour governments. For some, this represented the formation of a neoliberal hybrid (Hall, 2005) whose leading advocates were promoting welfare reform which invested in human capital rather than providing economic maintenance (Giddens, 2003: 117). This alters the narrative around welfare provision by the state. Rather than outright reduction and cutbacks, as advocated by the 1980s Conservative governments, it promoted investment in 'good' welfare provision (such as education and health) while cutting back on the 'bad' expenditure (such as social security) (Powell, 1999). Founded upon an integration into welfare narratives of the idea of reflexive individuals (Giddens, 2002), the analysis suggests that the expansion of choice, new risks in contemporary society, and disillusionment with traditional norms and social boundaries require a move towards reflexivity, where individuals manage their risk choices. Lord Freud, having advised Labour and the Conservative governments since 2002, is making an explicit link to such views in his argument around tackling risk-avoidance. Thus there is a drive to reform welfare to support positive risk-taking. This brings to the foreground wider narratives around active citizenship and the shift from a rights-based to a participatory narrative (Coffey, 2004; Lister, 2011). Such active and responsible citizens retain importance within the Conservative party analysis of 'Broken Britain' (discussed below), for this places individual action, in particular self-help, front and centre of efforts to manage social problems (Davies and Pill, 2012). Using the example of pensions, Langley (2008: 134) explores how such efforts to promote responsibility, create 'investor subjects' for whom: 'prudence and thrift are displaced by new moral and calculative self-disciplines of responsibility and entrepreneurially meeting, managing and manipulating ever-increasing obligations'.

This creates a context in which individual effort and entrepreneurialism creep into the redesign of welfare provision to manage the consequences of the contemporary social and economic context. There is a diminished effort to end social problems and a focus on helping citizens to manage their lives in a way which limits the potential impact of these problems.

To explore this in more detail, attention is now given to the repositioning of child poverty that has taken place over the last few years. Relating to efforts to alter the child poverty measure, the Conservative government drew attention to 'lifestyle factors'. Building on the earlier work of the Centre for Social Justice, this draws attention to family breakdown, debt and addiction as the main factors that impact on child poverty and the life chances these children will access as they transition to adulthood. Subsequently, Duncan Smith, writing with then Chancellor George Osborne (2014), set out an argument for tackling the 'real source' of child poverty: worklessness, family breakdown, educational failure, addiction and debt. As part of the Child Poverty Strategy this sought to shift the focus away from income, in particular relative income, as a government measure of child poverty. This presented, so they argued, an elusive target against which to achieve poverty reduction initiatives.

The Great Recession, they argued, reduced median incomes, lowering the poverty line, despite the fact that people's living conditions did not improve. Rather, the context in which a child grows up poor, 'entrenched worklessness, family breakdown, problem debt, drug and alcohol dependency' (Duncan Smith and Osborne, 2014), prevents children and their families from being lifted out of poverty.

A move to repeal the 2010 Child Poverty Act was mooted by Duncan Smith in 2015. This seemed to be reiterated in the conference speech by then leader David Cameron, referring to children growing up in 'chaos' and adding mental health problems and abuse to the list of 'root causes' of poverty. This discourse does little more than reinforce explanations of poverty based on pathology that have existed in debates since the reform of the Poor Law. It has been suggested that this illustrates the efforts of Duncan Smith (and the Centre for Social Justice) to reposition debates around poverty through a *terministic screen* designed to deflect attention from one set of causes to another. Slater (2014: 964, emphasis in original), in developing this argument, postulates:

> it is a *selection and deflection of reality* (bolstered by the strategic deployment of ignorance), which encourages all who encounter the screen to view society through its behavioural filters of family breakdown, out-of-wedlock childbirth, worklessness, dependency, anti-social behaviour, personal responsibility, addiction, and teenage pregnancies.

His argument suggests that the frequently stated social pathologies that are labelled as the root causes of poverty are invoked in order to manufacture ignorance of alternative ways of addressing poverty and low income. A single behavioural explanation takes centre stage, ignoring structural explanations, filtering into the policy debate and the public mind, and becomes increasingly difficult to challenge and shift. The solution put forward to address this challenge, Slater suggests, was the idea of the Big Society – local community activism, reinvigorated to tackle significant social problems (Blonde, 2010). The significance of this, however, does not rest just in efforts to rethink the role of the state, welfare state and citizens as part of a move to cut state expenditure during times of austerity. There is an additional concern with a move towards self-help as part of the wider austerity analysis which is relevant here.

Community self-help initiatives can be utilised by policy makers to (1) reduce demands on rising welfare budgets; (2) be a counterbalance to the breakdown of social cohesion (re-establishing moral and social responsibilities); and (3) help cushion the impact of poverty (Burns and Taylor, 1998). The obsession with moralistic and pathological explanations of poverty found within the New Right (going back to the 1980s) focuses interest around the first and second of these explanations. As Gregory (2014: 175) argues: 'The Big Society could be presented as a means [...] to promote localism, to foster the re-growth of moral/social responsibility, thus maintaining the state as a facilitator of self-help rather than a service provider.'

Relating to this debate, Taylor (2011: 10) suggests that the term 'self-help' is a reinterpretation of community by thinkers within neoliberal ideologies, which accommodates a wider narrative of pluralism in welfare provision that gives individuals the capability to take control of their services. Gregory (2015) draws out two broad narratives in relation to self-help. One attached to neoliberal economic ideas, supports the reduction of welfare provision by the state through a move towards welfare pluralism and the promotion of individual/private responsibility for addressing social problems (Drakeford, 2000). This is evidenced by changes in the mixed economy of welfare (Powell and Hewitt, 1998) and the politicisation of definitions of need (Langan, 1998). The second narrative seeks to utilise the concept of self-help as an alternative to market forces and neoliberal values found in a plethora of alternative economic practices which, to date, have had little impact on wider social policy debates (Williams and Windebank, 2001; McKillop and Wilson, 2003; Williams, 2011).

Consequently, the repositioning of the causes of social problems on individual over structural factors, as outlined above in relation to risk-avoidance and the MUD, creates a context in which solutions are also being reframed in relation to individual capabilities and a *willingness* to engage those capabilities. This draws out some important considerations for the focus upon the on-demand economy.

In a speech around the principles of welfare provision, Damien Green, Secretary of State for the Department for Work and Pensions, stated:

> Just a few years ago the idea of a proper job meant a job that brings in a fixed monthly salary, with fixed hours, paid holidays, sick pay, a pension scheme and other contractual benefits. But the gig economy has changed all that. We've seen the rise of the everyday entrepreneur. *People now own their time and control who receives their services and when. They can pick and mix their employers, their hours, their offices, their holiday patterns.* (Green, 2016, emphasis added)

The use of language to describe participation in the on-demand economy is especially interesting. It suggests an aspect of control. This is an idea highlighted earlier in this chapter, in relation to how payment of bills and direct debits need to be rethought in relation to control by the citizen-consumer (Clarke and Newman, 2012). Not only does this present a false idea of control (choice is often in a context not of one's own making), it also implies that the earning potential of citizens is increasingly under their control.

For decades, work as the main route out of poverty has maintained its centrality in social security reforms, despite increasing evidence of in-work poverty (Tinson et al, 2016). Here we are potentially seeing a refinement of this argument. Not only is work the best route out of poverty, the citizen now has greater control over their work – thus enhancing their responsibility for securing a sufficient income and ending their own poverty. Micro-enterprise and entrepreneurialism have been seen as way out of poverty within the context of the developing world (Kevane and Wydick, 2001; Shaw, 2004; Osalor, 2013) as well as the Western world (Sherrard Sherraden et al, 2004). Here narratives around individual aspiration and capability start to filter into the debates around poverty and social protection. It is possible to predict the sentiments that will start to emanate from this rhetorical construct: through individual effort, going beyond finding a job to actually creating one, it is possible to bring your poverty to an end! Simply exercise greater control over your time, who you work for and when. There are diminishing reasons to be in poverty when such opportunities for innovation exist, if only you are willing to take the chance. For some, this may be worrying, as this argument is embedded within a discussion of support for people with disabilities and those who are out of work. Are we to engage in this reimaging of employment, that is, as some form of DIY employment opportunities which the unemployed, but especially people with disabilities, are able to opt for in order to end their own poverty? The Taylor review (RSA, 2016) has an additional focus to those listed above: to reflect upon new opportunities for groups that are under-represented in the labour market, the elderly, people with disabilities and carers. It seems possible that new discourses around self-help will blend with new technological developments and the on-demand economy to find new ways to assert that citizens are failing to find their own routes out of poverty.

While it is too early to predict what developments may stem from the changes in employment patterns noted above, there is a shift in language here that is reinvigorating a focus on individuals and their own moral worth. What it potentially illustrates was well expressed by Jordan (2010: 191) when he argued that social policy has been 'hijacked by a version of individual self-realisation which subverts the whole basis of a viable collective life and social order'. The shift towards both the on-demand economy and zero-hours working, and the re-energised efforts to place the causes of social problems in an individualistic context where solutions can be found by aspirational, entrepreneurial, risk-takers, are increasing in prominence as we move towards the end of almost a decade of austerity politics and welfare cuts. Given the entrenched nature of these changes (Taylor-Gooby, 2013), it is difficult to see how it might be possible to successfully challenge this narrative and consequent policy changes.

Conclusion

This chapter has suggested that the context in which poverty and low income occurs is set to remain in place for the foreseeable future. Not only has the referendum vote to leave the EU resulted in significant revision of public and family finances, these also form part of a wider shifting context which could lead to further narratives around the individual as the author of their own fate, and their own escape route out of poverty. The perceived rise in on-demand employment has been drawn out in this chapter, for it offers a number of challenges for the design and implementation of both social protection for the relief of poverty and efforts to prevent poverty. What was noted, however, was that the language used around such developments could be easily blended with existing discourse around risk-avoidance and moralistic explanations of poverty creating a new *terministic screen*, whereby solutions, as well as problem definitions, are reshaped in significant ways. Universal Credit, as a form of 'social protection', may serve to reinforce such trends rather than offer a more genuine source of support for the unemployed.

Although there has not been the space here to engage in a discussion of possible alternatives and challenges to such developments, resistance to these trends may not be futile. Jordan (2010: 197) has argued for a need for 'a politics which motivates [citizens] to take collective action for change'. Lister (2016) has provided an articulate defence of social security around a series of progressive principles, while Gregory (2015) draws out a wider narrative around new values upon which alternatives to the current direction of policy development can be based. All three, from different starting positions draw attention to a universal basic income. Reflecting an ongoing debate in social policy and beyond, the basic income is not a new idea but may perhaps be one whose time has come. Lady Rhys Williams (1943) floated such an idea at the same time as Beveridge, but, it could be argued, the path dependency of social security had already been set. Insurance-based contribution systems may no longer be relevant to the contemporary social and economic context. While the basic income may offer one policy solution, it also generates more challenges and concerns in the short term; however, it does offer the potential to start a debate around framing of poverty and low income, as well as the mechanisms designed to address them.

References

Ben-Ami, D. (2012) *Ferraris for all: In defence of economic progress*, Bristol: Policy Press.

Blonde, P. (2010) *Red Tory: How left and right have broken Britain and how we can fix it*, London: Faber & Faber.

Bochel, C. (2016) 'The changing governance of social policy', in H. Bochel and M. Powell (eds) *The coalition government and social policy: Restructuring the welfare state*, Bristol: Policy Press.

Broughton, N. and Richards, B. (2016) *Tough gig: Tacking low-paid self-employment in London and the UK,* Social Market Foundation, http://www.smf.co.uk/wp-content/uploads/2016/10/Social-Market-Foundation-SMF-Tough-Gig-Tackling-low-paid-self-employment-in-London-and-the-UK-October-2016.pdf

Burns, D. and Taylor, M. (1998) *Mutual aid and self-help*, Bristol: Policy Press.

Clarke J. and Newman J. (2012) 'The alchemy of austerity', *Critical Social Policy*, 32: 299-319.

Coffey, A. (2004) *Reconceptualising social policy*, Maidenhead: Open University Press.

Corlett, A. and Finch, D. (2016) *Double take: Workers with multiple jobs and reforms to National Insurance*, The Resolution Foundation, http://www.resolutionfoundation.org/app/uploads/2016/11/Double-take.pdf

Corlett, A., Finch, D. and Whittaker, M. (2016a) *Living standards 2016: The experiences of low to middle income households in downturn and recovery*, The Resolution Foundation, http://www.resolutionfoundation.org/app/uploads/2016/02/Audit-2016.pdf

Corlett, A., Finch, D., Gardiner, L. and Whittaker, M. (2016b) *Bending the rules: Autumn Statement response*, Resolution Foundation, http://www.resolutionfoundation.org/app/uploads/2016/11/Bending-the-rules-AS.pdf

D'Arcy, C. (2016) *Self-employed workers earned more in the 90s: Now another pay squeeze looms*, New Statesman, http://www.newstatesman.com/politics/staggers/2016/10/self-employed-workers-earned-more-90s-now-another-pay-squeeze-looms

Davies, J.S. and Pill, M. (2012) 'Empowerment or abandonment? Prospects for neighbourhood revitalization under the Big Society', *Public Money and Management*, 32(3): 193–200.

Drakeford, M. (2000) *Privatisation and social policy*, Essex: Pearson Education.

Duncan Smith, I. and Osborne, G. (2014) 'The Conservatives' child poverty plan tackles poverty at source', *The Guardian*, 26 February, www.theguardian.com/commentisfree/2014/feb/26/conservative-child-poverty-strategy-george-osborne-iain-duncan-smith

Emmerson, C. and Pope, T. (2016) *Winter is coming: The outlook of public finances in the 2016 Autumn Statement*, IFS, www.ifs.org.uk/uploads/publications/bns/BN188.pdf

Farnsworth K. (2011) 'From economic crisis to a new age of austerity: the UK', in K. Farnsworth and Z. Irving (eds) *Social policy in challenging times: Economic crisis and welfare systems*, Bristol: Policy Press, pp 251–70.

Farnsworth, K. and Irving, Z. (eds) (2011) *Social policy in challenging times: Economic crisis and welfare systems*, Bristol: Policy Press.

Giddens, A. (2002) *Runaway world: How globalisation is reshaping our lives*, London: Profile Books.

Giddens, A. (2003) *The Third Way*, Cambridge: Cambridge University Press.

Green, D. (2016) 'From welfare state to welfare system', www.gov.uk/government/speeches/from-welfare-state-to-welfare-system

Gregory, L. (2014) 'Resilience or resistance? Time banking in the age of austerity', *Journal of Contemporary European Studies*, 22(2): 171–83.

Gregory, L. (2015) *Trading time: Can exchange lead to social change?* Bristol: Policy Press.

Gough, I. (2011) 'From financial crisis to fiscal crisis', in K. Farnsworth and Z. Irving (eds) *Social policy in challenging times: Economic crisis and welfare systems*, Bristol: Policy Press, pp 49–64.

Hall, S. (2005) 'New Labour's double-shuffle', *Review of Education, Pedagogy, and Cultural Studies*, 27: 319–35.

Hill, K., Davis, A., Hirsch, D. and Marshall, L. (2016) *Falling short: The experiences of families below the Minimum Income Standard*, Joseph Rowntree Foundation, www.jrf.org.uk/report/falling-short-experiences-families-below-minimum-income-standard

Intuit (2015) 'Intuit forecast: 7.6 million people in on-demand economy by 2020', http://investors.intuit.com/press-releases/press-release-details/2015/Intuit-Forecast-76-Million-People-in-On-Demand-Economy-by-2020/default.aspx

Jordan, B. (2010) *What's wrong with social policy and how to fix it*, Cambridge: Polity Press.

Kevane, M. and Wydick, B. (2001) 'Microenterprise lending to female entrepreneurs: Sacrificing economic growth for poverty alleviation?', *World Development*, 29(7): 1225–36.

Langan, M. (1998) 'The contested concept of need', in M. Langan (ed.) *Welfare: Needs, rights and risks*, London: Routledge, pp 3–34.

Langley, P. (2008) 'Financialization and the consumer credit boom', *Competition & Change*, 12: 133–47.

Levitas, R. (1998) *The inclusive society? Social exclusion and New Labour*, Basingstoke: Palgrave Macmillan.

Lister, R. (2011) 'The age of responsibility: social policy and citizenship in the early 21st century', in C. Holden, M. Kilkey and M. Ramia (eds) *Social Policy Review 23: Analysis and debate in social policy*, Bristol: Policy Press, pp 63–84.

Lister, R. (2016) 'Putting the security back into social security', in L. Nandy, C. Lucas and C. Bowers (eds) *The alternative: Towards a new progressive politics*, London: Biteback Publishing Ltd.

McKillop, D.G. and Wilson, J.O.S. (2003) 'Credit unions in Britain: A time for change', *Public Money and Management*, 23(2): 119–23.

Murray, C. (1990) *The emerging British underclass*, London: IEA Health and Welfare Unit.

O'Connor, S. and Holder, V. (2016) 'Tax systems struggles to cope with the rise of the gig economy', 24 November, www.ft.com/content/ba9dc7c8-b26d-11e6-a37c-f4a01f1b0fa1

OTS (Office of Tax Simplification) (2016) 'The "gig" economy', www.gov.uk/government/publications/the-gig-economy-an-ots-focus-paper

Osalor, P. (2013) *The entrepreneurial revolution: A solution for poverty eradication*, London: Posag International.

O'Sullivan, K.C., Howden-Chapman, P.L., Fougere, G.M., Hales, S. and Stanley, J. (2013) 'Empowered? Examining self-disconnection in a postal survey of electricity prepayment meter consumers in New Zealand', *Energy Policy*, 52: 277–87.

Powell, M. (1999) 'Introduction', in M. Powell (ed.) *New Labour, new welfare state?* Bristol: Policy Press, pp 1–27.

Powell, M. and Hewitt, M. (1998) 'The end of the welfare state?', *Social Policy & Administration*, 32(1): 1–13.

Rhys Williams, J. (1943) *Something to look forward to*, London: Macdonald.

Rowlingson, K. and McKay, S. (2016) *Financial inclusion annual monitoring report 2016*, University of Birmingham, http://www.birmingham. ac.uk/Documents/college-social-sciences/social-policy/CHASM/ annual-reports/financial-inclusion-monitoring-report-2016.pdf

RSA (2016) 'Matthew Taylor to lead independent review of employment practices in the modern economy', RSA, www.thersa. org/about-us/media/2016/matthew-taylor-to-lead-independent-review-of-employment-practices-in-the-modern-economy

Save the Children (2011) *The UK poverty rip-off*, Save the Children, www.savethechildren.org.uk/sites/default/files/docs/UK_Poverty_ Rip_Off_Brief_1.pdf

Seabrook, J. (2015) *Pauperland: Poverty and the poor in Britain*, London: C. Hurst.

Seymour, R. (2012) 'Lord Freud on welfare: making the poor pay for the risk-taking of the rich', 23 November, www.guardian.co.uk/ commentisfree/2012/nov/23/lord-freud-welfare-poor-risk

Shaw, J. (2004) 'Microenterprise occupation and poverty reduction in microfinance programs: Evidence from Sri Lanka', *World Development*, 32(7): 1247–64.

Sherrard Sherraden, M., Sanders, C.K. and Sherraden, M. (2004) *Kitchen capitalism: Microenterprise in low-income households*. Albany, NY: State University of New York Press

Slater, T. (2014) 'The myth of "Broken Britain": Welfare reform and the production of ignorance', *Antipode*, 46(4): 948–69.

SSAC (Social Security Advice Committee) (2014) *Social security and the self-employed*, www.gov.uk/government/uploads/system/uploads/ attachment_data/file/358334/Social_security_provision_and_the_ self-employed__FINAL_24_SEPT__.pdf

Taylor, M. (2011) 'Community organising and the Big Society: is Saul Alinsky turning in his grave?', *Voluntary Sector Review*, 2(2): 257–64.

Taylor-Gooby, P. (2013) *The double crisis of the welfare state and what we can do about it*. Basingstoke: Palgrave Macmillan.

Tinson, A., Ayrton, C., Barker, K., Born, T.B., Aldridge, H. and Kenway, P. (2016) *Monitoring poverty and social exclusion*, Joseph Rowntree Foundation, www.jrf.org.uk/report/monitoring-poverty-and-social-exclusion-2016

Williams, C.C. (2011) 'Socio-spatial variations in community self-help: a total social organisation of labour perspective', *Social Policy and Society*, 10(3): 365–78.

Williams, C.C. and Windebank, J. (2001) 'Paid informal work: a barrier to social inclusion?' *Transfer: European Review of Labour and Research*, 1(1): 25–40.

THREE

Revolutionary times? The changing landscape of prisoner resettlement

Emma Wincup

Reviews of contemporary debates and developments in criminal justice policy have rarely been included in previous editions of *Social Policy Review*. As I have noted elsewhere (Wincup, 2013), crime and its control has seldom been a key concern of social policy academics. Instead it has been left largely to criminologists, who too frequently have failed to explore the connections between crime and social policy. This chapter focuses on one aspect of criminal justice: prisoner resettlement. It has been deliberately chosen not only because it offer an opportunity to explore how developments in criminal justice policy mirror shifts in other social policy contexts but also because it allows an appreciation of the impact of social policies on the likelihood of (re)offending.

The chapter is structured as follows. We begin by looking at the numbers of prisoners released each year from the 117 prisons in England and Wales, their characteristics, and the main issues they face upon release. This will open up a discussion of the purpose of resettlement and the respective responsibilities of criminal justice and other agencies. Next, we will consider the notion of a 'rehabilitation revolution' which was initially conceived by the Coalition government (2010–15) and promised to have a far-reaching impact on the structure and delivery of resettlement services. In the next two sections, we will reflect critically upon the impact of the 'rehabilitation revolution', both in custody and in the community. The chapter ends with an exploration of how prisoner resettlement is shaped by a wider range of social policies, focusing on housing and social security in particular.

Our focus in this chapter is on England and Wales since other parts of the UK have their own criminal justice systems. For the most part, this discussion is limited to prisoners aged 18 and over. Those aged 17 and under are accommodated in young offender institutions and supervised by youth offending teams upon release. Different social policies also apply to this group; for example, the expectation that they will be in some form of education and training until they are aged 18 (see Fergusson, 2016).

Setting the scene: prison resettlement in the 21st century

Each year significant number of prisoners leave custody: in 2015, just under 70,000 prisoners were released from prison (Ministry of Justice, 2016). This number refers to sentenced prisoners and it is important to note that a significant number of people leave prison each year after being found not guilty by the courts or being given a community-based penalty (see Hucklesby, 2009; Prison Reform Trust, 2011). Placing the latest figures in context, since 2010 there has been a significant fall in the number of prisoners released from custody, largely due to the courts sentencing fewer offenders to immediate custody for short sentences (that is, less than 12 months) (Ministry of Justice and NOMS, 2016). Typically, release is an automatic process when prisoners reach the mid-point of a determinate sentence, but the overall figure includes approximately 800 prisoners given indeterminate sentences by the courts and approximately 8,000 medium-term prisoners who successfully applied for early release subject to agreeing to the conditions of a home detention curfew (that is, remaining at a specified address for a set period of time, typically overnight, which is monitored electronically by a contracted provider from the private sector).

A significant proportion of those released from prison have only served short sentences. In the first half of 2016, 29% of those released fitted into this category (Ministry of Justice, 2016). Until 2015 they were released from custody without any formal supervision from criminal justice agencies, although they may have been supported by voluntary or third sector organisations through ad hoc localised arrangements. Plans to extend supervision to this group as part of the development of a new sentencing framework were included in the Criminal Justice Act 2003 but were never implemented and this was repealed by the Coalition government in the Legal Aid, Sentencing and Punishment of Offenders Act 2012. After over a decade of delays, the Offender Rehabilitation Act 2014 provided the legislative framework for statutory supervision of short-sentence prisoners, which was implemented as part of the Transforming Rehabilitation (TR) agenda, which we will consider in the next section. Briefly, TR – described as a strategy for reform (Ministry of Justice, 2013b) – introduced far-reaching changes to the probation service through greater involvement of the private and voluntary sector. It is anticipated that savings resulting from the transformation would be sufficient to finance community-based supervision for short-sentence prisoners.

The majority of those released are male: in the first half of 2016, only 9% of those released were female (Ministry of Justice, 2016). This figure is striking not only because males outnumber females so significantly but also because the proportion of females among those released is almost twice as high as in the prison population because women typically serve short sentences (women currently make up around 4.75% of the prison population, Ministry of Justice et al, 2017). The full implications of this are beyond the scope of the chapter (see Carlton and Segrave's [2013] collection of essays focused on women exiting prison) but we will reflect upon the impact of the 'rehabilitation revolution' on female prisoners throughout the chapter.

The 'prison gate' for many is in practice a 'revolving door' (Padfield and Maruna, 2006). A likely outcome is that those released from prison will either be reconvicted for a further offence or recalled to prison for breaking the conditions of their licence or their home detention curfew. Reconviction rates among release prisoners are high. Almost half (45%) of those released from custody between April 2014 and March 2015 were reconvicted and this rate has remained relatively stable for some time despite a series of policy initiatives to reduce reoffending among this group (see Ministry of Justice, 2017 for a more detailed discussion of the methodology used). Levels of reconviction were highest among those sentenced to short periods in custody: three fifths of those released from prison during the same period after serving a sentence of 12 months or less were reconvicted (Ministry of Justice, 2017).

High levels of reoffending among former prisoners have been the focus of political attention since the turn of the 21st century when resettlement was 'rediscovered' (Hedderman, 2007). It formed part of the New Labour government's strategy of being 'tough on crime, tough on the causes of crime'. In practice, the focus was on the former (Wincup, 2013), but in relation to prisoners there was at least an attempt to explore the underlying reasons which led to their imprisonment, even if this was driven by a desire to reducing reoffending. The newly formed Social Exclusion Unit highlighted the social exclusion of prisoners (Social Exclusion Unit, 2002). It drew attention to the 'deep' social exclusion (see Levitas et al, 2007) faced by prisoners, whose lives are frequently characterised by multiple, complex and interacting problems which were often exacerbated by even a brief period in custody. The report painted a picture of the typical prisoner as workless with few qualifications and skills; dependent on social security; in poor health (physically and mentally), sometimes due to problem substance use; with precarious living arrangements, possibly homeless; and with weak family ties. There was little evidence that they possessed the levels of human and social capital which would support them to desist from crime (see Farrell, 2004) and plentiful evidence of 'risk factors' associated with crime (see Tanner-Smith et al, 2012). While social exclusion was widespread, the report drew attention to highest levels being among young adult prisoners (that is, those aged 18–20) and prisoners from black and minority ethnic backgrounds, who are over-represented in the prison population (see Ministry of Justice, 2015). A subsequent official review looked specifically at female prisoners and their 'vulnerabilities' (Corston, 2007), prompted by a higher than usual number of deaths in the female prison estate.

The extent to which the Social Exclusion Unit's work on prisoners was motivated by a desire to promote their social inclusion is a moot point. Undoubtedly the disproportionate number of offences committed by this relatively small group was a key concern since reoffending among ex-prisoners was seen as one of the main drivers of a rising prison population (see Ministry of Justice and NOMS, 2016), which New Labour needed to address. It had been elected on the basis of a general election campaign which promised to bring rising levels of crime under control and enhance community safety, distancing itself from 'Old' Labour who were seen as 'soft' on crime (Wincup, 2013).

Significant shifts in policy and practice occurred as the Social Exclusion Unit's (2002) report added to the policy momentum which was established the previous year by a HM Inspectorates of Prison and Probation (2001) thematic review of resettlement. The latter noted the absence of community supervision for short-sentence prisoners and the lack of a 'joined up' approach linking prison- and community-based support. As we noted in the previous section, post-release supervision was extended to all prisoners in 2003 but was only implemented 12 years later by a different government and via very different arrangements. The Social Exclusion Unit's 2002 report called for a 'National Rehabilitation Strategy' and this was introduced in 2004 in the form of the *Reducing reoffending: National action plan* (Home Office, 2004). As I have noted elsewhere, the explicit focus on social exclusion was lost in translation and it rarely appeared in this important strategic document (Wincup, 2013). A number of resettlement pathfinders were established and evaluated (Lewis et al, 2003; Clancy et al, 2006), which were designed to explore different approaches to working with prisoners, predominantly those serving short sentences.

Space precludes a more detailed discussion of the impact of the renewed emphasis on resettlement in the early part of the 21st century (see Hucklesby and Hagley-Dickinson, 2007), but it is worth emphasising that there was little evidence of sustained change. By 2010, when the Coalition government assumed power, the prison population was continuing to grow (Ministry of Justice and NOMS, 2016) and reconviction rates among former prisoners remained high (Ministry of Justice, 2012). A recent thematic review by HM Inspectorates of Prisons and Probation (2016) echoes the findings of the Social Exclusion Unit (2002) report. On the face of it, little has changed and many prisoners are released often to face similar, if not worse, circumstances than those which may have led them to offend in the first instance.

Before moving on to look at the latest developments in resettlement policy, we should pause for a moment and reflect upon some of the issues raised by the discussion above. It has been frequently noted that the concept of 'resettlement' is contested (see Hucklesby and Hagley-Dickinson, 2007; Moore, 2012). There is considerable debate about what activities might fall under this umbrella term (Raynor, 2007) and also the problematic assumptions it makes about the lives of those imprisoned prior to entering custody. Our brief review of the evidence above has demonstrated that the majority of prisoners have never experienced 'settled' lives and require considerable support to become 'included' in society. The nature of this support extends beyond the usual remits of criminal justice agencies. This opens up a debate about who might provide resettlement services. The nature of the problems faced by offenders suggests that the involvement of a wider range of statutory agencies is needed; for example, Jobcentre Plus or local authorities, but also points to the need to commission specialist expertise from voluntary and private sector organisations. The discussion also leads us to reflect upon the purpose of resettlement: should it be driven by criminal justice concerns (for example, to encourage desistance and reduce reoffending) or a commitment to social justice (for example, to promote opportunities for former prisoners to allow them to lead law-abiding lives without the associated shame and stigma of their past)? They are, of course, interlinked, but the selected emphasis influences both the nature of resettlement activities and the choice of key players.

The promise of a 'rehabilitation revolution'

A matter of days after the Conservative–Liberal Democrat Coalition government was formed, it published *The Coalition: Our programme for government* (Cabinet Office, 2010). This succinct document set out the ambitions of this unique government and among the 31 sections were two dedicated to criminal justice (crime and policing, and justice). Radical changes to work with offenders both in prison and the community were proposed as part of a 'radical reform of our criminal justice system' (Cabinet Office, 2010: 13).

> We will introduce a 'rehabilitation revolution' that will pay independent providers to reduce reoffending, paid for by the savings this new approach will generate within the criminal justice system. (Cabinet Office, 2010: 23)

Revolution, in this sense, refers to the process by which rehabilitation is structured rather than any distinct characteristics of the rehabilitation offered (Squires, 2016). Arguably, even by this definition, the terminology was misleading because there is a longer history of marketisation within both prison and probation. Voluntary sector involvement is long-standing and in recent times relationships have become more formalised (see Hucklesby and Corcoran, 2016). Similarly, private sector involvement has earlier roots, although, with the exception of private prisons, these are largely confined to peripheral services, for example, facilities management. There are two, albeit interrelated, important dimensions of the 'rehabilitation revolution'. The first is the organisation of 'offender management', a term formally adopted in 2004 to refer to correctional services in England and Wales when the National Offender Management Service (NOMS) was created to bring HM Prison Service and the National Probation Service into closer alignment (NOMS was replaced by HM Prison and Probation Service on 1st April 2017). The second dimension relates to the funding mechanism used to finance offender management. We will explore these two dimensions in turn.

The 'rehabilitation revolution' was operationalised through the TR agenda. A consultation paper was published early in 2013 (Ministry of Justice, 2013a) and a strategic document quickly followed (Ministry of Justice, 2013b). The first step was to split probation into a National Probation Service that would take responsibility for advising courts on the sentencing of *all* offenders and manage those assessed as at high risk of serious harm (to others) or with a prior history of domestic violence or sexual offences. The remainder, that is, those presenting with low or medium risk of harm were to be supervised by the newly created Community Rehabilitation Companies (CRCs). Initially established under public ownership in June 2014, they were transferred to new contracted providers eight months later. Around 80% of cases were initially allocated to the CRCs (National Audit Office, 2016) but there has been some movement since with reduced caseloads for the CRCs (and consequent financial implications) and higher than expected caseloads for the National Probation Service (NPS) (House of Commons Committee of Public Accounts, 2016).

TR is often conflated with the privatisation of probation and it is easy to understand why given the outcome of the extensive procurement exercise. From 19 bidders, 8 providers were selected to provide contracted services in 21 CRCs with a total lifetime contract value of £3.7 billion (National Audit Office, 2016). All but one of the 21 CRCs is controlled by private sector owners, who sometimes have responsibility for more than one company: for example, five are managed by Purple Futures, a partnership led by Interserve. The fact that through my study window I can look out at the construction work they are undertaking at the local secondary school provides an illustrative example of the breadth of their activities. The focus on private sector involvement downplays the contribution of others, including that of charities, public sector education providers, organisations formed by probation staff, a registered social landlord and social enterprises.

The extent of private sector involvement was far from unexpected, particularly given the financial package offered to contracted providers, which we will discuss shortly. Potentially, there was scope to create a 'mixed economy' of provision, fitting with the government emphasis at the time to create a 'Big Society'. This form of political ideology, popularised by David Cameron during his time as prime minister, emphasised the role of civil society in delivering community-based services and initiatives. The outcome of the procurement exercise echoes Morgan's (2012) warning that behind the notion of a 'Big Society' lurks a 'Big Market'. The lack of third (or voluntary) sector involvement was noted in a recent report commissioned by the House of Commons Committee on Public Accounts (2016). It criticises the Ministry of Justice and NOMS for failing to deliver on the pledge to support a varied market of providers and argues that it needs to do so to address gaps in services.

It is worth noting that these significant organisational changes followed soon after a series of attempts to modernise probation through changes in governance which have sought to extend central government control (Deering and Feilzer, 2015). Most significantly, the NPS was formed in 2001 via the Criminal Justice and Court Services Act 2001: 54 probation committees were replaced by 42 local probation boards, solely funded by the Home Office until 2007, when responsibilities were divided and oversight of offender management transferred to the Ministry of Justice. NPS became part of NOMS in 2004. From 2008, following the implementation of the Offender Management Act 2007, the process began of replacing the 42 local probation boards with 35 regional probation trusts responsible for both service provision and commissioning from voluntary and private sector organisations. Interested readers can explore the history of probation elsewhere (see Mair and Burke, 2012 for the most recent account). The backdrop to these changes is important but the scale of the changes introduced under the TR agenda was unprecedented. As Deering and Feilzer (2015) argue, the service has been split, partially privatised and no longer functions as an integrated public body.

Organisational changes also led to significant alterations to the prison estate. In November 2014, 80 out of 120 prisons in England and Wales, including all female prisons, were designated as resettlement prisons (HM Inspectorates of Prisons and Probation, 2016). CRCs assumed responsibility for delivering Through the Gate services in their allocated prisons, with work commencing within 72 hours of a prisoner being received into custody. This involves an initial screening and preparing a resettlement plan, alongside a series of other tasks including helping prisoners to find accommodation, which we will explore later in the chapter (NOMS, 2015). CRCs could choose whether to deliver these services 'in house' or to subcontract delivery to other organisations by setting up a supply chain.

The second dimension is the use of a payment-by-results (PbR) funding mechanism. This approach is not unique to criminal justice and has been used in a range of policy contexts, starting initially with the NHS (Gosling, 2016). It allows the government to commission services on the basis that the organisation will be paid according to the outputs (for example, reductions in reoffending) rather than the inputs (for example, the number of offenders supervised). The expectation is that a greater emphasis on outcomes will lead to more economic, efficient and innovative ways to working, encouraged by the tendering process as potential providers compete for contracts (Ministry of Justice, 2011). The use of PbR is an attractive option for governments, transferring risk and responsibility to the independent provider (Whitfield, 2012). However, in order to be successful it requires organisations to bid that are willing to accept the terms on offer. The model used to contract CRCs was diluted due to the lack of appetite among providers to accept anything other than one that allowed them to secure funding for outputs (for example, completing specified activities) rather than one focused on outcomes (for example, reductions in reoffending) (National Audit Office, 2016).

Prior to TR, there had been moves to introduce pilot PbR projects into prisons. HMP Peterborough – perhaps not coincidentally a privately run local prison for both female and male offenders – hosted the One Service. This operated on a philanthropic basis using Social Impact Bonds (see Fox and Albertson, 2011) with returns on investments (linked to reductions in reoffending (see Disley et al, 2011). This example illustrates how PbR mechanisms are not synonymous with attempts to pursue a privatisation agenda. However, the procurement process for managing CRCs was of a different scale, with far higher levels of risk. As a consequence, many voluntary organisations were unable to participate: the exceptions were those that were large and had a national base (for example, Addaction, NACRO, Shelter). Rodger's (2012: 19) fear that small-scale, locally based and often specialist services would be squeezed out as part of a 'industrialisation' of rehabilitation was realised in practice.

The drivers of the 'rehabilitation revolution' are a source of debate. It can be interpreted as an attempt to save money by a government keen to reduce public spending as part of its austerity measures. It was certainly the case that other parts of the criminal justice system were significantly affected by 'the cuts' (Garside and Ford, 2016). Reduced budgets for crime and justice are a significant departure from the past, when successive governments had been reluctant to scale back their efforts for fear of being seen as the party that is 'soft' on law and order matters (see Downes and Morgan, 2012 for an overview of law and order politics in general elections from 1945 to 2010). Equally it might be viewed in more ideological terms, forming part of a strategy to 'roll back the state' so that it retains direct responsibility only for those offenders judged to present the greatest risk to the public and where there is the strongest case for a clear line of accountability. We will now turn our attention to exploring whether a 'rehabilitation revolution' has occurred.

Through the prison gate: from prison to the community

The impact of TR was examined by the House of Commons Committee of Public Accounts late in 2016. Inevitably, given the remit of the committee which commissioned the report, its focus is on financial considerations. Nonetheless it provides an important early insight into the reforms, with the caveat that they were far from complete at that early stage. We focus here on the committee's findings in relation to the supervision of short-sentence prisoners but note the bigger picture, which suggests that the promise of a 'rehabilitation revolution' has yet to be fulfilled.

The report (House of Commons Committee of Public Accounts, 2016) questioned whether the extension of supervision to offenders sentenced to less than 12 months is having the desired impact, drawing attention in particular to the high rate of recalls among this group. It also drew attention to implementation problems surrounding the new Through the Gate resettlement services, which fell under the remit of the CRCs, highlighting the wide variation in the quality of these services across England and Wales. The report identified the challenge of companies contracted by NOMS working in partnership with housing, education and employment agencies (which may also be operating under contract) which lie outside the direct control of NOMS. One of the promises of TR was that it would encourage innovative practice. Contracted providers were given space to do so by the adoption of a deliberately unprescriptive approach to service delivery. It was hoped that that would provide sufficient flexibility to develop services more appropriate to the needs of minority groups of prisoners, such as women, in a way that would be impossible through the insistence on a 'one size fits all model'. In practice, this more targeted approached has yet to be implemented and instead there has been an over-reliance on group-based activities, believed to be a negative outcome of the existing commercial arrangements.

During the early stages of implementation, the number of recalls to prison for breaking licence conditions increased (House of Commons Committee of Public Accounts, 2016). This might be seen as evidence of success, in that more extensive supervision was resulting in a greater awareness of behaviour deemed to be unacceptable although not necessarily criminal. Equally, it might point to unsatisfactory supervision arrangements. Either way, it puts additional pressure on the prison estate which is already struggling to cope, reducing the likelihood that prisoners will receive quality resettlement support prior to their release, leading to negative outcomes when they return to the community.

A recent joint inspectorate report by HM Inspectorates of Prisons and Probation (2016) sheds some light on why this might be the case. Published in October 2016, it found evidence to support the concern that it had flagged ten months earlier that Through the Gate expectations were not being given priority 'on the ground', despite it being a flagship government policy which aimed to bring about a step change in rehabilitation practice and thus reducing the risk of reoffending. This was attributed to the funding model, which steered CRCs to prioritise work with more immediate results (and thus payments) and which is less challenging. This strategy – known as 'cherry picking' – is well documented in the literature on the implementation of PbR in other contexts (see Monaghan and Wincup, 2013). As we will explore in the next section, many factors linked to reoffending are beyond the control of CRCs, and indeed criminal justice agencies. As a consequence, the needs of individual prisoners were not properly identified and planned for, and not enough was done to help prisoners get ready for release. The review (HM Inspectorates of Prisons and Probation, 2016) identifies a series of problems culminating in a poor level of service for prisoners but also the wider community. It tries to maintain a positive tone, for example pointing to better service provision for female prisoners, but its recommendations point to the need for significant change if the strategic vision for Through the Gate services is to be realised.

Beyond criminal justice: prisoner resettlement in austere times

In the final section of this chapter, we examine some of the broader shifts in social policy over the past decade which have impacted upon prisoners. As many others have noted, the global fiscal crisis, which peaked in 2008, resulted in a series of austerity measures with greatest impact on those who rely upon the state for financial support. Like the criminal justice reforms considered earlier in this chapter, it is misleading to view them solely as an economic solution. Instead, it is important to recognise that how states responded to this crisis is a matter of political choice, and that governments may exploit such opportunities for political ends (see also Squires, 2016). Deficit reduction combined with a series of other aspirations around welfare reform which centred around tackling dependency. We focus here on two areas of social policy: social security and housing, both areas where there has been significant change as documented in previous volumes of *Social Policy Review* and most recently by Dwyer (2016) and Stephens and Stephenson (2016).

Social security policy and prisoners

Two features of the changing social security landscape over the past decade are worthy of note to set the scene for an exploration of a social security policy targeted at prisoners. The first is a 'deepening' and 'widening' of the obligation to work, from which only a minority are excused, and the second is a commitment to conditionality, interweaving support with discipline in the form of financial sanctions. Two flagship policies have emerged from this. In 2011, a Work Programme was introduced, a welfare-to-work initiative targeted in particular at the long-term unemployed. In 2013, Universal Credit was incrementally introduced: an attempt to simplify the benefits system through replacing six means-tested benefits with a single one. The chequered history of its implementation has been described elsewhere and attention has been paid to its most controversial aspects, including the move towards monthly payments and the extension of conditionality to those in work currently receiving 'tax credits' (Sainsbury, 2014). The former is likely to pose a significant challenge to those leaving prison with little experience of monthly budgeting.

A bespoke Work Programme for prison leavers was announced in March 2012 (Department for Work and Pensions, 2012) to operate in prisons across England, Wales and Scotland. Pilots were introduced two months later. Rather than having to fulfil the usual eligibility criteria relating to long-term unemployment, prisoners were expected to join the Work Programme immediately after release. This was in recognition of the considerable barriers to employability faced by offenders and the strong likelihood that their work histories were characterised by lengthy periods of unemployment (Fletcher, 2016). This intervention had high aspirations, defining success in terms of obtaining and retaining employment for two years. One anomaly is that the incentive payments offered to providers to work with prisoners were less than those offered to the most seriously disadvantaged in the labour market (see Wincup, 2013).

An evaluation of this targeted Work Programme was published late in 2014 (George et al, 2014). It describes in detail the implementation process but data were not available to determine how many released prisoners were helped to find work by the Work Programme (Black, 2016). What the evaluation reveals is high rates of sanctioning among this group because of their failure to comply with the conditions of the Work Programme. Over a quarter (28%) of those surveyed lost their benefits in part or in full, and rates were highest among those aged 25 and under. Fletcher (2016) found higher rates among his sample of offenders: 56% of the sample had been sanctioned, sometimes on more than one occasion. The use of sanctions escalated criminality as those without benefits, sometimes for long periods of time, engaged in survival crimes (Fletcher, 2016). Similarly, sanctioning was perceived as linked to family conflict, worsening mental health and homelessness – all known risk factors for (re)offending (Fletcher, 2016). Unsurprisingly, offenders viewed the social security system in terms of discipline rather than support (Fletcher, 2016).

The evaluation (George et al, 2014) also raises some fundamental questions about the 'work- first' approach, suggesting that some prisoners may need intensive support for long-term problems such as poor mental health, drug and alcohol dependency, and poor basic skills. It also drew attention to lack of housing as a considerable barrier to employability.

Housing policy and prisoners

The role of appropriate housing in the successful resettlement of prisoners is widely acknowledged (see, for example, Maguire and Nolan, 2007). I have documented elsewhere the challenges faced by prisoners in their attempts to secure housing as they negotiate a series of eligibility criteria and frequently find themselves excluded from social, private and voluntary sector housing (Wincup, 2013). Here I wish to draw out the implications of recent and planned future housing policy reforms on prisoners, which are only likely to exacerbate the problems faced by prisoners upon release.

The local housing allowance (LHA) which determines housing benefit entitlement was introduced in 2008. It applies solely to individuals who are renting accommodation from a private landlord. This applies to a significant number of former prisoners. Among this group, levels of home ownership are very low (Williams et al, 2012) and many will not be eligible for social housing, which is subject to strict eligibility criteria. Since 2002, ex-prisoners who can prove they are vulnerable have been included on the list of those in priority need and thus will be considered statutorily homeless. However, most prisoners (who are typically young, male and without dependents) will not meet the eligibility criteria (see Lund, 2011).

LHA is typically paid direct to tenants, although there is provision for it to be paid direct to a landlord if it there is a history of poor money management and it is judged that a direct payment might help an individual to retain their tenancy. This is a particular issue for former prisoners since the evidence points to problems such as debt and insufficient legitimate sources of income, but also financial exclusion (for example, lack of access to a bank account) (Citizens Advice, 2010). The rules relate to LHA are complex, but among the factors considered are the benefits already received by an individual. A benefits cap was announced by the Coalition government in the 2010 spending review and implemented in

2013 following provisions laid out in the Welfare Reform Act 2012. Age is also relevant. Those who are single (without dependents) and aged 35 and under are only eligible for a shared housing allowance rate, extending earlier provision to restrict the housing benefit for young people under 25 introduced in 1985. Some former prisoners will be 'excused' from a reduced level of financial support for housing. Care leavers are exempt until they are aged 22, and this is significant given the disproportionate number of care leavers among the prison population (Social Exclusion Unit, 2002). Similarly, those aged 25–35 who have lived in homeless hostels for at least three months and are accessing rehabilitation or support services before moving to the private rented sector are also exempt. Again, a number of former prisoners may fit within this category due to high levels of homelessness among those released (Williams et al, 2012). Finally, there are exemptions for former prisoners managed under the multi-agency public protection arrangements, that is, those with histories of sexual and/or violent offending.

We noted above the challenges of securing social housing for prisoners. Those most likely to be awarded tenancies are female prisoners, since they are more likely to be classified as in priority need due to pregnancy, responsibility for dependents, or experiences of domestic violence. Social housing tenants have also been subject to welfare reform measures; most controversially, the so-called 'bedroom tax'. This is an under-occupancy charge introduced in the Welfare Reform Act 2012, targeted at working-age tenants. It reduces the amount of benefit paid to individuals with a spare bedroom. How a spare bedroom is defined is a source of debate but it is worth noting that 'sanctuary rooms' count as spare bedroom. These are rooms adapted to make them secure for those who have experienced domestic violence. A significant proportion of the female prison population are victims of this form of crime (Corston, 2007). A further change affecting social housing tenants is the introduction of Universal Credit. Once this is fully implemented, the expectation is that social housing tenants will receive money for rent directly and are expected to transfer it to their housing provider, which could be problematic for the reasons described earlier in this chapter. Finally, the LHA is being extended beyond private sector accommodation to social housing. This will take place in April 2018 but applies to all new tenants from April 2016. For those in supported housing, a year's grace has been granted to allow time for decisions to be made about the allocation of additional 'top up' funding, which will be determined at a local level.

The potential impact of changes to the financing of supported housing is worthy of further discussion. At the time of writing, the government is consulting on funding for supported housing (Department for Communities and Local Government and Department for Work and Pensions, 2016). Ex-offenders are specifically referred to in the documentation alongside other groups who are over-represented among the known offender population: for example, those with drug or alcohol problems, vulnerable young people (citing care leavers as an example), homeless people and those experiencing mental health problems. The consultation document identifies the role of supported housing in what it terms 'recovery', helping ex-offenders to integrate back into the community. The details have still to be worked out, particularly in relation to short-term transitional supported accommodation, but service providers have expressed their concerns about the viability of supported housing provision (see, for example, Anders, 2016).

Conclusion

In this chapter we have explored some of the significant recent policy shifts with reference to released prisoners. We have considered points of disjuncture from the past alongside evidence of continuity. Criminal justice reforms have been contextualised so that parallels with policy developments in other areas of social policy have been noted. We have reflected upon how the experience of leaving prison is influenced by both criminal justice and social policies. Whether these are revolutionary times is a source of debate, but it is evident that the landscape has changed beyond recognition and the government has yet to make good on its promise of addressing the seemingly intractable high rates of reoffending among released prisoners. Moreover, the climate in which it is seeking to do so has grown colder. The pursuit of an austerity politics has made it more difficult for those released to desist from crime and, for many, the prison gate continues to be revolving door.

The state of our prisons is also far from conducive to effective preparation for release. Arguably prisons in England and Wales are in a state of perpetual crisis. At this particular point in time, the term 'crisis' appears to be an appropriate one to deploy but has been devalued by its overuse. Cavadino et al (2013) suggest that it is more accurate to refer to a series of interlocking crises, but largely stemming from a crisis of resources. There is ample evidence of crisis at the present moment in time. The prison population shows no sign of decreasing; there has been a series of violent disturbances, which in one case culminated in a private prison being returned to public control; deaths in custody have reached unprecedented levels; drug use within prisons, particularly the use of novel psychoactive substances, is widespread; and prisoners being locked up for extensive periods of time has become the norm in many prisons (see Prison Reform Trust, 2016). In such circumstances, it is hard to imagine that any meaningful work on helping prisoners work towards release can be undertaken and more likely that a period of imprisonment will do more harm than good.

References
Anders, P. (2016) 'Supporting supported housing', 15 September, www.revolving-doors.org.uk/blog/supporting-supported-housing

Black, C. (2016) *An independent review into the impact on employment outcomes of drug or alcohol addiction, and obesity*, www.gov.uk/government/uploads/system/uploads/attachment_data/file/573891/employment-outcomes-of-drug-or-alcohol-addiction-and-obesity.pdf

Cabinet Office (2010) *The Coalition: Our programme for government*, London: Cabinet Office.

Carlton, B. and Segrave, M. (2013) *Women exiting prison: Critical gender, post-release support and survival*, Abingdon: Routledge.

Cavadino, M., Dignan, J. and Mair, G. (2013) *The penal system: An introduction* (5th edn), London: Sage.

Citizens Advice (2010) *Improving the financial capability of offenders: A guide for Citizens Advice Bureaux and others*, www.citizensadvice.org.uk/Global/Migrated_Documents/corporate/improving-the-financial-capability-of-offenders-briefing.pdf

Clancy, A., Hudson, K., Maguire, M., Peake, R., Raynor, P., Vanstone, M. and Kynch, J. (2006) *Getting out and staying out: Results of the resettlement pathfinders*, Bristol: Policy Press.

Corston, J. (2007) *The Corston report: A report by Baroness Jean Corston of a review of women with vulnerabilities in the criminal justice system*, London: Home Office.

Deering, J. and Feilzer, M. (2015) *Privatising probation: Is transforming rehabilitation the end of a probation ideal?*, Bristol: Policy Press.

Department for Communities and Local Government and Department for Work and Pensions (2016) *Funding for supported housing: Consultation*, www.gov.uk/government/uploads/system/uploads/attachment_data/file/571013/161121_-_Supported_housing_consultation.pdf

Department for Work and Pensions (2012) 'Government launches employment support for prisoners', Press Release, 6 March, www.gov.uk/government/news/government-launches-employment-support-for-prisoners

Disley, E., Rubin, J., Scragg, E., Burrowes, N. and Culley, D. (2011) *Lessons learned from the planning and early implementation of the social impact bond of HMP Peterborough*, Research Series 5/11, London: Ministry of Justice.

Downes, D. and Morgan, R. (2012) 'Overtaking on the left? The politics of "law and order" in the "Big Society"', in M. Maguire, R. Morgan and R. Reiner (eds) *The Oxford Handbook of Criminology* (5th edn), Oxford: Oxford University Press.

Dwyer, P. (2016) 'Citizenship, conduct and conditionality: sanction and support in the 21st-century UK welfare state', in M. Fenger, J. Hudson and C. Needham (eds) *Social Policy Review 28: Analysis and debate in social policy, 2016*, Bristol: Policy Press.

Farrell, S. (2004) 'Social capital and offender reintegration: making probation desistance focused', in S. Maruna and R. Immarigeon (eds) *After crime and punishment: Pathways to offender reintegration*, Cullompton: Willan Publishing.

Fergusson, R. (2016) *Young people, welfare and crime: Governing non-participation*, Bristol: Policy Press.

Fletcher, D. (2016) 'First wave findings: offenders', May, www.welfareconditionality.ac.uk/wp-content/uploads/2016/05/WelCond-findings-offenders-May16.pdf

Fox, C. and Albertson, K. (2011) 'Payment by results and Social Impact Bonds', *Criminology and Criminal Justice*, 11(5): 395–413.

Garside, R. and Ford, M. (2016) *UK Justice Policy Review*, vol. 5, 6 May 2014 to 5 May 2015, www.crimeandjustice.org.uk/sites/crimeandjustice.org.uk/files/UK%20Justice%20Policy%20Review%205,%20Mar%202016.pdf

George, A., Metcalf, H., Hunter, G., Bertram, C., Newton, B., Skrine, O. and Turnbull, P. (2014) 'Evaluation of day one mandation of prison leavers to the Work Programme', London: Department for Work and Pensions.

Gosling, H. (2016) 'Payment by results: challenges and conflicts for the therapeutic community', *Criminology and Criminal Justice*, 16(5): 519–33.

Hedderman, C. (2007) 'Rediscovering resettlement: narrowing the gap between policy rhetoric and practice reality', in A. Hucklesby and L. Hagley-Dickinson (eds) *Prisoner resettlement: Policy and practice*, Cullompton: Willan Publishing.

HM Inspectorates of Prisons and Probation (2001) *Through the prison gate: A joint thematic review by HM Inspectorates of Prison and Probation*, London: Home Office.

HM Inspectorates of Prisons and Probation (2016) *An inspection of Through the Gate resettlement services for short-term prisoners*, www.justiceinspectorates.gov.uk/cjji/wp-content/uploads/sites/2/2016/09/Through-the-Gate.pdf

Home Office (2004) *Reducing reoffending: National action plan*, London: Home Office.

House of Commons Committee of Public Accounts (2016) *Transforming rehabilitation: Seventeenth report of session 2016–17*, www.publications.parliament.uk/pa/cm201617/cmselect/cmpubacc/484/484.pdf Hucklesby, A. (2009) 'Keeping the lid on the prison remand population: the experience in England and Wales', *Current Issues in Criminal Justice*, 21(1): 3–23.

Hucklesby, A. and Corcoran, M. (eds) (2016) *The voluntary sector and criminal justice*, London: Palgrave Macmillan.

Hucklesby, A. and Hagley-Dickinson, L. (eds) (2007) *Prisoner resettlement: Policy and practice*, Cullompton: Willan Publishing

Levitas, R., Pantazis, C., Fahmy, E., Gordon, D., Lloyd, E. and Patsios, D. (2007) *The multi-dimensional nature of social exclusion*, London: Cabinet Office.

Lewis, S., Vennard, J., Maguire, M., Raynor, P., Vanstone, M., Raybould, S. and Rix, A. (2003) *The resettlement of short-term prisoners: An evaluation of seven pathfinders*, RDS Occasional Paper 83, London: Home Office.

Lund, B. (2011) *Understanding housing policy* (2nd edn), Bristol: Policy Press.

Maguire, M. and Nolan, J. (2007) 'Accommodation and related services for ex-prisoners', in A. Hucklesby and L. Hagley-Dickinson (eds) *Prisoner resettlement: Policy and practice*, Cullompton: Willan Publishing.

Mair, G. and Burke, L. (2012) *Redemption, rehabilitation and risk management: A history of probation*, Abingdon: Routledge.

Ministry of Justice (2011) *Competition strategy for offender services*, London: Ministry of Justice.

Ministry of Justice (2012) *Proven re-offending statistics quarterly bulletin, January to December 2010, England and Wales*, www.gov.uk/government/statistics/proven-reoffending-earlier-editions

Ministry of Justice (2013a) *Transforming rehabilitation: A revolution in how we manage offenders*, https://consult.justice.gov.uk/digital-communications/transforming-rehabilitation/supporting_documents/transformingrehabilitation.pdf

Ministry of Justice (2013b) *Transforming rehabilitation: A strategy for reform*, https://consult.justice.gov.uk/digital-communications/transforming-rehabilitation/results/transforming-rehabilitation-response.pdf

Ministry of Justice (2015) *Statistics on race and the criminal justice system 2014*, www.gov.uk/government/uploads/system/uploads/attachment_data/file/480250/bulletin.pdf

Ministry of Justice (2016) *Prison release: Q2 2016*, www.gov.uk/government/statistics/offender-management-statistics-quarterly-april-to-june-2016

Ministry of Justice (2017) *Proven reoffending statistics bulletin, April 2014 to March 2015*, www.gov.uk/government/statistics/proven-reoffending-statistics-april-2014-to-march-2015

Ministry of Justice and NOMS (National Offender Management Service) (2016) *Story of the prison population 1993 to 2016*, www.gov.uk/government/statistics/story-of-the-prison-population-1993-to-2016

Ministry of Justice, NOMS (National Offender Management Service) and HM Prison Service (2017) *Population bulletin: weekly 29 January 2017*, www.gov.uk/government/statistics/prison-population-figures-2017

Monaghan, M. and Wincup, E. (2013) 'Work and the journey to recovery: exploring the implications of welfare reform for methadone maintenance clients', *International Journal of Drug Policy*, 24(6): e81–86.

Moore, R. (2012) 'Beyond the prison walls: some thoughts on prisoners "resettlement" in England and Wales', *Criminology and Criminal Justice*, 12(2): 129–47.

Morgan, R. (2012) 'Crime and justice in the "Big Society"', *Criminology and Criminal Justice*, 12(5): 463–81.

National Audit Office (2016) *Transforming rehabilitation*, www.nao.org.uk/wp-content/uploads/2016/04/Transforming-rehabilitation.pdf

NOMS (National Offender Management Service) (2015) *A guide to 'Through the Gate' resettlement services*, London: National Offender Management Service.

Padfield, N. and Maruna, S. (2006) 'The revolving door: exploring the rise in recalls to prison', *Criminology and Criminal Justice*, 6(3): 329–52.

Prison Reform Trust (2011) *Innocent until proven guilty: Tackling the overuse of custodial remand*, www.prisonreformtrust.org.uk/Portals/0/Documents/Remand%20Briefing%20FINAL.PDF

Prison Reform Trust (2016) *Bromley briefings prison factfile, autumn 2016*. www.prisonreformtrust.org.uk/Portals/0/Documents/Bromley%20Briefings/Autumn%202016%20Factfile.pdf

Raynor, P. (2007) 'Theoretical perspectives on resettlement: what it is and how it might work', in A. Hucklesby and L. Hagley-Dickinson (eds) *Prisoner resettlement: Policy and practice*, Cullompton: Willan Publishing.

Rodger, J. (2012) 'Rehabilitation revolution in the Big Society', in A. Silvestri (ed.) *Critical reflections: Social and criminal justice in the first year of the Coalition government*, London: Centre for Crime and Justice Studies.

Sainsbury, R. (2014) 'Universal Credit: the story so far', *Journal of Poverty and Social Justice*, 22(1): 11–13.

Social Exclusion Unit (2002) *Reducing reoffending by ex-prisoners*, London: Cabinet Office.

Squires, P. (2016) 'The Coalition and criminal justice', in H. Bochel and M. Powell (eds) *The Coalition government and social policy: Restructuring the welfare state*, Bristol: Policy Press.

Stephens, M. and Stephenson, M. (2016) 'Housing policy in the austerity age and beyond', in M. Fenger, J. Hudson and C. Needham (eds) *Social Policy Review 28: Analysis and debate in social policy, 2016*, Bristol: Policy Press.

Tanner-Smith, E., Wilson, S. and Lipsey, M. (2012) 'Risk factors and crime', in F. Cullen and P. Wilcox (eds) *The Oxford handbook of criminological theory*, Oxford: Oxford University Press.

Whitfield, D. (2012) 'The payment-by-results road to marketisation', in A. Silvestri (ed.) *Critical reflections: Social and criminal justice in the first year of the Coalition government*, London: Centre for Crime and Justice Studies.

Williams, K., Poyser, J. and Hopkins, K. (2012) *Accommodation, homelessness and reoffending of prisoners: Results from the Surveying Prisoner Crime Reduction (SPCR) survey*, Ministry of Justice Research Summary 3/12, www.gov.uk/government/uploads/system/uploads/attachment_data/file/278806/homelessness-reoffending-prisoners.pdf

Wincup, E. (2013) *Understanding crime and social policy*, Bristol: Policy Press.

FOUR

Confronting Brexit and Trump: towards a socially progressive globalisation

Chris Holden

On 23 June 2016, British citizens voted to leave the European Union (EU). Less than five months later on 8 November, American citizens elected Donald Trump as the President of the United States of America (USA). A consensus quickly emerged that both votes represented a reaction against 'globalization' by 'dispossessed', 'left behind' population segments (Harris, 2016). Guy Ryder, the director general of the International Labour Organization (ILO), called it 'the revolt of the dispossessed', arguing that: 'The societies we all live in are distributing the benefits of globalisation and economic processes extraordinarily unfairly and people think they are getting a raw deal' (cited in Allen, 2016). The consensus also identified 'global elites' as the target of this vote of dissatisfaction (although in some of the right-wing media coverage this was cleverly repackaged as a rejection of an undefined 'liberal elite', thus implying a rejection of 'liberal' politics rather than the inequalities associated with neoliberal globalisation). President Barack Obama, for example, observed that: 'When we see people, global elites, wealthy corporations seemingly living by a different set of rules, avoiding taxes, manipulating loopholes … this feeds a profound sense of injustice' (cited in Smith, 2016).

There are clearly idiosyncratic aspects of each vote. In the UK, for example, a deeply Eurosceptic national press sustained a discourse over a number of years prior to the referendum, in which the EU was portrayed overwhelmingly as a foreign threat to British sovereignty rather than as a common European project (Hawkins, 2012). The complexities of EU membership, let alone those pertaining to an exit process, were never properly explained to the British electorate. Furthermore, while Trump has promoted deeply protectionist politics in the USA, the dominant discourse in the UK has been one of the need for continuing liberalised trade outside of the EU (albeit without free movement of people). While recognising these specificities, however, it seems credible that both votes reflect a deep dissatisfaction among particular population groups with the outcomes of neoliberal globalisation. These outcomes are simultaneously economic, social, political and cultural, and it is difficult to disentangle the interaction between these elements, especially since they may not be separated in the minds of voters themselves. The perceived impact of immigration was a key element in both cases. Here, I focus primarily on the economic and social, rather than the cultural, aspects of neoliberal globalisation, particularly the trend towards greater inequality and the reaction against it.

The neoliberal globalisation process was set in train in large part by US President Ronald Reagan and British Prime Minister Margaret Thatcher in the 1980s, in reaction to the perceived failures of nationally-regulated 'Keynesian' capitalism. Yet this neoliberal globalisation is just one possible template for transnational cooperation and integration. The post-war international settlement hammered out at Bretton Woods and elsewhere managed to significantly lower trade barriers and facilitate high levels of global integration without leading to wholesale restrictions on national policy space (Rodrik, 2011). Neoliberal globalisation has gone beyond this in reducing to a minimum national regulations on finance and capital flows, and in instituting forms of 'trade' liberalisation that have little to do with tariffs or quotas, but which strip governments of their powers to regulate and support domestic industry. Such developments have been implemented side by side with welfare state retrenchment, privatisation policies and a substantial growth in inequality.

Belatedly, erstwhile proponents of neoliberal globalisation are beginning to realise the social damage caused by that model. President Barack Obama, who for most of his period in office had promoted continuing trade liberalisation, called for a 'course correction' of the 'path of globalization', in order to 'make sure that the benefits of an integrated global economy are more broadly shared by more people, and that the negative impacts are squarely addressed' (cited in Smith, 2016). *The Economist* magazine ran a supplement arguing against a turn away from economic liberalisation, but conceded that 'The strains inflicted by a more integrated global economy were underestimated, and too little effort went into helping those who lost out' (O'Sullivan, 2016: 5). The World Economic Forum (2017: 6) identified rising income and wealth disparity as the most important trend determining global developments over the next ten years, noting that 'the growing mood of anti-establishment populism suggests we may have passed the stage where [reviving economic growth] alone would remedy fractures in society: reforming market capitalism must also be added to the agenda'.

Global social policy scholars have been analysing the social aspects of globalisation for some years now, and have often made the case for socially just forms of globalisation (Townsend and Donkor, 1996; Yeates, 2001; George and Wilding, 2002; Deacon, 2006, 2007). In a period when technological advance makes the world seem smaller regardless of political processes, the only alternative to some form of international cooperation and global integration is a destructive turn towards populist nationalism, although the optimum balance between national and global forms of governance is not an obvious one (Rodrik, 2011). Nevertheless, the horrors of the 1930s and 1940s were a calamitous lesson as to where nationalism can lead. Below I make a case for a socially progressive globalisation as an alternative to the shift towards nationalism that is currently in train.

The dangers of writing six months ahead of publication, in what is a fast moving political environment, are evident. It is too soon to know what the outcome of Brexit negotiations will be, or just how damaging a president Donald Trump will prove to be for the USA and the world. My intention is not to foresee future events, however, but rather to analyse some of the underlying economic, social and political factors explaining the two votes, identify the inherent dangers of a retreat to nationalism, and suggest an alternative way forward. I first review the relevant economic and social factors underlying the two votes, with a focus upon the growth of inequality during the period of neoliberal globalisation. I then discuss the apparent nationalist backlash against neoliberal globalisation. Finally, I discuss the elements of a socially progressive globalisation. The focus throughout is on high-income countries, where the backlash against neoliberal globalisation has most recently manifested itself. Yet this should not lead us to ignore the needs of the global South. While China has made impressive gains, it has often been low-income countries that have got the worst deal from the current form of globalisation. A socially progressive globalisation must also foreground the needs of the global South, although that is not the main topic of this article.

Neoliberal globalisation and inequality

Until 2008, the era of neoliberal globalisation following the 1970s was accompanied by continuing, if erratic, growth for high-income countries and high rates of growth for some low- and middle-income countries. However, high-income countries' growth rates have not matched those of the 'long boom' of the post-war period, and many low-income countries did not benefit from the neoliberal policy prescriptions imposed upon them. Furthermore, the neoliberal deregulation of finance led to an unstable model of capitalism, which has resulted in repeated financial crises, culminating in that of 2007–08. Neoliberal globalisation increases the opportunity for the rich to avoid or evade taxes via tax havens and for transnational corporations (TNCs) to profit from cheap labour overseas and to avoid taxes via transfer pricing. A globally mobile transnational capitalist class sees less need to maintain a social contract at home in the form of a welfare state, and welfare states are seen as costly impediments to attracting investment.

Where growth has occurred, the wealth produced has rarely been distributed in an equitable way. Piketty suggests that, while there have been fluctuations in levels of inequality, a key tendency of capitalist economies, particularly during periods of low growth, is for returns to capital to outpace growth of the economy itself, thus leading to greater inequality (Piketty, 2014). In this context, the post-Second World War reduction of inequality in the advanced welfare states, Piketty argues, should be understood principally as the result of the two world wars themselves and of post-war political settlements involving welfare state development, but not as an enduring shift towards greater equality.

The post-war reduction of inequality in high-income countries increasingly looks like a temporary blip in an overarching process of widening inequalities of wealth and income. The Organisation for Economic Co-operation and Development (OECD) reports that income inequality increased in 17 of the 22 OECD countries for which long-term data series were available between 1985 and 2008, with the average Gini coefficient rising from 0.29 to 0.316 (OECD, 2011: 22). Gough (2011) notes how consumer debt rose extensively during this neoliberal period, in order to provide the demand necessary to sustain high levels of output, which could no longer be provided by the limited growth of wages. This extension of debt accompanied deregulation of the financial sector, was in part a product of it and in turn enhanced its growth, thus creating an unsustainable 'financialised' capitalism (Gough, 2011). According to Stiglitz (2013: 120), prior to the 2008 financial crisis, 40% of all corporate profits in the US went to the financial sector.

Responses to the financial crisis and resulting recession have only exacerbated the general trend towards greater inequality. Government bailouts of failing banks, large fiscal stimulus in the immediate wake of the crisis, growing unemployment and recession, followed by slow growth, have led to a massive increase in government indebtedness (Gough, 2011). Governments have responded, in varying degrees, with austerity programmes that cut benefits and public services, with little in the way of additional taxation of the wealthiest – who gained most during the period of neoliberal expansion – thus forcing those on the lowest incomes to pay for the crisis.

OECD data show that higher-income households have benefited more from the partial economic recovery since 2008 than have middle- and low-income households (OECD, 2016a). The persistence of long-term unemployment and slow wage growth meant that labour incomes of poorer households have remained low in many countries. In the UK, real wages have remained low despite job growth. The data show that across OECD countries, the average Gini coefficient of disposable household income reached 0.318 in 2013/14, only slightly higher than in 2007, but higher than any point since the mid-1980s (OECD, 2016a). In 2014, the latest year for which data are available, household disposable incomes remained below pre-crisis levels, especially for the bottom decile. While redistribution largely offset the increase in market income inequality in the early post-crisis period, the turn to austerity has hit those with low wages or without labour incomes particularly hard. Redistribution has decreased in a majority of OECD countries since 2010.

The extreme nature of contemporary inequality, involving the concentration of wealth in the hands of a tiny elite, is often overlooked. A number of scholars have noted how the wealthy elite in the US has captured the political process, using it to reinforce their own accumulation of wealth at the expense of the vast majority of citizens (Hacker and Pierson, 2010; Stiglitz, 2013). The 'Occupy' movement in the US and other countries adopted as its slogan 'we are the 99%', and indeed Hacker and Pierson (2010: 155) show that in the US the richest 1% increased its share of pre-tax income from about 8% in 1974 to more than 18% in 2007, and from 9% to 23.5% during the same period when investment and dividend income is included. Yet even these figures obscure the actual level of concentration, with the share of the top 0.1% (the richest 150,000 families) increasing from 2.7% to 12.3%, and the share of the top 0.01% (the richest 15,000 families) increasing from 'less than one in every one hundred dollars in 1974 to more than one of every seventeen – or more than 6 percent of national income accruing to 0.01 percent' (Hacker and Pierson, 2010: 155).

That inequality has been growing during the period of neoliberal globalisation is now widely accepted. However, until recently, few governments or international organisations accepted that this was in itself a serious problem, and even now few accept that it is their responsibility to tackle it (Holden, 2014a). As long as economies were growing, increasing disparities of income and wealth could be ignored. That changed after 2008, with the OECD and International Monetary Fund (IMF) now warning of the dangers inherent in increasing social polarisation, yet no coherent plan for a more equitable globalisation has been forthcoming. Without it, a slide into regressive nationalism threatens to drown the gains from globalisation rather than its injustices.

Into the fire? Global markets and the nationalist trap

As Held and McGrew (2007: 28) point out, for most of human history most people lived out their lives in extremely localised cultures. Nation states have been the world's primary political units for little more than a couple of hundred years. Prior to this, and coterminous with the development of nation states in Europe, polities took a variety of forms, the most widespread and persistent being city states and empires. In the period of neoliberal globalisation, the state has continued as the world's main political unit, underpinning other forms of organisation, but has increasingly ceded power 'upwards' to international organisations and 'downwards' to subnational regions, cities and localities (Hirst and Thompson, 1999: 270; Agnew, 2005: 444). The EU is perhaps the most developed example of the ceding 'upwards' of powers, via a partial pooling of national sovereignty, but 'downward' disaggregation of the national state is also apparent in the creation of special economic zones (SEZs) and in the ceding of more autonomy to subnational political units (Holden and Hudson, in press). This process has been overlaid with a variety of international and transnational organisations and agreements, as the territory and functions of the state have been partially 'unbundled' (Ruggie, 1993), giving rise to what Grande and Pauly (2005) call 'complex governance'. In some ways, the current period resembles the medieval world, where populations were subject to a range of overlapping authorities, but in this case on a global scale (Cerny, 1998).

Yet the nation state remains at the centre of social, political and economic life in two ways: it is the organisational foundation upon which other (supranational, subnational and crosscutting) organisational forms usually rest; and it provides the cultural 'glue' and the basis for the identity of the majority of its citizens. As Rodrik (2011) makes clear, the appropriate balance between global markets, global governance and national sovereignty is not an obvious one, but a strong case can be made that global market liberalisation has gone too far. That overreaching may well give rise to a nationalist backlash that goes too far in the opposite direction, with profound consequences for economic growth and stability and for social tensions.

Unsurprisingly, a number of groups and organisations have for some time posited a return to a more robust nationhood as a response to the cultural disruptions and material inequities of neoliberal globalisation (Held and McGrew, 2007: 198–99). The Brexit vote and Trump's victory in the US presidential election in some ways represent just the most recent of such tendencies. With reference to the growth of the 'precariat', Standing (2011: 148) has observed how insecurity can breed anger and how such anger can render people susceptible to the messages of populists and demagogues. He notes how former Italian prime minister Silvio Berlusconi and his colleagues 'called the judiciary "a cancer" and dismissed Parliament as "a useless entity"', a tendency reflected in the *Daily Mail*'s labelling of the UK's High Court judges, who ruled that only Parliament could invoke Article 50 to leave the EU, as 'the enemies of the people' (Slack, 2016). Standing (2011: 151) calls this 'a politics of inferno', noting that: 'Unless mainstream parties offer the precariat an agenda of economic security and social mobility, a substantial part will continue to drift to the dangerous extreme.'

Trump's election, in particular, poses a profound threat to the global liberal order, precisely because it demonstrates how millions of people who feel disenfranchised can assert themselves through the democratic institutions of liberal capitalist states in ways that, at their most worrying, threaten to undermine some of the most cherished aspects of those institutions. Trump's demagoguery and apparent disregard for some aspects of the rule of law, such as his refusal during the election campaign to commit to accepting the outcome of the election should he lose, are one example of this. The targeting of migrants is a particularly dangerous aspect of this politics, with Trump threatening to seek out and deport undocumented Latin American migrants.

In economic policy, Trump's nationalism manifests itself in a commitment to trade protection, yet this is married to an incongruous set of other economic policies, including deregulation of the financial sector, borrowing for infrastructure investment and sweeping tax cuts. Arguing that trade liberalisation has led to the substitution of millions of American manufacturing jobs by those in Mexico or China, Trump has pledged to renegotiate or even scrap the North American Free Trade Agreement (NAFTA) and a series of bilateral free trade agreements (FTAs), raise tariffs on Mexican goods to 35%, raise tariffs on Chinese goods to 45%, and even to withdraw from the World Trade Organization

(WTO). Such measures could provoke a trade war, which the Peterson Institute for International Economics estimates would lead to the loss of between 1.3 million and 4.8 million American jobs, depending on its severity (Noland et al, 2016). The termination of NAFTA and FTAs with Central American countries could lead to economic disruption that would increase incentives for migration and illicit flows into the USA (Noland, 2016). Trump's statements during the election also suggest that other international agreements and institutions may be under threat, most importantly the Paris climate agreement. Trump's nomination of Rex Tillerson, the chief executive of ExxonMobil, as his secretary of state suggests both his lack of concern about climate change and the nature of his government as one that will work for the corporate elite, not for those on low and moderate incomes who voted for him. Those already nominated for Trump's Cabinet at the time of writing constituted the richest US Cabinet in history (Neate, 2016).

On tax, Trump argued for reductions in income tax rates for all income brackets, including the wealthiest, the scrapping of federal estate and gift taxes, and for reducing corporation tax from 35% to as low as 15%. He may offer an amnesty to companies willing to repatriate billions of dollars worth of profits currently held abroad. The Tax Policy Center (2016) estimates that the plan would reduce annual federal tax revenue by about 4% of GDP, with the federal debt rising by at least $7 trillion over ten years. The plan would much favour the rich. The top 0.1%, those earning more than $3.7 million a year, would gain a tax cut of nearly $1.1 million, or 14% of their after-tax income on average. The poorest fifth would gain just $110 a year, or 0.8% of their income. Planning to cut taxes for the wealthy while borrowing for investment, in a context of massive and growing inequalities, is both inequitable and economically risky. In terms of fiscal stimulus, it would make much more sense to reduce taxes for those on low incomes, who spend a greater proportion of their incomes, and to use taxation of the wealthy to part-fund infrastructure investment.

In the UK, the new Conservative Prime Minister Theresa May sought to strike an uneasy balance between recognising dissatisfaction with inequality and insecurity, allying herself to nationalist sentiment, and promoting a global, neoliberal, vision of the UK outside of the EU. In her speech to the Conservative Party conference following the referendum, for example, May empathised with the sense 'that many people have today that the world works well for a privileged few, but not for them'; derided cosmopolitanism by arguing that 'if you believe you're a citizen of the world, you're a citizen of nowhere. You don't understand what the very word "citizenship" means'; and asserted that her government would build 'a Global Britain' and always act 'as the strongest and most passionate advocate for free trade right across the globe' (May, 2016).

The actual likely emphasis of May's government, beyond rhetoric, was hinted at in a speech to the Confederation of British Industry (CBI). In a classic example of the 'race to the bottom', she suggested that corporation tax, already reduced by George Osborne when Chancellor from 28% to 20%, and due to be cut further to 17% by 2020, might be lowered still further to 15% so as not to be undercut by Trump's tax plans (Syal and Walker, 2016). If a favourable deal was not forthcoming from the EU following Article 50 negotiations, it was suggested that the rate could be cut still further to 10%, to undercut the rates of the vast majority of EU member states (Mowat, 2016). Simultaneously, May appeared to row back on a commitment to place worker representatives on company boards (Syal and Walker, 2016). It was even suggested by one Conservative MP that the government might open up a series of free ports (a form of SEZ) across the UK (Sunak, 2016). SEZs represent the ultimate form of neoliberal globalisation, in which, at its worst, social conditions and effective regulations are sacrificed in an attempt to compete economically (Holden and Hudson, in press).

For British Conservatives, an a priori commitment to neoliberalism means that their nationalism is usually subordinated to the needs of the global market, whatever the rhetoric. While opposing free movement of labour, they therefore aggressively support most other forms of liberalisation. This is not the case for Trump, nor for Marine Le Pen of the French National Front, who, at the time of writing, was likely to attain a place in the run-off for the French presidency in May 2017. I argue below that there is an alternative to a globalised neoliberalism with its gross inequalities, on the one hand, and a reactionary nationalism (perhaps with equally gross inequalities) on the other.

Towards a socially just globalisation

In the contemporary world political economy, social justice must rest on both national and global measures. Some aspects of the recent 'unbundling' of the nation state may need to be 'reterritorialised', 'reshored' or 'onshored' (Urry, 2014). National economic and social policies are crucial, and some international institutions and agreements will need reforming. Whether, to what extent, and how this is done is a matter of the utmost importance. Getting it wrong risks a lowering of national income for all countries, a potential trade war, an increase in global instability, and an increase in jingoism and intolerance. Yet, as *The Economist* (2016a) succinctly puts it, 'Unless the share of GDP in the developed world shifts in favour of labour and away from capital, populists will be elected'.

Comprehensive welfare states at the national level are not incompatible with international trade. The trend in high-income countries to scale back welfare states has been part of the neoliberal package, which sees liberalisation in all areas as necessary and positive. In this vision, free trade, liberalised labour markets, welfare retrenchment, privatisation and reduction (or at least containment) of state expenditure go together. Yet robust welfare states are necessary to protect workers from the effects of the greater economic instability, industrial restructuring and occasional economic shocks that accompany increased trade openness (Holden, 2014b). Welfare states act also as macroeconomic 'automatic stabilisers' in times of recession, increasing expenditure (and thus demand) by the unemployed, as well as ensuring they have incomes sufficient to meet their needs.

In the current period of continuing slow growth, globally and in most national economies, following the 2007–08 financial crisis, nationally based programmes of infrastructure investment may well be warranted. To ward off continuing recession, central banks have maintained near zero interest rate policies and, in some cases, resorted to effectively printing money via 'quantitative easing'. The problem with such policies is that it would be difficult to extend them much further should another shock hit the relevant economies, and they worsen inequality by inflating the price of assets. In that context, and when interest rates remain low, it makes sense for governments to borrow and invest in 'Keynesian' fashion. This policy, in one form or another, has a remarkable level of consensus behind it, being supported by those as diverse as Donald Trump, the UK Labour Party, *The Economist* magazine and economists such as Joseph Stiglitz and Paul Krugman. Nevertheless, there are important differences in the various policy prescriptions, with different implications for their economic effectiveness and for social justice. Reducing taxes for, or subsidising, those on the lowest incomes, while introducing higher taxes for the wealthy, and borrowing where necessary to invest in educational, health and transport infrastructure, would optimise the mix of economic and social effectiveness.

One problem with this kind of fiscal stimulus in an integrated world economy is that it can 'leak' out of the country, creating demand for foreign goods and services rather than domestic ones. The way round this is international coordination, something achieved in the early days following the 2007–08 crisis, before governments flipped self-defeatingly into austerity mode. Keynesian measures may seem easier to implement in Trump's protectionist vision, but protectionism is likely to choke off growth, increase prices for all (including those who can least afford it) and lead ultimately to economic failure. Unfortunately, the immediate effect of Trump's version of fiscal stimulus might well be a temporary growth spurt, facilitating his re-election in 2020, before eventual economic ruin (Krugman, 2016; Elliott, 2016).

To tackle the vast inequalities that have been facilitated by neoliberal globalisation, it is essential to readjust tax systems to make them more progressive. Much can be done here by national governments acting alone. In addition to a more progressive income tax system, wealth taxes should be considered. There is a strong case for strengthening estate or inheritance taxes (Prabhakar, 2011), something both Trump and the UK's Conservative Party would like to see reduced or even abolished. Piketty (2014: 524–27) makes a strong case for a combination of progressive taxes on income, inheritance and wealth.

Yet, while many progressive tax and other measures can be implemented by governments acting alone, taming the neoliberal global economy and its inequities will require international cooperation if a damaging retreat into nationalism and/or a 'race to the bottom' in tax rates are to be avoided. Piketty (2014: 515–39) argues that the goal should be to work towards a global wealth tax. Doing so would require much greater financial transparency and sharing of bank data than currently exists, something which is necessary even for an effective nationally implemented wealth tax. The activities of tax havens, which facilitate the massive evasion and avoidance of taxation, need to be severely curtailed. The use of transfer pricing by TNCs to ensure that their profits are declared in jurisdictions where they pay least tax also needs to be tackled. The OECD has begun work on combatting tax evasion and avoidance under its 'base erosion and profit shifting' (BEPS) programme, work that needs to be intensified and built upon. As the OECD points out, only TNCs can make use of such measures, giving them 'a competitive advantage over enterprises that operate at a domestic level' and undermining the compliance of all taxpayers (OECD, 2016b). The aim is to give countries 'the tools to ensure that profits are taxed where economic activities generating the profits are performed and where value is created' (OECD, 2016b). Yet we need to go further than the OECD's current initiative and, for example, conclude an international agreement to set minimum rates of taxation, particularly for corporations.

The deregulation of finance is a significant factor explaining the growth of inequality, both because of the excessive incomes in the sector and as a result of the 2007–08 crisis, which caused the 'great recession' and led to a substantial transfer of wealth from taxpayers to the banks via government bailouts and subsequent austerity policies. While the financial sector needs to be properly regulated, it could also be taxed in innovative ways. This could include an international financial transaction tax, which would levy a small percentage on every financial transaction. A tax of this kind was proposed by James Tobin in the 1970s (Tobin, 1978). Such a tax could potentially discourage excessive risk taking and recover some of the costs of the economic crisis from the financial institutions that carry such a large responsibility for it (Burman et al, 2016). With sufficient international political will, such a tax would be easier to implement than a global wealth tax, although it could be complementary to such a tax.

It is instructive that while we have a World Trade Organization, we do not have a world tax organisation. Liberalised trade has been the focus for much of the current reaction against globalisation, principally because it can make jobs less secure. In a period when neoliberals have insisted that labour regulations are also liberalised and welfare states cut back, this has led to deep insecurity. This in turn has fed demands for trade protection, particularly in the USA, where social protection is less developed than in Europe. It is in this context, also, that we need to understand the shift of opinion against migration. Selective protection of domestic industries, at least temporarily, is sometimes warranted. Both high-income countries and East Asian 'tiger' economies used such measures during the period of their industrialisation (Chang, 2003). However, blanket protection is highly likely to lead to falls in national income for all countries, and unilateral resort to protectionism risks a trade war. The latter would be disastrous, not least because it would undermine the multilateral system.

The US and the EU have already partially undermined the WTO system by initiating a series of trade and investment agreements outside of its auspices, in an attempt to outmanoeuvre China following the stalling of the WTO's Doha round of negotiations. The most important of these agreements are the Trans-Pacific Partnership (TPP), an agreement between the USA and 11 countries in the Pacific Rim, and the Transatlantic Trade and Investment Partnership (TTIP) between the US and the EU. These agreements have been highly controversial, both because negotiations have been highly secretive and because they focus not only on 'traditional' trade barriers such as tariffs and quotas, but on 'behind the border' provisions. The most important of these are regulatory cooperation and investor–state dispute settlement (ISDS) mechanisms. The former aims to harmonise regulations in order to lower trade costs, but has raised fears that regulatory standards on health and other areas will be lowered. ISDS is highly controversial because it provides a legal mechanism whereby TNCs can directly initiate disputes with governments where they claim to have been treated in a manner that is not 'fair and equitable' (in contrast to the WTO, where only member states may initiate disputes). Such mechanisms already exist in thousands of bilateral investment treaties (BITs), and have been used to demand compensation where public policy overrides the needs of TNCs (Hawkins and Holden, 2016). As a result of Trump's election victory, it is highly likely that TPP will not be signed by the US and that negotiations on TTIP will be stalled indefinitely. Rather than decrying the loss of these agreements, as *The Economist* (2016b) and others have done, it would be better to welcome the abandonment of unnecessarily pro-corporate provisions. Negotiations held in secret to agree treaties that give exclusive rights to TNCs and close down governments' policy space are a major reason for opposition to globalisation.

Instead, there should be a return to multilateralism, initially via the WTO where trade is concerned. However, the WTO system itself could be reformed in various ways. While it provides a multilateral venue for resolving trade disputes, the organisation's relentless drive towards ever increasing liberalisation should be re-evaluated. One important way to reform the WTO system would be to build social clauses into trade agreements. For example, minimum labour standards could be brought back onto its agenda, something favoured by the USA (though not by the UK) in the WTO's early years. Such moves proved controversial within the WTO, with its 1996 Singapore Ministerial naming the ILO as the competent body with regard to labour standards. Yet, both the US and the EU have since included labour provisions within bilateral and plurilateral trade agreements (Peels and Fino, 2015).

Low-income countries have generally opposed such social clauses in trade agreements because they fear that they could be used as a form of disguised protection by the high-income countries, so undermining their comparative advantage in lower-cost labour. Such fears might be allayed by the adoption of the kind of process proposed by Mishra (1999), whereby lower-income countries are permitted lower standards (but above a minimum floor), while an 'escalator' requires the adoption of higher standards above certain levels of GDP per capita. If calibrated effectively, this could guard against 'social dumping' and afford a degree of competitive protection to workers in high-income countries, while simultaneously affording workers in low-income countries a level of social protection that did not unduly undermine their comparative advantage in labour costs. In return, the EU and the US could also offer to reduce their current levels of agricultural protection. Such protection is a major impediment to the economic development of many low-income countries and has been a significant reason for the stalling of the Doha round. While reductions in agricultural subsidies and tariffs would be politically contentious in the EU and the US, and would not have uniformly beneficial effects for low-income countries, they should be carefully considered as part of a new settlement that would benefit high-income country consumers and low-income country farmers alike.

Piketty (2016) has further argued for trade agreements to include 'quantified and binding measures to combat fiscal and climate dumping [...] For example, there could be common minimum rates of corporation tax and targets for carbon emissions which can be verified and sanctioned'. Such measures could guard against the damaging race to the bottom in corporate tax rates that is currently in train.

The WTO and the wider global trade and investment regime could also be reformed to ensure the maintenance of adequate policy space for national governments. Current exceptions to trade rules that protect public health, for example, could be clarified and strengthened to ensure that trade agreements do not unduly constrain governments' ability to protect the health and social welfare of their citizens. Rodrik (2011: 252–59) has suggested that the WTO's Agreement on Safeguards, which already permits member states to raise tariffs in certain restricted circumstances when a sudden surge in imports threatens domestic firms, could be expanded to protect domestic labour and environmental standards. In a similar vein, ISDS clauses in BITs and other agreements should be repealed across the board.

Conclusions

The results of the UK's referendum on EU membership and the US presidential election in 2016 have caused many commentators to re-evaluate the assumptions of neoliberal globalisation. Trump's election, in particular, poses a challenge not only to neoliberal economics, but also to liberal democratic politics and the rule of law (both domestically and internationally). I have argued here for an alternative vision to that of neoliberal globalisation on the one hand, and a resort to reactionary nationalism on the other: a clear commitment to tackle the gross inequalities that have characterised the period of neoliberal globalisation and to work towards socially just forms of global governance. To argue for this direction of travel is not to underestimate the political obstacles and constraints that would impede it. Effective international cooperation is difficult at the best of times, and the process of negotiating new standards and institutions can be painfully slow. The greater the number of countries involved in any such process, the more likely it is that global standards will take the form of a 'lowest common denominator'. Avoiding such minimalism to establish effective forms of supranational governance often requires some pooling of national sovereignty and the placing of some constraints on national policy space. Current forms of opposition on both the right and the left to the EU and to the wider global trade regime are testament to what can happen when elites build supranational institutions without the consent of their populations.

Beyond Brexit, the problems currently confronting the EU provide a lesson in this regard. The 2007–08 financial crisis and the sovereign debt crisis that followed in 2010 have led member states to swing towards an austerity policy, so that the Euro has become a stick with which to discipline countries like Greece, with profound consequences both for welfare within the relevant countries and for Europe's broader 'social model' (Papadopoulos and Roumpakis, 2012). In some ways this merely reflects the inbuilt pro-market bias of the EU (and the European Community before it), which has always been premised upon market-led integration, resulting most recently in the agreement to create the single market. Yet the EU could have a crucial role to play in constructing more socially just forms of supranational governance, both among its own member states and more globally. The EU's size means that it is large enough to implement measures such as a minimum corporate tax rate within its own borders, where insufficient agreement exists more widely. Significant progress has already been made within the EU towards the establishment of a financial transaction tax (Burman et al, 2016: 178–79). The EU also has the power to negotiate with the weight of 28 economies in international forums, so that it could be an important voice for socially just forms of governance at the global level. The persistence of advanced welfare states in most member states, and public support for these, provides a political and social basis for it to play such a role. For all its weaknesses, the EU is an impressive experiment in supranational governance, with the potential to do much good by placing a firmer social floor under the excesses of the global (and the internal) market. Beginning to shift the mission of the EU from a mainly market building one to one concerned equally with sustaining social security across Europe, and effectively regulating and taxing TNCs, could help to ward off current challenges to its legitimacy.

Acknowledgements

My thanks to Ben Hawkins, John Hudson, Sophie Mackinder and Antonios Roumpakis for helpful comments on an earlier draft of this chapter. The final result is, of course, entirely my responsibility.

References

Agnew, J. (2005) 'Sovereignty regimes: territoriality and state authority in contemporary world politics', *Annals of the Association of American Geographers*, 95(2): 437–61.

Allen, K. (2016) 'Economic frustration has spawned Trump and Brexit, warns UN labour chief', *The Guardian*, 14 November 2016, https://www.theguardian.com/business/2016/nov/14/economic-frustration-spawned-trump-brexit-warns-ilo-chief?CMP=Share_iOSApp_Other

Burman, L.E., Gale, W.G., Gault, S., Kim, B., Nunns, J. and Rosenthal, S. (2016) 'Financial transaction taxes in theory and practice', *National Tax Journal*, 69(1): 171–216.

Cerny, P. (1998) 'Neomedievalism, civil war and the new security dilemma: globalisation as durable disorder', *Civil Wars*, 1(1): 36–64.

Chang, H.J. (2003) *Kicking away the ladder*, London: Anthem Press.

Deacon, B. (2006) 'Global social policy reform', in P. Utting (ed.) *Reclaiming development agendas: Knowledge, power and international policy making*, Basingstoke: Palgrave, pp 144–75.

Deacon, B. (2007) *Global social policy and governance*, London: Sage.

The Economist (2016a) 'Buttonwood: déjà vu all over again', 12 November, p 68.

The Economist (2016b) 'Pacific trade: try, persist, persevere', 19 November, pp 14–16.

Elliott, L. (2016) 'Donald Trump's economic policies could go badly wrong – but not soon enough', *The Guardian*, 19 November, https://www.theguardian.com/business/2016/nov/19/trump-economic-policies-growth-us-economy?CMP=Share_iOSApp_Other)

George, V. and Wilding, P. (2002) *Globalization and human welfare*, London: Palgrave.

Gough, I. (2011) 'From financial crisis to fiscal crisis', in K. Farnsworth and Z. Irving (eds) *Social policy in challenging times: Economic crisis and welfare systems*, Bristol: Policy Press, pp 49–64.

Grande, E. and Pauly, L.W. (2005) 'Complex sovereignty and the emergence of transnational authority', in E. Grande and L.W. Pauly (eds) *Complex sovereignty: Reconstituting political authority in the twenty-first century*, Toronto: University of Toronto Press, pp 285–99.

Hacker, J.S. and Pierson, P. (2010) 'Winner-take-all politics: public policy, political organization and the precipitous rise of top incomes in the United States', *Politics & Society*, 38(2): 152–204.

Harris, K. (2016) 'The reasons for Trump were also the reasons for Brexit', *The Guardian*, 10 November, https://www.theguardian.com/commentisfree/2016/nov/10/donald-trump-brexit-us?CMP=Share_iOSApp_Other

Hawkins, B. (2012) 'Nation, separation and threat: an analysis of British media discourses on the European Union treaty reform process', *Journal of Common Market Studies*, 50(4): 561–77.

Hawkins, B. and Holden, C. (2016) 'A corporate veto on health policy? Global constitutionalism and investor-state dispute settlement', *Journal of Health Politics, Policy and Law*, 41(5): 969–95.

Held, D. and McGrew, A. (2007) *Globalization/anti-globalization*, Cambridge: Polity Press.

Hirst, P. and Thompson, G. (1999) *Globalisation in question* (2nd edn), Cambridge: Polity Press.

Holden, C. (2014a) 'Global poverty and inequality', in N. Yeates (ed.) *Understanding global social policy* (2nd edn), Bristol: Policy Press, pp 21–51.

Holden, C. (2014b) 'International trade and welfare', in N. Yeates (ed.) *Understanding global social policy* (2nd edn), Bristol: Policy Press, pp 105–28.

Holden, C. and Hudson, J. (in press) 'Global competitiveness and the rescaling of welfare: rescaling downwards whilst competing outwards?', in D. Horsfall and J. Hudson (eds) *Social policy in an era of competition: From global to local perspectives*, Bristol: Policy Press.

Krugman, P. (2016) 'Trump slump coming?', *The New York Times*, 14 November, mobile.nytimes.com/2016/11/14/opinion/trump-slump-coming.html?_r=0&referer=

May, T. (2016) 'Conservative Party conference speech', *The Independent*, 5 October, www.independent.co.uk/news/uk/politics/theresa-may-speech-tory-conference-2016-in-full-transcript-a7346171.html

Mishra, R. (1999) *Globalization and the welfare state*, Cheltenham: Edward Elgar.

Mowat, L. (2016) 'Corporation tax to be halved to persuade banks to stay in UK', *The Express*, 23 October, www.express.co.uk/news/uk/724329/Theresa-May-to-cut-corporation-tax-half-persuade-banks-stay

Neate, R. (2016) 'Donald Trump faces Senate backlash over "cabinet of billionaires"', *The Observer*, 18 December, https://www.theguardian.com/us-news/2016/dec/18/donald-trump-senate-backlash-cabinet-of-billionaires?CMP=Share_iOSApp_Other

Noland, M. (2016) 'A diminished leadership role for the United States', in M. Noland, G.C. Hufbauer, S. Robinson and Tyler Moran, *Assessing trade agendas in the US presidential campaign*, Washington, DC: Peterson Institute for International Economics.

Noland, M., Robinson, S. and Moran, T. (2016) 'Impact of Clinton's and Trump's trade proposals', in M. Noland, G.C. Hufbauer, S. Robinson and Tyler Moran, *Assessing trade agendas in the US presidential campaign*, Washington, DC: Peterson Institute for International Economics.

OECD (2011) *Divided we stand: Why inequality keeps rising*, Paris: OECD Publishing, dx.doi.org/10.1787/9789264119536-en

OECD (2016a) *Income inequality update: Income inequality remains high in the face of weak recovery*, November, www.oecd.org/social/OECD2016-Income-Inequality-Update.pdf

OECD (2016b) *About BEPS and the inclusive framework*, www.oecd.org/tax/beps/beps-about.htm

O'Sullivan, J. (2016) 'An open and shut case: special report on the world economy', *The Economist*, 1 October.

Papadopoulos, T. and Roumpakis, A. (2012) 'The Greek welfare state in the age of austerity: anti-social policy and the politico–economic crisis', in M. Kilkey, G. Ramia and K. Farnsworth (eds) *Social Policy Review 24*, Bristol: Policy Press, pp 205–30.

Peels, R. and Fino, M. (2015) 'Pushed out the door, back in through the window: the role of the ILO in EU and US trade agreements in facilitating the decent work agenda', *Global Labour Journal*, 6(2): 189–202.

Piketty, T. (2014) *Capital in the twenty-first century*, Cambridge, MA: The Belknap Press of Harvard University Press.

Piketty, T. (2016) 'We must rethink globalisation, or Trumpism will prevail', *The Guardian*, 16 November, https://www.theguardian.com/commentisfree/2016/nov/16/globalization-trump-inequality-thomas-piketty

Prabhakar, R. (2011) 'Debating the "death tax": the politics of inheritance tax in the UK', in C. Holden, M. Kilkey and G. Ramia (eds), *Social Policy Review 23*, Bristol: Policy Press, pp 85–102.

Rodrik, D. (2011) *The globalization paradox: Why global markets, states, and democracy can't coexist*, Oxford: Oxford University Press.

Ruggie, J.G. (1993) 'Territoriality and beyond: problematizing modernity in international relations', *International Organization*, 47(1): 139–74.

Slack, J. (2016) 'Enemies of the people: fury over "out of touch" judges who have "declared war on democracy" by defying 17.4m Brexit voters and who could trigger constitutional crisis', *Mail Online*, 3 November, www.dailymail.co.uk/news/article-3903436/Enemies-people-Fury-touch-judges-defied-17-4m-Brexit-voters-trigger-constitutional-crisis.html

Smith, H. (2016) 'Obama calls for course correction to share spoils of globalisation', *The Guardian*, 17 November, https://www.theguardian.com/us-news/2016/nov/16/obama-calls-for-course-correction-to-share-spoils-of-globalisation?CMP=Share_iOSApp_Other

Standing, G. (2011) *The precariat: The new dangerous class*, London: Bloomsbury Academic.

Stiglitz, J. (2013) *The price of inequality*, London: Penguin.

Sunak, R. (2016) *The free ports opportunity: How Brexit could boost trade, manufacturing and the North*, Surrey: Centre for Policy Studies.

Syal, R. and Walker, P. (2016) 'May hints at further cuts to corporation tax to placate business', *The Guardian*, 21 November, https://www.theguardian.com/politics/2016/nov/21/theresa-may-cuts-to-corporation-tax-cbi-speech?CMP=Share_iOSApp_Other

Tax Policy Center (2016) *An analysis of Donald Trump's revised tax plan*, Urban Institute and Brookings Institution, www.taxpolicycenter.org/publications/analysis-donald-trumps-revised-tax-plan

Tobin, J. (1978) 'A proposal for international monetary reform', *Eastern Economic Journal*, 4(3–4): 153–59.

Townsend, P. and Donkor, K. (1996) *Global restructuring and social policy: The need to establish an international welfare state*, Bristol: Policy Press.

Urry, J. (2014) *Offshoring*, Cambridge: Polity Press.

World Economic Forum (2017) *The global risks report 2017*, Geneva: World Economic Forum.

Yeates, N. (2001) *Globalization and social policy*, London: Sage.

Part Two

Contributions from the Social Policy Association Conference 2016

Catherine Needham

The title of a round table at the 2016 Social Policy Association conference – What can and should the Social Policy Association do to resist radically and resolutely? – highlights the commitment to practices of resistance and critique within the academy. The contributions in this section of the book draw attention to different aspects of critique, as well as to the importance of ideas in understanding how policies change.

Garthwaite's chapter on food banks focuses on the discourses around deservingness, choice and gratitude in emergency food provision. Food banks, she reminds us, are located in a government narrative of 'shirkers and scroungers', with many MPs going on record to express doubts about people's level of neediness. Her participant observer data, generated through two years of volunteering at a food bank, gives a powerful insight into the lived experience of food bank users. She draws attention to the role that welfare professionals have to play in assessing deservingness in relation to allocating food vouchers. Narratives of being 'genuine' versus 'undeserving' also feature in the attitudes of volunteers at the food bank, suggesting – Garthwaite argues – the pervasiveness of media representations of poverty in general and food banks in particular.

A particularly powerful section of her chapter relates to the extent to which people should be allowed choice over what is contained within their food package. As she puts it, 'why should it be frowned upon when people express distaste or desire for a certain brand of food?' There is a strong sense that this contravenes the gratitude that food bank volunteers (and perhaps some readers) expect. She ends the chapter with an affirmation that every individual deserves food, irrespective of their supposed behavioural 'choices'.

Natalie Booth's chapter on maternal imprisonment is infused with the same undertone of critique of the ways in which penal arrangements remain prisoner-centric and fail to recognise a women's maternal status and familial responsibilities. She draws on in-depth semi-structured interviews with 15 imprisoned mothers, exploring the impact on their identities and practices of mothering, and the implications for children and families. The powerful statistic that only 5% of children remain in their own homes once their mother is removed to prison dramatically underlines the framing of imprisonment as a family sentence.

Her data brings out what it means to do 'mothering in prison' and the extent to which mothers must cope with the 'internalised stigma' of being a 'failed mother' because of the dichotomy between their prisoner and motherhood identities. She draws attention to the marked difference between the policy rhetoric from the Ministry of Justice about improved support for family ties and the reality of maintaining those ties while in prison. The inadequacy of prison processes regarding use of the telephone and visitation make the practical challenges of keeping in touch extremely difficult.

Katherine Smith's chapter discusses the role of ideas in policy making, highlighting the need to discuss ideas in a 'post-truth' era where existing notions of expertise and evidence are discredited. She characterises a 'perfect storm' surrounding evidence-based policy as the public grows more distrustful of academic and policy expertise. She uses tobacco control and health inequalities as two public health interventions which help to illuminate the contribution of evidence-informed ideas in building momentum for policy change.

Ideational theories have grown in importance within social policy through the work of Béland (2005) and others. Smith's contribution is to explore why some ideas and not others are transformative of public policy. She contrasts the effective intervention on tobacco control in the last decade with the lack of progress on addressing health inequalities. Her primary data draws from a large corpus of interviews with researchers, journalists, academics and others over ten years. She argues that for ideas to be effective in changing policy they need to be institutionalised, but they also need to be charismatic, in the sense of being imbued with a creative transformative power. She contrasts the charismatic ideas put forward by the tobacco control community to develop a package of ideas around control which would have been unthinkable a decade earlier (such as the banning of smoking in public places) with the inability of health inequalities researchers to articulate charismatic ideas.

Betzelt and Bode's work on German welfare reform brings together the focus on welfare stigma and shame of the Garthwaite and Booth chapters with the interest in hegemonic ideas, linking to Smith's argument. The chapter is a contribution to understanding the emotional states of those experiencing welfare retrenchment. Drawing on case studies of labour market and pension policies they explore the ways in which the liberalization of the German social model has prompted emotional states of fear which enforce compliance but also endanger social integration. This they characterise as a 'new German Angst', evidenced in an 'anxiety epidemic' as people are pressured to take more individual responsibility for risks previously understood to be social and collectively shared. This 'politics of fear' has been discussed elsewhere (for example, Furedi, 2005), but here it is discussed particularly in relation to welfare state change. In a commentary that resonates with patterns in the UK's Brexit vote and in the Trump victory in the USA, Betzelt and Bode highlight the way in which cultural alienation can be more salient than fears of future job insecurity or enhanced competition in the labour market.

The chapter's focus on the hidden poor and the stigma of welfare dependence has clear resonances with the arguments made by Garthwaite and Booth. Betzelt and Bode's discussion of the way in which pension reform and the growth of private pensions has been based on a new hegemonic discourse link to Smith's arguments about the role of ideas in policy change. What Betzelt and Bode suggest is remarkable is the degree of compliance with welfare changes, enabling the move towards de-securitisation without any substantial political resistance. However they express their own angst about the future, noting that structural uncertainty combined with cultural alienation can lead to racism and destroy social integration. Their chapter, like the others, highlights the need for social policy scholars to be engaged in critique and resistance as well as recording and theorising social change.

References

Béland, D. (2005) 'Ideas and social policy: an institutionalist perspective', *Social Policy and Administration*, 39(1): 1–18.

Furedi, F. (2005) *Politics of fear: Beyond left and right*, London: Continuum International.

FIVE

Rethinking deservingness, choice and gratitude in emergency food provision

Kayleigh Garthwaite

Introduction and context

In the UK, the most well-known charity operating foodbanks is the Trussell Trust, a large, national, Christian franchise which operates a voucher system for people seeking emergency food provision. Their network issued more than half a million emergency food parcels in the first six months of 2016. This staggering number means that the Trussell Trust foodbank network is on course to distribute the highest number of food parcels in its 12-year history during 2016–17 (Trussell Trust, 2016). Overall, however, it is difficult to quantify the exact number of foodbanks in existence as there are many organisations and independent groups that offer charitable food aid.

As foodbank use has risen, the idea that more people are using foodbanks due to their availability has become a popular one within some sections of the mass media and the government. In April 2016, the All-Party Parliamentary Group (APPG) on Hunger warned that there is evidence of serious and growing hunger in Britain, particularly affecting children, but that many voters 'no longer believe' some claims about foodbank demand (APPG, 2016). In reality, people are largely using foodbanks as a last resort, due to factors such as benefit delays, sanctions, debt and low pay. Almost half of the reasons people cite for using foodbanks can be attributed to austerity-led welfare reform (Trussell Trust, 2016). Empirical evidence from academics and frontline charities has further shown how benefit sanctions and delays, fuel poverty and low-paid, insecure work drive people towards foodbanks (see Lambie-Mumford, 2014; Perry et al, 2014; Loopstra et al, 2015; Garthwaite, 2016a).

This growth in food banks has coincided with a popularisation of the genre of 'poverty porn' television shows, together with an ever-present government narrative which blames and shames people using food banks for their own situation, resulting in many 'hidden costs' (Purdam et al, 2015) of using a foodbank. Such ideological myths of 'shirkers and scroungers' (Garthwaite, 2011), 'troubled families' (Shildrick et al, 2016) and the 'abject' citizen (Tyler 2013) have become increasingly visible as welfare reform and austerity has gone on. Wells and Caraher (2014) note how a frequent theme of newspaper articles from Conservative politicians characterised people using a foodbank as 'unable to manage their personal finances, [they are] freeloaders abusing the service the foodbank offers or they are opportunistically taking advantage of the burgeoning network of foodbanks offering free food' (2014: 1436).

People accessing a foodbank are then perceived as the 'undeserving poor', seeking out free food so that they can spend their money on 'luxury' items such as alcohol, cigarettes and large televisions. Explanations for rising foodbank use from some Conservative MPs have therefore focused upon individualised behaviour, specifically poor financial management, addiction and, in some cases, selfish and neglectful behaviour. Vale of Glamorgan MP Alun Cairns blamed an 'inability to manage money and to budget, addiction to alcohol or substance misuse, bullying at home, neglect by the benefit recipient and a range of other reasons' (cited in Shipton, 2013). Wrekin MP Mark Pritchard has questioned whether some people using foodbanks could be spending some of the money they save on alcohol and cigarettes. The MP made his comments on Twitter, asking: 'Foodbanks serving a need – but how many folks can still find funds to pay for alcohol and cigarettes but not food?' Guto Bebb, Conservative MP for Aberconwy, has said: 'There are some who appear to use foodbanks while being able to smoke and pay for a Sky TV package' (cited in Monroe, 2013). Conservative councillor Julia Lepoidevin deemed foodbank users 'selfish' and suggested that they 'make a conscious decision not to pay their rent, their utilities or to provide food for their children because they choose alcohol, drugs and their own selfish needs' (cited in Elgot, 2014). Speaking about foodbank use in January 2014, former Tory MP Edwina Currie stated:

> 'I get very, very troubled at the number of people who are using food banks who think that it's fine to pay to feed their dog, their dog is in good nick and beautiful, but they never learn to cook, they never learn to manage and the moment they've got a bit of spare cash they're off getting another tattoo. We should feel cross about this, all of us.' (cited in Bennett, 2014)

Perhaps unsurprisingly, this political rhetoric has had a strong influence on beliefs about foodbank use and deservingness, and can lead to stigma, shame and embarrassment for the people who need to use them (Garthwaite, 2016b).

Understandably, the rise of emergency food aid provision in the UK has become increasingly well documented by social policy academics (Dowler and Lambie-Mumford, 2014; Loopstra et al, 2015), but relatively less attention has focused on the lived experiences of seeking charitable food provision from a foodbank. In this context, this chapter is based on ethnographic research inside a Trussell Trust foodbank in north-east England. It offers a new perspective on who is (or who should be) considered 'deserving' or 'undeserving', drawing on the opinions of foodbank volunteers, staff at referral agencies, people who donated food, and people who used the foodbank themselves. The chapter then links these perspectives to choice and the anticipation of gratitude, alongside expected behaviours of people accessing emergency food. Finally, the chapter argues that every individual deserves access to food, irrespective of supposed behavioural 'choices'. It concludes that replacing the social security safety net with charitable food provision should not become an accepted and unchallenged norm.

Research design

This chapter draws on data from the project 'Local Health Inequalities in an Age of Austerity: The Stockton-on-Tees Study', a five-year, mixed methods project examining localised health inequalities in an era of austerity in the town of Stockton-on-Tees, in north-east England. Stockton-on-Tees has the highest health inequalities within a local authority in England, with life expectancy gaps of 17.3 and 11.4 years among men and women respectively between the least and most deprived wards (Public Health England, 2015). Taking an ethnographic approach to studying health inequalities, weekly volunteering and participant observation began at a Trussell Trust foodbank in November 2013. Once fully trained, the volunteering role included preparation of food parcels; distributing food parcels; liaising with referring agencies; and administration of the vouchers that all foodbank users are required to obtain in order to receive emergency food provision. My identity as a researcher was made known to all foodbank users, volunteers and staff at referring agencies involved in the research. Volunteering allowed for a detailed insight into the way the foodbank was used and how it operated. Not only did volunteering demonstrate commitment to 'the cause' and the local area, it also provided a space in which to form relationships that did not solely focus on the researchers' needs and objectives. Instead, importance was shifted towards what the foodbank users and volunteers needed (see Garthwaite, 2016b for further details).

Field notes were taken before, during and immediately after volunteering in the foodbank and included observations, conversations and the researcher's reflections. Eighty-two in-depth interviews with people who used the foodbank (n = 60), foodbank volunteers (n = 12), and foodbank referrers (n = 10) were also carried out. Ten of the 60 foodbank users were then interviewed again in their own homes up to two weeks after the receipt of their food parcel to explore their experiences of the food given. For the 60 foodbank users interviewed (38 men and 22 women), the age range of the sample varied from 16 to 63 years old. The gender patterning of the sample reflects the wider demographics of people who used the foodbank. Interviews that took place in the foodbank were not digitally recorded, but detailed notes were taken immediately afterwards. Participants were asked to discuss topics relating to: why they came to the foodbank; daily budgeting practices; employment; experiences of social security benefits, including sanctions, appeals and delays; their health; their local area; and their hopes for the future.

Observational notes and interview transcripts were analysed with the assistance of qualitative data analysis software (NVivo 10). Participation was voluntary, confidential and secured by either verbal or written informed consent. Data were fully anonymised before thematic analysis was undertaken. The findings of the qualitative interviews were then compared with the observations that had previously been noted. Ethical considerations were respected throughout the research, with the research being approved in advance by Durham University Department of Geography Ethics Committee. The names used below are pseudonyms.

Deservingness and the foodbank encounter

The general view among the volunteers was that most people who used the foodbank were there due to genuine need, but ideas of who was deemed to be 'deserving' or 'undeserving' were regularly discussed. In some ways, foodbank organisations such as the Trussell Trust play an integral part in this question of 'who deserves help', and the Trust's use of care professionals to issue vouchers for use in foodbanks could be viewed as upholding a distinction between deserving and undeserving service users. Cloke et al (2016: 10) explain this by arguing: 'the Trust risks capture by wider political ideologies and practices that subjectify deservingness and undeservingness, and thereby opens itself up to claims that it subscribes to and re-enforces the moral landscapes of poverty promulgated by neoliberal governance'.

A key reason why I chose to volunteer in a Trussell Trust foodbank was their referral system. Other independent food banks can require evidence of personal identification or hardship, in the form of bank statements or household bills. As I was going to be carrying out the volunteer role as well as that of a researcher, it would be highly unethical to make judgements as to whether someone should be given emergency food assistance or not. Nor was that something I wanted to do, on a personal level. May (2014) has called this process 'moral outsourcing', whereby foodbank volunteers are freed from the moral responsibility of having to decide who is and who is not deserving of assistance, enabling them to claim a more comfortable, 'non-judgemental' stance because these decisions are made for them in advance by trained 'welfare professionals'.

Nevertheless, the reality of the often complex administrative bureaucracy involved in accessing emergency food jars with the common misconception that anyone can turn up at a foodbank and get 'free food'. The research presented here counters this perception. Accessing emergency food involves already working with an agency that can issue a voucher, which can then be exchanged for three days' worth of food during foodbank opening hours (in the case of the Stockton-on-Tees foodbank, this is twice a week, 10:00–13:00). The voucher contains information about the reasons for referral, how many people at the address are 'workless', the ages of their children, and the name and address of the person seeking support. Staff at the referral agency must sign the voucher, which is then checked against a list of signatories the foodbank has for each individual agency.

Many vulnerable people may not be in contact with referral agencies, such as Citizens Advice Bureau (CAB), their local housing office or the council, therefore accessing support from a foodbank may not be possible. Further, the stigma associated with accessing a voucher can also deter people from seeking help, leaving them without food, potentially worsening pre-existing health conditions (Garthwaite, 2016b). On occasion, people came to the foodbank and would not realise they needed a red voucher to access support. There were several instances when I had to refuse people who didn't have the required red voucher, the first being James, as the following extract from my field notes shows:

Field notes
20 June 2014

Today was the first day where I've had to actually turn someone away. James, in his 30s, said that he has been working with a drug and alcohol service in the town, and that they were going to ring us here at the foodbank to say he needed a food parcel. We haven't had a phone call. Sometimes this happens if an agency has run out of red vouchers, so I said I would go and give them a ring. I tried calling three times but found no answer, and after looking online I couldn't find another number for the agency. I felt really bad and asked Angie what we should do. We both wanted to help him, but Angie said, 'If we do it for one person, word will get around and everyone will turn up without a voucher.' Following the rules is always the best thing to do, I've been told many times. Looking at the clock, it was 12.30 pm and we close the foodbank at 1 pm. I said to James if he could run up to CAB maybe they could help him out? About 15 minutes later he came through the door, out of breath from running all the way there and back, red voucher in hand.

Although the church itself can issue a red voucher, the volunteers agreed that James had time to go and get a voucher from CAB and "if he really needs food he'll go and get one [a voucher]". As I chatted to Maureen about this later, saying I felt uneasy about what just happened, she said:

'I would say on the whole you get genuine people you sometimes get the odd one who will try it when they haven't got a voucher. If they really are in need they'll go and get a voucher like we suggest and then they'll come back.'

The voucher system was largely seen by the volunteers as a way of separating the 'genuine', deserving cases out from the 'undeserving', who may be trying to abuse the system. Foodbank manager Angie put it like this:

'I like the voucher system. Generally speaking it's an agency who is already working with people that refer them so they know a bit about their background. It doesn't always happen but generally speaking the agency will know them and so know their situation. I think that's good. Also if somebody does come in and say "Can I have some food?" you can say "Have you got a voucher?" because that's the rules.'

People using the foodbank also said they thought the red voucher was a good idea as it ensured the "genuine people" were receiving help. Tracey, 49, came to the foodbank for the first time after her and her husband were experiencing problems with his zero-hours contract. Tracey said: "I mean anyone could go if they didn't have that voucher, but if they've got that voucher they can't get food without it, it is a good idea."

Others, such as David, 42, felt that the voucher system is not a well-advertised fact about foodbanks, leading to deserving/undeserving stereotyping. I met David when he came to the foodbank for the first time after his marriage had broken down. David was dealing with multiple issues; he had suffered several family bereavements, including his mother, father and grandparents, he had lost his job as a graphic designer and was now "drinking heavily". As soon as David walked into the foodbank, he stood at the back of the room, stiff with fear. I went and took the red voucher from David, which was crumpled up in his hand as if to make it invisible. One of the first things he said to me was: "People don't realise you have to go and get a voucher to come here. That's hard enough. I'm sick of everyone thinking you can just turn up and get free food. I feel like I'm begging."

For David, the fear of using the foodbank was almost too much to overcome. He sat, regularly in tears, telling me how he felt as though he was begging for food – "Well, I am" – he said.

During the research, a general view that the red voucher system acted as a safety net for volunteers, who could say "we have to follow the rules" if somebody tried to access emergency food without the required voucher, was a popular one. Foodbank manager Angie said:

'It's not you saying no to that person so I mean we can give vouchers out from here if we felt somebody was genuine but there are so many agencies out there but it's a safeguard I think for the volunteers that we're not saying no, we've got to follow the rules and that helps hopefully the more genuine people.'

The voucher system was offered as a reason for donation on more than one occasion. In accessing support via the red voucher, people donating food could be sure what they deemed to be genuine people were receiving a food parcel. "We wanted to give it to somewhere where you need a referral," two teachers from a local primary school told me as they brought a donation to the foodbank, boxes of food wrapped in pretty ribbons, decorated with drawings and wrapping paper by the children in their class. They were worried about people abusing the system, and told me, "You see it in the papers, don't you?" It is clear how media representations of foodbanks, and of poverty more generally, is being internalised by food donors, as well as by others associated with the foodbank, as the following section explores (see also Garthwaite, 2016b).

Cycles of dependency?

As mentioned earlier, the Trussell Trust system aims to prevent foodbank dependency; if someone has been to the foodbank over three times, then volunteers must contact the agency that referred them to see why they need additional vouchers. It is interesting here to flag up how the Trussell Trust has said they want to avoid 'cycles of dependency' (Garthwaite, 2016a). Peter, the manager at a drug and alcohol support service in the town centre (and one of the most frequent referral agencies to the foodbank) shared his perspectives on dependency and the red voucher system:

> 'It works but the problem that we have is word gets round so everyone wants a red food parcel as there's more in them [than some of the other emergency food providers' parcels] and obviously it's on the worker to find out who … you can't say who deserves but who's got the more needs for the red voucher, and that's what we try to do. But some people come in and they demand the red voucher but I won't give them it, so that's how generally it works. We look at more so … we know family units need food so you'll find the referrals we send through tend to be more than one person y'know, we need to be a bit more stringent with them.'

Peter highlighted the complexities of administering the red voucher, and told me how he tried to avoid labelling people as 'deserving' or 'undeserving'. Yet despite this, his perspectives are falling in line with these divisions, and he seems to be characterising certain people as making demands of the service. Why should family units be prioritised over single adults? Arguably, Peter's behaviour is an example of 'moral outsourcing' (May, 2014) by a voluntary sector organisation rather than the state or the foodbank itself. This was clearly evident when talking to Gillian, a support worker at the Citizen's Advice Bureau, who said:

'I'm not afraid of saying no. There was a woman the other day, she'd had all the vouchers and she turned up wanting more. She was still drinking [alcohol], so I just said no. The foodbank isn't there as a long-term thing. People are using the foodbank instead of doing their food shopping. She put a letter of complaint in about me but I'm not bothered, it's my job. If someone isn't helping themselves, if they're still making those choices then what can you do? It's lifestyle choices at the end of the day.'

Throughout the research, I met people who could have fitted into Gillian's rigid definition of an 'undeserving' foodbank user. Paul, in his late 30s, was a long-term recovering heroin addict who had been to the foodbank at least nine times. Paul explained how he was on a three-month sanction for failing to turn up to an appointment at a private sector welfare-to-work company. I asked why he missed his appointment, and he replied: "I couldn't be arsed to get out of bed." He told me that he spent what little money he had on drugs, alcohol, his Xbox 360 and his dog. At a basic level, Paul could slot into the many stereotypes surrounding foodbank (mis)use. But Paul wasn't exactly enjoying a lavish lifestyle on benefits. He was bored, but had no realistic job prospects. He thought his history of being in and out of prison over a period of 20 years didn't help with that. One of the reasons why Paul struggled to get out of bed in the morning was due to his mental health problems and tiredness, which were worsened by the heroin he had been taking for over half of his life.

Paul's story could be regarded as a persuasive example of the imagined stereotype of the 'undeserving' foodbank user. Yet questioning Paul's apparent behavioural choices is hugely divisive and only seeks to further ingrain the idea that he does not deserve help. Debates over whether people are genuine are powerful ways to distract from the more important story that should be told about foodbank use, and about living in poverty more generally. Food is a basic human right that shouldn't be denied to someone just because they take drugs, smoke or drink alcohol; every individual deserves access to food, irrespective of these supposed behavioural 'choices'. 'Food insecurity' and 'food poverty' have been related to the concept of a 'right to food' (see Dowler and O'Connor, 2012; Lambie-Mumford 2013, 2015; Riches, 2002). Lambie-Mumford (2013: 87) argues this 'could provide social policy researchers and policymakers with an important framework and imperative for approaching and prioritising food experiences'. Rights-based approaches stress that access to safe, nutritious food is a basic human right, and above all a requirement for health, well-being and dignity (Douglas et al, 2015). Creating distinctions between deserving and undeserving foodbank users also allows state responsibility to be seen as a secondary issue; adopting a right-to-food approach 'sets out clearly that the state is the duty-bearer' (Lambie-Mumford, 2015: 2). It is therefore clear how, in creating these 'un/deserving' stereotypes of people using a foodbank, the right to food is eroded, with moral judgements instead being used as a justification for the denial of this right. Ideas surrounding the right to food and deservingness are further called into question when considering choice and gratitude in a foodbank setting.

Choice and gratitude

Williams et al (2016: 11) have drawn attention to 'the emotional nexus of shame, stigma, and gratitude' involved when thinking critically about foodbank use. In discussing the red voucher system, dependency and ideas of deservingness, the issue of gratitude emerges as key for the way people accessing a foodbank express their thoughts on asking for emergency food, and in the perspectives of the volunteers.

It was not uncommon to meet people who were so overcome with emotion at being given their emergency food that they cried, hugged me and promised to donate to the foodbank once they were back on their feet. Denise, 49, was a clear example of this. For Denise, this was the first spell of unemployment she had encountered in her working life, having previously worked in pubs, hotels and restaurants. Since she separated from her husband three months before, her health (both physical and mental) had deteriorated and the difficulties she faced in gaining employment again were worsening her health even further. Interviewing Denise a fortnight after meeting her in the foodbank, she told me: "When I got home and was unpacking it my mam was laughing at me cos I was amazed, I got corned beef and I said 'Mam I got corned beef, it's too expensive.'"

The extract from my field notes further illustrates this complex relationship:

Field notes
12 December 2014

Peter, 26, came in today. He was a heroin addict who had managed to get clean for a year, then the past few months he has relapsed again. He was talking to Maureen when I brought his food over to him and he happened to mention he liked muesli, so I said I'd swap the Rice Krispies in his parcel for some muesli as I knew we had some upstairs. He was so grateful it made me feel awkward. I was bringing him a packet of own brand muesli, but he was so pleased about it that he thanked me about three times, tears in his eyes. It just feels all wrong.

For people coming to the foodbank, choice is not something they are likely to be used to. Growing conditionality, such as the requirement that jobseekers must spend 35 hours per week searching for paid employment, erodes choice and increases surveillance. There is little choice involved in paying the bedroom tax, or finding an appropriate time to have a Jobcentre appointment. Choice is also absent for people accessing emergency food; people are handed a parcel of food that a volunteer has already picked out for them. There is little choice involved in any of these decisions. So maybe, when faced with the charitable food aid from a foodbank, in an environment that is (or at least aims to be) warm, welcoming and non-judgemental, why should it be frowned upon when people express distaste or desire for a certain brand of food? Mckenzie (2015) draws on an argument put forward by George Orwell in *The Road to Wigan Pier*: 'You don't want to live in absolute hardship with no comfort. Struggling to make ends meet is endless misery, and, as Orwell surmised, lots of sugar in your tea and a warm fire goes some way to relieving, even if just for a minute, the endless misery.'

Power, choice and expectations all play a part in the foodbank experience for both volunteers and people coming with their red voucher. These expectations may or may not be met during a visit to the foodbank, as the following field notes show:

Field notes
17 January 2014

We had a woman come in today who said 'I'm from the DWP [Department for Work and Pensions].' We all assumed she meant she was here to collect some vouchers for the Jobcentre. Rebecca – in her 40s, I'd say – was dressed in fancy black lacy tights, pencil skirt, a beige belted mac, and had a full face of makeup – not the usual clothing choices of people I've seen in here in the past four weeks, to be honest. Maureen went to sit with her and it transpired she had a voucher from DWP for food. She didn't want to say anything about her circumstances. 'What will I get in the food parcel?' Rebecca asked me when I went over to get her red voucher. I talked her through one of our printed sheets detailing what a single person gets. She asked what brands we had, and I told her sometimes brands like Heinz, John West, but usually Tesco's or Sainsbury's own make. She looked pretty outraged and said 'You don't get things from Marks and Spencer's'?' I told her we didn't tend to. When I went upstairs and made her parcel I didn't pay particular attention to the brands I gave her, as I don't do that for anyone else. I gave Rebecca the food and she left.

24 January 2014

I found out Rebecca (the woman in the mac) came back in and brought some of the food back that we'd given her! Corned beef, tinned vegetables, and tinned fruit, the volunteers told me. 'I won't eat just anything' Rebecca had said to Maureen. After the initial shock, we all agreed that at least she'd brought them back so someone else could have them ...

These extracts show the expectations of both the foodbank volunteer and person using the foodbank are sometimes unmet. Tarasuk and Eakin (2003) discuss how such expectations of gratitude play an important role in foodbank provision in their research in Canada. Their findings show how volunteers state that "everything in the food parcel should be appreciated" and they doubt the seriousness of the need for food assistance if people are critical about the content of the food parcel. Similar findings are reported by Caplan (2016: 8) who wrote:

Clients who return items saying 'I want something better. Give me Waitrose, not Tesco value' are thought to be behaving inappropriately. Yet this demand to have a modicum of choice in what they take away may be understood as a claim to be treated, at least to some degree, like everyone else, who does have a 'choice' in what they eat. But this response was relatively rare. More common reactions from clients were repeated thanks, even hugs and tears.

Taste and preference tend not to be addressed with a visit to the foodbank. Douglas et al. (2015) found that: 'It was striking (sadly so) that participants were not receiving food they normally ate or enjoyed from the food bank, but were taking what they were given. In addition, they all indicated general reluctance about asking staff for food items they liked.'

As foodbanks rely on donations based on a suggested shopping list, sometimes more 'obscure' items are donated that ended up being left on the shelf. Lumpfish caviar, Thai green curry paste, make-your-own jam kits, and a jar of capers in Prosecco remained on the shelves for months on end. As Janet Poppendieck (1998: 214, emphasis in original) has asked 'Why am I choosing *for* people whose tastes and preferences I may not share?' In the Netherlands, van der Horst et al. (2014) have shown how emotions of gratitude and shame can play a role in the foodbank encounter:

> Some receivers conform religiously to such implicit social rules in order to gain some status. Others instead are aware of what is expected of them, but choose not to conform. As conforming would suggest that they are to blame for their situation, which they want to make clear they are not.

Tarasuk and Eakin argue that food banks 'render the unmet need invisible' (2003: 1513). They found that:

> Those who attempted to gain greater access to food by circumventing distribution policies were labelled 'abusers' and risked being banned from the food bank indefinitely. The dissociation of food distribution from need and the suppression of evidence of unmet need among clients through the discourses of abuse and gratitude effectively rendered clients' food needs invisible.

Douglas and colleagues use the term 'compulsory gratitude' to indicate the relationship between the food giver and receiver. As receiving food from a foodbank is not a socially acceptable means of consumption, the shift from entitlement to charitable provision brings increased stigma, conditionality and surveillance for people who are seeking food aid (Garthwaite, 2016a, 2016b). Silvasti (2015: 478, 480) has commented that 'it should be underlined that charity food is never an entitlement, it is a gift' that does not 'offer legitimate access to all citizens, equally'. This is heightened by the refusal of the state to officially recognise the evidenced extent and causes of food insecurity in the UK. Charity is not offered to social equals, thus recipients remain separate from volunteers in terms of both status and expectations, while 'social honour accrues to those who volunteer; stigma to those who are clients' (Poppendieck, 1998: 254).

Conclusion

Set against a backdrop of rising foodbank use, and an increased stereotyping of people living on a low income, this chapter has explored the relationship between deservingness, choice and gratitude and foodbank use in the UK.

Volunteers, staff at referral agencies, and food donors and people who used the foodbank regularly discussed ideas of who is (or who should be) considered 'deserving' or 'undeserving'. This is then closely linked to choice and the anticipation of gratitude, and, more specifically, the expected behaviours of people accessing emergency food. Deservingness is arguably inbuilt into the foodbank referral scenario, which requires staff at referral agencies to decide whether to issue a red voucher required to access a food parcel.

The Trussell Trust aims to avoid 'cycles of dependency', a key point raised by staff at referral agencies when discussing foodbank use. Dependency is then woven into ideas around the temporariness of foodbank use. At present, the balance between the longer-term institutionalisation of foodbanks and the inbuilt structural inequality sending people towards foodbanks in the first place, is skewed. There has been an insistence that the government must address issues such as benefits sanctions, delays and the bedroom tax, all of which contribute to large numbers of people needing emergency food. Yet at present, the government continue to deny a link between their ongoing reforms and rising foodbank use. It is therefore difficult to imagine a future without foodbanks, given the continual dismantling of the social security safety net. Above all, charitable food provision should not become an accepted and unchallenged norm.

As foodbank use continues to become an ever-present feature of austerity Britain, it is critical to avoid assigning distinctions of 'deserving' or 'undeserving' to those who use them. The findings emphasise the importance of the idea that every individual deserves access to food, irrespective of supposed behavioural 'choices'. Employing ethnographic techniques to study foodbank use has allowed for a more nuanced understanding of the complexity of accessing emergency food provision and associated ideas of dependency, as Paul's story shows. It is therefore crucial to humanise the lived experiences of using a foodbank, to ensure they are viewed as shocking and outrageous, rather than allowing them to become an accepted and inevitable feature of society.

References

APPG (All-Party Parliamentary Group on Hunger) (2016) 'Britain's not-so-hidden hunger', http://www.frankfield.com/upload/docs/Britain's%20not-so-hidden%20hunger.pdf

Bennett, A. (2014) 'Edwina Currie says "pernicious" food banks make people poorer', www.huffingtonpost.co.uk/2014/01/28/ edwina-currie-food-banks-_n_4680965.html

Caplan, P. (2016) 'Big society or broken society? Food banks in the UK', *Anthropology Today*, 32(1): 5–9.

Cloke, P., May, J. and Williams, A. (2016) 'The geographies of food banks in the meantime', *Progress in Human Geography*, p.0309132516655881.

Douglas, F., Sapko, J., Kiezebrink, K. and Kyle, J. (2015) 'Resourcefulness, desperation, shame, gratitude and powerlessness: common themes emerging from a study of food bank use in northeast Scotland', *AIMS Public Health*, 2(3): 297–317.

Dowler, E. and Lambie-Mumford, H. (2014) 'Food aid: living with food insecurity', Working Paper of the Communities & Culture Network+ Food Aid Call, http://www.communitiesandculture.org/files/2013/01/Living-with-Food-Insecurity-CCN-Report.pdf

Dowler, E. and O'Connor, D. (2012) 'Rights-based approaches to addressing food poverty and food insecurity in Ireland and UK', *Social Science & Medicine*, 74 (1): 44–51.

Elgot, J. (2014) '"Selfish" food bank users spent money on booze and drugs, says Tory Julia Lepoidevin', Huffington Post, 27 June, www.huffingtonpost.co.uk/2014/06/27/food-banks-_n_5536359.html

Garthwaite, K. (2011) 'The language of shirkers and scroungers? Talking about illness, disability and coalition welfare reform', *Disability & Society*, 26(3): 369–72.

Garthwaite, K. (2016a) *Hunger pains: Life inside foodbank Britain*, Bristol: Policy Press.

Garthwaite, K. (2016b) '"Stigma, shame and 'people like us'": an ethnographic study of foodbank use in the UK', *Journal of Poverty and Social Justice*, 24(3): 277–89.

Lambie-Mumford, H. (2013) '"Every town should have one": emergency food banking in the UK', *Journal of Social Policy*, 42(1): 73-89.

Lambie-Mumford, H. (2014) 'Food bank provision and welfare reform in the UK', SPERI Policy Brief, No. 4, http://speri.dept.shef.ac.uk/wp-content/uploads/2014/01/SPERI-British-Political-Economy-Brief-No4-Food-bank-provision-welfare-reform-in-the-UK.pdf

Lambie-Mumford, H. (2015) *Addressing food poverty in the UK: Charity, rights and welfare*, Sheffield: Sheffield Political Economy Research Institute.

Loopstra, R., Reeves, A., Taylor-Robinson, D., Barr, B., McKee, M., and Stuckler, D. (2015) 'Austerity, sanctions, and the rise of food banks in the UK', *British Medical Journal*, 350: h1775.

May, J. (2014) 'Secular reflections on the challenges of food banking and the language of deservedness and dependency for Christian discipleship', paper presented at the London Churches Social Action Theological Enquiry in to Food Banking Forum, June, www.londonchurches.org.uk/12.html

Mckenzie, L. (2015) *Getting by: Estates, class and culture in austerity Britain*, Bristol: Policy Press.

Monroe, J. (2013) 'Let's debate our need for food banks – a national disgrace', *The Guardian*, https://www.theguardian.com/society/2013/dec/18/food-banks-parliamentary-debate-scandal

Perry, J., Williams, M., Sefton, T. and Haddad, M. (2014) *Emergency use only: Understanding and reducing the use of food banks in the UK*, London: CPAG, Church of England, Oxfam GB and the Trussell Trust.

Poppendieck, J. (1998) *Sweet charity? Emergency food and the end of entitlement*, Harmondsworth: Penguin.

Public Health England (2015) 'Stockton-on-Tees health profile 2015', APHO, www.apho.org.uk/resource/item.aspx?RID=50336

Purdam, K., Garratt, E.A. and Esmail, A. (2015) 'Hungry? Food insecurity, social stigma and embarrassment in the UK', *Sociology*, 50(6).

Riches, G. (2002) 'Food banks and food security: welfare reform, human rights and social policy. Lessons from Canada?', *Social Policy & Administration*, 36(6): 648–63.

Shildrick, T.A., MacDonald, R. and Furlong, A. (2016) 'Not single spies but in battalions: a critical, sociological engagement with the idea of so-called "Troubled Families"', *Sociological Review*, online first, doi: 10.1111/1467-954X.12425

Shipton, M. (2013) 'Vale of Glamorgan MP Alun Cairns in food bank row after claims drug addicts use them', 19 September, www.walesonline.co.uk/news/wales-news/vale-glamorgan-tory-mp-alun-6060730

Silvasti, T. (2015) 'Food aid – normalising the abnormal in Finland', *Social Policy and Society*, 14(3): 471–82.

Tarasuk, V. and Eakin, J.M. (2003) 'Charitable food assistance as symbolic gesture: an ethnographic study of food banks in Ontario', *Social Science & Medicine*, 56(7): 1505–15.

Trussell Trust (2016) 'Half a million emergency food parcels distributed by Trussell Trust foodbanks in six months', https://www.trusselltrust.org/2016/11/08/half-million-emergency-food-parcels-distributed-trussell-trust-foodbanks-six-months/

Tyler, I. (2013) *Revolting subjects: Social abjection and resistance in neoliberal Britain*, London: Zed Books.

van der Horst, H., Pascucci, S. and Bol, W. (2014) 'The "dark side" of food banks? Exploring emotional responses of food bank receivers in the Netherlands', *British Food Journal*, 116(9): 1506–20.

Wells, R. and Caraher, M. (2014) 'UK print media coverage of the food bank phenomenon: from food welfare to food charity?', *British Food Journal*, 116(9): 1426–45.

Williams, A., Cloke, P., May, J. and Goodwin, M. (2016) 'Contested space: the contradictory political dynamics of food banking in the UK', *Environment and Planning A*, 48(11): 2291–316.

SIX

Maternal imprisonment: a family sentence

Natalie Booth

Introduction

The Criminal Justice System (CJS) may only be charged with the responsibility of the prisoner – but when that prisoner is also a mother then we need to acknowledge that their custodial sentence will also interfere with family life (Loucks, 2005; Codd, 2008; Enroos, 2011). Viewing these women in isolation from their maternal status fails to recognise how they are embedded in social and familial networks, relationships and responsibilities, and generally perform a primary caregiving role to their dependent children (Caddle and Crisp, 1997). Not only does this have implications for female prisoners as they attempt to remain connected to motherhood, but it also has a substantial effect on the large number of innocent children and family members left behind during maternal imprisonment. Prisoners' children have been called the 'hidden victims of imprisonment' (Cunningham and Baker, 2004: 2) and the 'orphans of justice' (Shaw, 1992: 41) within the literature because they, and their family members, are continually disregarded within the political and policy sphere, academic studies and society more generally (Murray, 2005).

This is despite statistics indicating that over half of all the women in prison in England and Wales are mothers; most of whom were actively involved in caretaking prior to their imprisonment (Caddle and Crisp, 1997; Williams et al, 2012). Estimates suggest that this leaves 18,000 children every year in England and Wales separated from their mother following her custodial sentence (Corston, 2007). Immediate care of these children must be assumed by someone else when the mother is remanded into prison custody and in most instances family members adopt these responsibilities (Caddle and Crisp, 1997). Consequently, the everyday practices of several family members are subjected to significant renegotiations in response to these changes, while roles and responsibilities are adapted to accommodate the different domestic circumstances (Hairston, 2009). The extent of these readjustments can be better appreciated in light of only 5% of children remaining in their own homes once their mother is removed into prison (Caddle and Crisp, 1997). Thus, it is evident that the nature of this mother–child separation has repercussions that ripple through the wider family, punishing even those members who have not been legally accused or sentenced. It is these implications that suggest how maternal imprisonment may be experienced as a 'family sentence'.

The purpose of this chapter is to develop this concept of a 'family sentence' by providing new empirical evidence that draws on in-depth interviews with mothers detained in the female prison estate in England. The chapter first explores the policy and penal landscape in England and Wales to contextualise the position of prisoners' families in wider society and government discourses. Following this, the family context will be introduced, specifically drawing attention to social and cultural constructs of 'good mothers' and how the dominant gendered expectations around motherhood are juxtaposed against a prisoner identity. It also examines the limited research attention that maternal imprisonment has received to date, and the paucity of knowledge about family life under these challenging circumstances. The research approach and data collection methods are briefly detailed in the methodology section, before exploring the research findings and implications.

The policy context

As part of a global trend, the prison population in England and Wales has grown in recent years (Wacquant, 2002; Ministry of Justice [MoJ], 2013). Although it is difficult to pinpoint exactly what has caused this dramatic increase, many commentators have suggested it is related to the more punitive stance of successive governments and their policies since the 1980s and the 'tough on crime' rhetoric which has filtered into popular discourse and legislations (see Cavadino and Dignan, 2002; Liebling, 2004). Yet women are generally imprisoned for short sentences and non-violent crimes, such as theft and handling (MoJ, 2016a) and are less represented among serious offenders – although it is acknowledged that some will have been involved in serious or dangerous criminal activities that means their removal from the home may improve the lives of her children and families (see Codd, 2008). Nevertheless, it is important to note that the higher number of women in prison – around 2,000 more than twenty years ago on any one day (MoJ, 2015, 2016b) – will have resulted in more families experiencing maternal imprisonment.

In parallel with these changes, there has been a growing interest in prisoners' families (Codd, 2008). This has occurred as families were identified as an effective source of support – practically, financially and emotionally – for prisoners both during their sentence and release, with a wealth of government documents advocating these relationships (Social Exclusion Unit, 2002; Home Office, 2004; MoJ and Department for Children, Schools and Families [DCSF], 2009; Criminal Justice Joint Inspection (CJJI, 2014). Specifically, the emphasis on maintaining prisoners' family ties has fixated on the ways in which families can help to reduce reoffending. The link between familial relationships and recidivism was formally recognised following a decision to include 'Children and Families' as one of the seven pathways to rehabilitate prisoners in the *Reducing re-offending: National action plan* (Home Office, 2004). Since then, this rhetoric has filtered from policy to practice as operational guidelines issued to prison establishments in *Prison service instructions*[1] (NOMS, 2011: 2) stated that prisoners are 'less likely to reoffend if they have had received family visits whilst in custody'. More recently, Her Majesty's Inspectorate of Prisons (HMIP, 2014) reported that family ties were the most effective route to help prisoners desist from criminal behaviour on their re-entry into the community from prison.

However, this prisoner-centric focus has failed to recognise that prisoners' families have vulnerabilities and needs in their own right as they attempt to manage the mother's detainment while assuming her domestic and caregiving role and responsibilities. The limited awareness of a prisoner's status as a mother also means that no consideration is given to her dependent children or their possible welfare needs at any stage in the CJS process. For instance, within the current system these children are rendered invisible at court because nobody is responsible for identifying them or establishing what (if any) care has been arranged *before* the mother is incarcerated. In response to this, a joint campaign called 'Families left behind' (PACT, 2015), led by the voluntary sector has tried to introduce legislation that requires the courts to ask defendants about their dependents so that appropriate steps can be taken to ensure provisions are made for them – though so far, this has met with little success. Yet a small-scale study at HMP Holloway[2] in London found that most family members assumed responsibility for the mothers' children at the last minute, and without any prior preparations having been put in place (Boswell and Wood, 2011). Arguably, this sudden uptake of care can exacerbate what is already a stressful familial event – even precipitating a familial crisis – as the mother is detained without provisions or arrangements for her children having been decided or organised.

Many of these procedural failures occur because there is no formal agency or organisation responsible for prisoners' families in England and Wales (Williams et al, 2012) – either within the CJS or in other institutions, such as schools. This means that no official body routinely identifies family members, collects information about them or represents them in social and policy contexts. It also means that there are no statutory interventions or services focused on supporting prisoners' families. Responsibility for this population instead falls to voluntary sector organisations, such as Prison Advice and Care Trust (PACT), Barnardo's, Partners of Prisoners (POPS) and many more. Yet the current economic climate means that these organisations are faced with financial challenges as they attempt to secure long-term funding, functioning with extreme anxieties around the next tenure (Codd, 2008; Mills and Codd, 2008; de Las Casas et al, 2011). Raikes (2016) has also hinted at how national provisions are in pockets across the country, creating a 'postcode lottery' when it comes to the services available for these families. Therefore, given this context, it is evident that successive governments have failed to show a genuine commitment for the welfare and needs of the individuals with a prisoner in their family. The so-called support for family ties in policy and in prison establishments appears to be more of a smokescreen for wider anxieties around reducing reoffending rather than arising out of a concern for family life during a mother's imprisonment. Indeed, this discourse barely acknowledges that families may be motivated to maintain contact for the sake of its members. A report undertaken by New Philanthropy Capital (Brookes, 2005: 3) aptly summarised how, within the policy landscape, 'rhetoric from government ministers in this area is commendable, but action has been poor'.

The family context

As motherhood is socially and culturally constructed, it has been subjected to highly prescriptive discourses in recent years, which work to reflect implicit assumptions about the function of the mother and, alongside this, appropriate mothering practices in society (Oakley, 1976; Hays, 1996; Enos, 2001). Within this frame of reference motherhood is deemed incompatible with a criminal identity. Or, to be more specific, the literature indicates that the concept of a '*good mother*' is incompatible with a criminal identity (Teather et al, 1997; Corston, 2007). For these women, criminality assumes a failure on their part in fulfilling the gendered roles ascribed to them through feminine norms in the gender contract: those pertaining to their responsibilities in childbearing and childrearing (Carlen, 1983). This explains why a 'bad mother' identity is ascribed to mothers in prison as a result of their seemingly 'doubly deviant' transgressions – first, as a result of their law-breaking behaviour as a citizen and, second, with regard to the undermining of gendered expectations placed on them as mothers (Teather et al, 1997; Corston, 2007; Baldwin, 2015). In other words, these women are 'bad mothers' by virtue of their imprisoned status (Enos, 2001) and consequently inhabit a stigmatised positionality as their criminality is 'incongruous with our stereotype of what a given type of individual (and in this case a mother) should be' (Goffman, 1963: 13).

Yet it is these socially idealised notions of motherhood that have generated unease around the use of prison as a punishment for mothers (Worrall, 1990; Matthews, 1999; Carlen, 2002; Chesney-Lind and Pasko, 2003; Gelsthorpe and Morris, 2008; Corston, 2007; Enroos, 2011). In particular, this is because women continue to play a central role in the domestic sphere, and with regard to caregiving (Gabel and Johnson, 1995; Huebner and Gustafson, 2007). David Cameron's speech on prison reform in February 2016 echoed some of these anxieties as he touched on the issues of babies born to imprisoned women (Cameron, 2016). Similarly, many commentators argue that maternal imprisonment is more disruptive and distressing than paternal imprisonment (Myers et al, 1999; Hardwick, 2012). Mostly this is because, when a father is imprisoned, in 90% of cases his children continue to be cared for by their mother in the community (Dodd and Hunter, 1992) rather than being faced immediately with the need for a new caregiver. Mostly female family members, such as aunts and sisters as well as grandparents, adopt these responsibilities when a mother is imprisoned (Caddle and Crisp, 1997; Boswell and Wood, 2011). It is important to note, though, that being in prison does not necessarily remove a mothers' legal parental responsibility or indeed her willingness to continue mothering. However, by virtue of her detainment, being imprisoned will significantly alter and compromise the roles and practices which she can adopt within the penal context.

The family's response to maternal imprisonment may vary depending on how they confront a mother's imprisonment, and when taken-for-granted understandings and practices are challenged (Enos, 2001). The way families conceptualise and enact obligations in their relationships may be drawn upon, for instance basing their response on the quality of past relationships, their familial history, and their expectation of reciprocity and interdependence in the future (Finch and Mason, 1993). This feeds into recent sociological conceptions of 'the family', which have pointed to its fluid and active meaning, responding to circumstances and emphasising the 'doing' of routine and regular everyday 'family practices' (Morgan, 1996, 1999, 2011) as opposed to 'being' within a family unit. Overall, though, it is difficult to ascertain an accurate picture of family life during parental imprisonment because this population has not received much attention (Murray, 2005; Codd, 2008), and specifically when a mother is imprisoned in England and Wales. Consequently, the research on which this chapter is based attempts to bridge the substantial gap in our knowledge about these circumstances by focusing on and advocating for the voices and experiences of family members with this lived experience in the form of a family-centred perspective.

Methodology

This chapter reveals the findings from a qualitative study[3] that conducted in-depth, interviews with 30 families experiencing maternal imprisonment in England and Wales[4] between May and November in 2015. The sample is made up of two cohorts; the first is comprised of 15 family members caring for children following their mothers' imprisonment (referred to as caregivers), while the second cohort is made up of 15 imprisoned mothers. The decision to recruit two groups of unrelated family members was made to ensure the focus of the research remained on the familial experience of maternal imprisonment, rather than comparing within-family narratives and dynamics. In this chapter, it is the experiences of the cohort of imprisoned mothers that are examined.

In accordance with guidelines set out in *Prison service instructions (PSI) 22* (NOMS, 2014), permission to undertake research within and across the prison estate was gained from the National Research Council (NRC) and from the governor of the women's prison where the cohort of mothers was recruited. A purposive sampling strategy was used (Bryman, 2012) so that insights into maternal imprisonment where the mother was convicted and had served at least two months of her sentence at the time of interview could be identified. These eligibility criteria were chosen so that all the mothers would have completed their court proceedings, and have been sentenced and incarcerated for long enough to enable them to reflect on the prison environment and their experiences of negotiating their changed familial circumstances. The mothers also had to have at least one child under 18 years to participate, as this coincides with most legal thresholds of adulthood and the cut-off for parental responsibility of dependants, although it is appreciated that mothering is not just limited to this age category.

The research conformed to ethical guidelines; it had received approval from the researcher's university before its commencement and was continually reassessed throughout the research process. Informed consent was secured verbally and in writing, and was returned to several times within the interview process and out of an awareness of the sensitivity of research subject. No incentives were offered for participation, and family members were clearly told that the research had no influence over the formalities or operationalisation of their custodial sentence. They were also made aware of the parameters of confidentiality that could be afforded as prisoner participants and because of their positionality within the prison institution, for instance around disclosures of harm and contraband (in line with guidelines in NOMS, 2012). Permission was gained from all participants to audio-record and transcribe the interviews, and during this process the data was anonymised and participants' names were changed to pseudonyms.

The mothers were not asked to disclose the nature of their criminal offence at any stage in the research process. Nevertheless, many offered this detail in the interview setting, feeling it was an important piece of information within their narrative. Consequently, it is known that the mothers were in prison for a range of different offences; from perverting the course of justice and burglary, to drug-related crimes, fraud and violent crimes, including Grievous Bodily Harm (GBH) – although all the mothers were serving sentences of four years or less. As Table 6.1 shows, most (n = 12) mothers identified as white British when asked to self-report their ethnicity, were aged between 25 and 30 years old (n = 8) and had on average two children, although there was one mother who had a larger family of seven children.

The interviews were specifically interested in understanding what happens when a mother receives a custodial sentence, asking how this process impacts her identity and status as a mother, as well as her perspectives of mothering in prison. In doing so, the mothers were asked to describe family life before coming into prison – their living arrangements, childcare arrangements, relationships and daily routines and practices – before asking them to discuss these since being received

Table 6.1: Demographics of mothers in sample (n=15)

Age	
25–30	8
31–34	1
35–40	1
41–44	2
45–50	3
Ethnicity	
White British	12
Romany Gypsy	1
Other*	2
Number of children	
1	3
2	6
3	3
4	2
More than 5	1

Note: *Other includes one mother who preferred not to record her ethnicity and a second mother who stated she was British.

into prison custody. Inductive thematic data analysis was used to organise and identify patterns and themes in the data as having originated from the participants own descriptions of their lives and experiences (Braun and Clarke, 2006). Findings from the research have provided rich data on the mothers' own understandings of their familial lives since being imprisoned, and it is to these experiences that the chapter now turns.

Family life: the view from behind bars

Within the sample of 15 mothers, two distinct groups of mothers were identified. The crucial differences between these groups were observed through the mothers' positionality and mothering role *before* coming into prison, which are outlined briefly below:

The disconnected group – is made up of 10 mothers who were actively involved in their children's lives before their custodial sentence. Most of them lived with their children (n = 8), of whom six were sole carers. The two mothers who did not live in the same household as their children reported having frequent and daily contact with their children. None of the mothers had served a custodial sentence before, were separated from their children for the first time and were named as such because they felt disconnected from their children as a result of these substantial changes in their familial lives.

The rebuilding group – includes the remaining five mothers in the sample who described distanced familial relationships as they had not lived with their children for many years. All the rebuilding mothers reported substance use issues, and four had been in prison before. These mothers had already endured lengthy separations from their children prior to their imprisonment, but viewed their current sentence as an opportunity to rebuild these relationships and their maternal role.

The substantial differences observed in the mothers' participation in their children's lives before being imprisoned were also found to shape their experiences of mothering *in prison* and their self-perceptions as mothers. Given these different familial contexts, the experiences of and repercussions for children and families during the mother's imprisonment were disparate. For this reason, the chapter explores the experiences of the disconnected group of mothers. Two themes were identified and are revealed in this section to illuminate the mothers' descriptions of their familial lives since being imprisoned; 'doing mothering in prison' and 'internalised stigma'.

Doing mothering in prison

The mothers discussed how their absence in the household and their children's daily lives was preventing them from engaging in their previous role, practices and responsibilities as mothers. As Eve explains, being unable to do routine activities like cooking a meal or telling her children off made her feel isolated from her children's everyday lives.

'Being in here [I'm] sort of isolated from their everyday issues; not
being able to see them when they're happy, sad and to celebrate,
or maybe when they're down and their angry, not being able to
help them. Just kind of the issues that you would think, like not
being able to cook them a meal, not being able to tell them off
when they've been naughty – all of those things I've taken for
granted and now I miss all of those things.' (Eve, two children,
aged 19 and 13)

Similarly, Esther describes missing "normal" things that she would have
done at home and with her daughters, including routine tasks such as
supporting them with their homework as well as sharing stories and
experiences from their day. It is these activities that her daughters would
like her to be able to do again in the future – as these were the everyday
practices she could not participate in during her custodial sentence.

'They want to do their homework with me, tell me about their
day, they might want to show me a little dance routine that
they've done, plait their hair, they just want me to cook them a
meal. Just normal things that I would have been doing, it doesn't
have to be anything overly exciting, just something normal. Put
them to bed; wash their hair, something like that.' (Esther, two
children, aged 10 and 7)

Put more briefly, Keira also asserts how she does not feel as knowledgeable
about her daughter's every life because she is no longer involved in her
daily practices, despite having been sole caregiver prior to her arrest.
"I don't know stuff; I couldn't, because I'm not with my daughter day
to day" (Keira, one child, aged 5).

To understand the nuances around doing 'normal' daily tasks, it is
necessary to contextualise these findings within recent sociological
definitions of family life, which have emphasised the importance of
'doing' family, rather than 'being' a family. A core tenet of Morgan's
(1996, 1999, 2011) conception of 'family practices' illuminates the
significance of the everyday and the sense of regularity in activities,
showing how being active and involved in certain responsibilities
allows the individual to adopt particular familial roles. Thus, for the
mothers to engage in everyday mothering practices, such as cooking
or bedtime routines, was to be 'doing' motherhood. Such perspectives
also feed into wider societal expectations and conceptualisations of an
idealised mothering role in which 'good' mothers suspend their own

needs and prioritise their children's by being protective and nurturing, and providing support to them.

Respondents indicated how access to doing mothering practices was not only affected by virtue of the physical separation that constitutes incarceration, but also because the available routes to sustain contact with family members from prison were inadequate. Prisoners are allowed contact with their family through prison processes such as visitation, telephones and mail (HMIP, 2016), although accessing and sustaining these forms of contact was identified as an ongoing battle for the mothers. Betty had been the sole caregiver to her three teenage children before her arrest, and explains how being separated from them for the first time was particularly difficult as she was struggling to maintain daily contact. "The main challenge as a Mum is to day in, day out, keep communication" (Betty, three children, aged 15, 13 and 11).

This study like other research, found that prisoners experienced problems accessing telephones on the prison wings (HMIP, 2016) and being able to pay for the phone calls (Sharratt, 2014). Visitation was also hampered because families must undertake long journeys, as mothers are detained in institutions on average 50 miles from their homes (NOMS, 2013), arriving to stringent search procedures (Condry, 2007) and an environment which does not foster meaningful contact (Sharratt, 2014; Booth, 2016). Although there is not the space to unravel these circumstances in more detail in this chapter, it was clear that the mothers felt that the prison processes did little to help them perform their mothering role. As Kelly explains, the contact which she can sustain from prison is not enough to overcome her absence in the family or allow her to support them. "I know I can speak to them on the phone and I can speak to them on the visit but I can't be there for them" (Kelly, four children, aged 27, 16, 12 and 9).

Similarly, Esther considers how the infrequency of this contact prevents her from being a part of her children's lives but emphasises the importance of communicating as often as possible.

'You're not part of it [family life] at the end of the phone or on a visit every couple of weeks, you're not seeing it, you're not there for it ... I just think the biggest thing you can do is just keep contact with them ... that's the biggest thing you can try to do.' (Esther, two children, aged 10 and 7)

These findings not only point towards a substantial disruption to family life when a primary carer is imprisoned, but indicates that the prison environment and its processes do little to support the mothers as they attempted to cling on to some – albeit a substantially reduced – aspect of their maternal role and identity in prison.

Internalised stigma

Building on the previous section, some links between being unable to continue performing their mothering role were understood to correspond with an erosion of the mother's self-identification with a 'good mother' identity. This is because they showed an awareness of their 'spoiled identity' (Goffman, 1963) as they recognised the dichotomy between their prisoner and motherhood identities. The extract below illustrates how Eve holds herself responsible for being absent, and describes how she feels the overwhelming need to make up for her perceived failures on release; illuminating feelings of guilt and inadequacy.

> 'I've let myself down and that is hard to deal with sometimes ... when I went to prison my son had just come out of primary school and was going to secondary school and so she [my daughter] was there on his first day, she was there making sure he had a uniform, making sure he had money for lunches, making sure that he had all the stationery he needed – she was doing everything that I should have been doing so yeah, I owe a lot to her ... I'll do everything I can to support them and help them [when I am released], hopefully for my son through the rest of school and my daughter to get her own life 'cause she's been so busy stepping into my shoes that she's given up her own life for me, so that's what I'm hoping ... my relationship with them is damaged and I need to prove myself to them, that I'm not going to do that again.' (Eve, two children, aged 19 and 13)

This shows feelings akin to Herek's (2009) definition of *internalised stigma*, in which the individual accepts society's discrediting of their stigmatised positionality and begins to internalise these negative beliefs in their own narrative and self-concept. What can be seen in Eve's narrative is that being in prison is affecting her maternal identity as she explains how her daughter – as caregiver to her younger brother – adopted the practices which she had previously engaged in, and would have ordinarily undertaken in the home. Her descriptions illuminate the difference in her idealised mothering role as she describes what she *should* have been doing, and comparing this against the actual circumstances – and also what she *expects* from herself in the future. Inevitably, she is measuring her own mothering practices against the dominant discursive conceptualisations of motherhood – and 'good mothers' in wider society.

Internalised stigma also involves a process of self-stigma – in which an individual facing a spoiled identity displays negative attitudes towards themselves (Herek, 2009). As with Eve, most of the mothers' assumed responsibility for their challenging familial circumstances – acknowledging how they were to blame for the prison sentence and thus for the widespread and damaging implications this had on their loved ones. This is articulated by Leanne as she recognises how her 8-year-old son is being punished despite being innocent of any crime, while identifying herself as being to "blame". "I feel like my eldest son has been punished and he hasn't even been naughty, but the only person to blame is myself and that's a fact" (Leanne, two children, aged 8 and 1).

Evidence of this self-stigma is also found in Betty's narrative as she recites the different aspects of her children's lives that had been "lost" because of her incarceration. "They lost their Mum, their home, their schools, their friends and even the animals; they lost everything so you couldn't blame them if they didn't want to know me" (Betty, three children, aged 15, 13 and 11).

These accounts indicate how the mothers were struggling to identify with their 'good mother' identity, as their critical assessments and acute awareness of their own, and their familial situations, led them to allocate this self-blame. For instance, Kathleen similarly engages in this self-stigma as she perceives her imprisonment to have much worse implications for the husband and children because of the domestic and financial adjustments they were struggling to manage in her absence.

> 'My husband didn't work but obviously he's had to find part-time work so he can support the kids ... he's really anxious, he's really stressed and he can't cope with it all ... I used to do everything, literally everything ... it has an effect on them because they've got less money, they haven't got their Mum around, the way they have their life, my husband is finding it difficult so I think it is worse for them than it is for me, most definitely.' (Kathleen, two children, aged 15 and 14)

The process of benchmarking their mothering practices and engaging in this self-stigma led the mothers to appreciate and comprehend how being imprisoned had amounted to a serious punishment, not just for them but also for their children and families outside. Taken to the extreme, the extent of this internalised stigma and the disconnectedness it brought from their former role and identity could substantially undermine the mother's ability to feel a part of their family unit and consequently identify as mothers. As Eve reveals, her positionality in prison and the poor contact available to 'do' mothering is reducing her self-identification and confidence as her children's mother.

> 'You're cut off from your children; you're not able to deal with the everyday things that you would deal with when you're outside … I feel very distanced, disconnected from them, even though I speak to them, and I see them, I don't feel like I'm their mother at the moment.' (Eve, two children, aged 19 and 13)

Discussion

The findings offer strong empirical support for the argument that a mother's incarceration is experienced as a family sentence, as the mothers' narratives illuminate how they – as the ones in receipt of the prison sentence – perceived and understood the punishment to have extended past them and rippled throughout their families (Loucks, 2005; Codd, 2008). The mothers' own critical and insightful evaluation of their difficult familial circumstances showed how the practical and relational effects of being absent were found to permeate the lives of several family members. The mothers appreciated how many aspects of their family's lives were subjected to reorganisations and negotiations, in their daily routines and practices in the home and in their social worlds. The mothers' narratives also suggest a marked difference between policy rhetoric that pledged support for family ties (see NOMS 2004; MoJ and DCSF, 2009; NOMS, 2011), and the challenges of maintaining these relationships in practice. Although to some extent the challenges facing the mothers occurred because they were in prison (Enos, 2001), their situation was made more difficult by the infrequent contact that could be sustained using the inadequate prison processes, such as telephone and visitation. Importantly, these findings point towards an emphasis on the *familial* experience of maternal imprisonment, which is juxtaposed against the prisoner-centric focus within the CJS in England and Wales. Within this framework there is therefore an inherent risk that the 'hidden' status of prisoners' children and families (Murray, 2005) within policy and penal discourses – as well as wider society – will endure, despite these relatives also being recipients of the prison punishment.

Other commentators have considered there to be substantial gendered implications when a mother is imprisoned, and have communicated unease at this process because of the central role that mothers generally have within the family unit (Gabel and Johnston, 1995; Huebner and Gustafson, 2007). Previous research exploring maternal imprisonment has been effective in identifying some of the larger upheavals for family members – such as, moving home and schools, changing work patterns and financial situations (Caddle and Crisp, 1997; Huebner and Gustafson, 2007; Hairston 2009). Adding further insights into these circumstances, the findings in this study indicate how removing a primary caretaker also has significant repercussions for the mothers' children and families in their daily lives and family practices (Morgan, 1999). The mothers' narratives showed the differences in their maternal role before custody and the struggles of continuing this in prison, which illuminated the importance of intricacies of 'doing': for instance, bedtime routines, homework and cooking meals. Indeed, the findings also demonstrate the significance of minutiae; those everyday, routine and 'normal' activities and tasks within the home. This improves our understanding of the nature and severity of the family sentence which is experienced when the mother is being detained – and especially when she had previously been the primary caregiver.

Following previous research (see Caddle and Crisp, 1997), the majority of women in the cohort of mothers (n = 10) had been centrally involved in their children's caregiving prior to their conviction. A smaller number of mothers in the cohort (n = 5), positioned in the rebuilding group, had been less directly involved in caretaking following previous spells in prison, and consequently reported different family circumstances from those experienced by the disconnected group. This supports Rowe's (2011) assertion that women in prison should not be viewed as a homogeneous group. The different characteristics of the disconnected and rebuilding groups also correspond with findings presented by Enos (2001), as she considered that mothers serving their first sentence are more likely to have been involved in their family, whereas when women persist in their offending careers their place within the family becomes increasingly peripheral. Within this framework, it could be argued that the nature and severity of the family sentence varies depending on the family's existing and historical caregiving circumstances and formation. In particular, this study has shown that when a mother is incarcerated for the first time as the primary carer, then this directly, immediately and adversely affects the day-to-day practices of their children and families.

The gendered insights produced in this qualitative study are also relevant against the backdrop of strong prescriptive expectations around motherhood – and especially 'good mothers' – as their internalised stigma indicated an awareness of their 'spoiled identities' (Goffman, 1963). The incongruence was noticed in the mothers' narratives as they measured themselves against idealised notions of motherhood. This led to a deconstruction in their self-perception of and identification with their maternal status. The research showed how this process of internalised stigma was so profound that it evoked feelings of disconnectedness, guilt and inadequacy. The mothers considered their families to be disadvantaged by their absence and suffering to a further extent, highlighting the pervasiveness of the family sentence. Yet it is less obvious how this process may unfold and affect relationships over time. Future research that examines maternal imprisonment longitudinally may evaluate whether this process could weaken familial relationships, having implications for the mothers' release. Statistics indicate that nearly half (48%) of women reoffend within one year (MoJ, 2014), and, considering that most women in prison have children (Caddle and Crisp, 1997), it is likely that these numbers also represent a high proportion of mothers. Building on these research findings and interpretations, it may be interesting to explore whether there are any links between the deconstruction of the mothers' identity and familial relationship during their first custodial sentence and their experiences of resuming care on release, including an examination of reoffending behaviour. Future research that explores these trajectories may provide insights into the longevity of the family sentence, which is something that this study does not offer.

Conclusion

This chapter has introduced the limitations of contemporary political, policy and penal arrangements in England and Wales, which remain prisoner-centric. It has explored the issue of failing to take into account the wider implications of removing an individual – and especially a mother – from society, and from their former role and status within the family. In doing so, it provided evidence for the argument that maternal imprisonment is experienced as a family sentence, as the mothers recognised how their imprisonment was also severely punishing family members. Drawing on sociological conceptions of contemporary family life, it was clear how the 'doing' of everyday family practices (Morgan, 1999) was a substantial aspect of what the imprisoned mothers were missing from their children's lives. Such insights improve our understanding of the multiple disadvantages and the severity of the family sentence experienced when a primary caretaker is removed. Under these circumstances, the findings offer support for gendered anxieties around the use of custodial sentences for women with children (Gabel and Johnson, 1995; Corston, 2007; Hardwick, 2012).

The substantial deconstruction of the mothers' ability to identify with their maternal role through the process of internalised stigma (Herek, 2009) was set against dominant expectations of 'good mothering'. This brings into question the longevity of the family sentence and, in particular, the potential future implications for the family once the mother is released back into the community. This evidence further suggests that evaluations of the prison environment may provide interesting insights into the familial experience, as the mothers revealed how the inadequate communicative process in the establishments did little to alleviate the challenges of doing mothering in prison. Therefore, given that the female prison population is larger than it once was (MoJ, 2013), it may be that investing time and effort in considering the wider implications of the custodial sentence on the family once a mother is removed is both timely and appropriate – and in doing so, begins to appreciate that the punishment of a custodial sentence is experienced as a 'family sentence'.

Acknowledgements

Special thanks to Professor Tess Ridge for her insightful comments on an earlier version of this chapter, and to the Economic and Social Research Council for funding the research [Award number 1229348].

Notes

[1] There are a number of rules, regulations and guidelines by which the prisons are run, and these are outlined in published Prison Service Instructions (PSIs).

[2] HMP Holloway was a female prison establishment in London which was closed in 2016.

[3] The research was funded by the Economic and Social Research Council (ESRC), award number: 1229348.

[4] Because there are no female prison establishments in Wales, Welsh mothers are detained in England and were therefore involved in the research as recruitment took place in English prison establishments.

References

Baldwin, L. (eds) (2015) *Mothering justice; Working with mothers in criminal and social justice settings*, Hook: Waterside Press.

Booth, N. (2016) *Families separated by bars: The home truths about sending mothers to prison*, http://theconversation.com/families-separated-by-bars-the-home-truths-about-sending-mothers-to-prison-56626

Boswell, G. and Wood, M. (2011) *An evaluation of the effectiveness of PACT's kinship care support service at HMP Holloway*, Kinship Care, PACT.

Braun, V. and Clarke, V. (2006) 'Using thematic analysis in psychology', *Qualitative Research in Psychology*, 3(2): 77–101.

Brookes, M. (2005) 'Investing in family ties: reoffending and family visits to prisoners', New Philanthropy Capital, www.thinknpc.org/publications/measuring-together-2/

Bryman, A. (2012) *Social Research Methods*, 4th ed, Oxford: Oxford University Press.

Caddle, D. and Crisp, D. (1997) *Imprisoned women and mothers*, London: Home Office Research Study 162.

Cameron, D. (2016) 'Prison reform', Prime Minister's speech, Westminster: London, www.gov.uk/government/speeches/prison-reform-prime-ministers-speech

Carlen, P. (1983) *Women's Imprisonment*, London: Routledge.

Carlen, P. (2002) *Women and punishment: The struggle for justice*, Cullumpton: Willan Publishing.

Cavadino, M. and Dignan, J. (2002) *The penal system: An introduction* (3rd edn), London: Sage.

Chesney-Lind, M. and Pasko, L.J. (2003) *The female offender: Girls, women and crime*, London: Sage.

CJJI (Criminal Justice Joint Inspection) (2014) *Resettlement provision for adult offenders: Accommodation and education, training and employment*, London: HMIP.

Codd, H. (2008) *In the shadow of prison: Families, imprisonment and criminal justice*. Cullumpton: Willan Publishing.

Condry, R. (2007) *Families shamed: The consequences of crime for relatives of serious offenders*, Cullumpton: Willan Publishing.

Corston, J. (2007) *The Corston report: A review of women with particular vulnerabilities in the criminal justice system*, London: Home Office.

Cunningham, A. and Baker, L. (2004) *Invisible victims: The children of women in prison*, Centre for Children and Families in the Justice System, www.lfcc.on.ca/Voices_Report-Invisible_Victims.pdf

de Las Casas, L., Fradd, A, Heady, L and Paterson, E. (2011) *Improving prisoners' family ties: Piloting a shared measurement approach*, New Philanthropy Capital, www.thinknpc.org/publications/measuring-together-2/

Dodd, T. and Hunter, P. (1992) *The national prison survey 1991,* London: HMSO, Office of Population Censuses and Surveys, Social Survey Division.

Enos, S. (2001) *Mothering from the inside*, Albany, NY: SUNY Press.

Enroos, R. (2011) 'Mothers in prison: between the public institution and private family relations', *Child and Family Social Work*, 16: 12–21.

Finch, J. and Mason, J. (1993) *Negotiating family responsibilities*, London: Routledge.

Gabel, K. and Johnston, D. (1995) *Children of incarcerated parents*, New York: Lexington Books.

Gelsthorpe, L. and Morris, A. (2008) 'Women's imprisonment in England and Wales: a penal paradox', in K. Evans and J. Jamieson (eds) *Gender and crime: A reader,* Maidenhead: McGraw-Hill, Open University Press.

Goffman, E. (1963) *Stigma: Notes on the management of spoiled identity*, Englewood Cliffs, NJ: Prentice-Hall.

Hairston, C.F. (2009) *Kinship care when parents are incarcerated: What we know, what we can do,* Baltimore, MD: Annie E. Casey Foundation.

Hardwick, N. (2012) 'Women in prison: Corston five years on', Issues in Criminal Justice Speech at University of Leicester.

Hays, S. (1996) *The cultural contradictions of motherhood*, New Haven, CT: Yale University Press.

Herek, G.M. (2009) 'Sexual stigma and sexual prejudice in the United States: a conceptual framework', in D. Hope (eds) *Contemporary perspectives on lesbian, gay, and bisexual identities*, Nebraska Symposium on Motivation 54, New York: Springer, pp 65–111.

HMIP (Her Majesty's Inspectorate of Prisons) (2014) *Resettlement provision for adult offenders: Accommodation and education, training and employment,* London: HMIP.

HMIP (2016) *Life in prison: Contact with families and friends.* London: HMIP.

Home Office (2004) *Reducing re-offending: National action plan*, London: Home Office Communication Directorate.

Huebner, B. and Gustafson, R. (2007) 'The effect of maternal incarceration on adult offspring involvement in the criminal justice system', *Journal of Criminal Justice*, 15: 283–96.

Liebling, A. (2004) *Prison and their moral performance: A study of values, quality and prison life*, Oxford: Oxford University Press.

Loucks, N. (2005) *Keeping in touch: The case for family support work in prison*, London: Prison Reform Trust.

Matthews, R. (1999) *Doing time: An Introduction to the sociology of imprisonment*, Basingstoke: Macmillan.

Mills, A. and Codd, H. (2008) 'Prisoners' families and offender management: mobilising social capital', *Journal of Community and Criminal Justice*, 55(1): 9–24.

MoJ (Ministry of Justice) (2013) *Story of the prison population 1993–2012: England and Wales*, London: Ministry of Justice.

MoJ (2014) *Women and the criminal justice system*, London: Ministry of Justice.

MoJ (2015) *Offender management statistics prison population 2015*, London: Ministry of Justice.

MoJ (2016a) *Offender management statistics annual tables 2015*, London: Ministry of Justice.

MoJ (2016b) *Offender management statistics quarterly: July to September 2015*, London: Ministry of Justice.

MoJ and DCSF (Department for Children, Schools and Families) (2009) *Reducing re-offending: Supporting families, creating better futures. A framework for improving the local delivery of support for the families of offenders*, London: HMSO.

Morgan, D.H.J. (1996) *Family connections*, Cambridge: Polity Press.

Morgan, D.H.J. (1999) 'Risk and family practices: Accounting for change and fluidity in family life', in E.B. Silvia and C. Smart (eds) *The new family?*, London: Sage.

Morgan, D.H.J. (2011) *Rethinking family practices*, London: Palgrave Macmillan.

Murray, J. (2005) 'The effects of imprisonment on families and children', in A. Liebling and S. Maruna (eds) *The effects of imprisonment*, Cullompton: Willan Publishing.

Myers, B.J., Smarsh, T.M., Amlund-Hagen, K. and Kennon, S. (1999) 'Children of incarcerated mothers', *Journal of Child and Family Studies*, 8(1): 11–25.

NOMS (National Offender Management Service) (2011) *Prison service instructions (PSI) 16/ 2011*, London: NOMS.

NOMS (2012) *Prison service instructions (PSI) 13/ 2012*, London: NOMS.

NOMS (2013) *Women's custodial estate review*. London: HMSO.

NOMS (2014) *Prison service instructions (PSI) 22/ 2014*, London: NOMS.

Oakley, A. (1976) *Woman's work: The housewife, past and present,* New York: Vintage Books.

PACT (Prison Advice and Care Trust) (2015) 'Families left behind' campaign, www.prisonadvice.org.uk/our-services/supporting-prisoners-children-and-families/campaigns-and-advocacy/left-behind

Raikes, B. (2016) *Guest blog: Ben Raikes on grandmothers' care for children of mums in prison.* Barnardo's I-Hop, www.i-hop.org.uk/app/answers/detail/a_id/820

Rowe, A. (2011) 'Narratives of self and identity in women's prisons: stigma and the struggle for self-definition in penal regimes', *Punishment and Society,* 13(5): 571–91.

Sharratt, K. (2014) 'Children's experiences of contact with imprisoned parents: a comparison between four European countries', *European Journal of Criminology,* 11(6): 760–75.

Shaw, R. (1992*)* 'Imprisoned fathers and the orphans of justice', in R. Shaw (ed.) *Prisoners' children: What are the issues?,* London: Routledge.

Social Exclusion Unit (SEU) (2002) *Reducing re-offending by ex-prisoners,* London: Social Exclusion Unit, http://webarchive.nationalarchives.gov.uk/+/http:/www.cabinetoffice.gov.uk/media/cabinetoffice/social_exclusion_task_force/assets/publications_1997_to_2006/reducing_summary.pdf

Teather, S., Evans, L. and Sims, M. (1997) 'Maintenance of the mother–child relationship by incarcerated women', *Early Child Development and Care,* 131 (1): 65–75.

Wacquant, L. (2002) 'The curious eclipse of prison ethnography in an age of mass incarceration', *Ethnography,* 3(4): 371–91.

Williams, K., Papadopoulou, V. and Booth, N. (2012) *Prisoners' childhood and family backgrounds: Results from the Surveying Prisoner Crime Reduction (SPCR) longitudinal cohort study of prisoners,* London: Ministry of Justice Research Series 4/12.

Worrall, A. (1990) *Offending women: Female lawbreakers and the criminal justice system,* London: Routledge.

SEVEN

German *Angst* in a liberalised world of welfare capitalism: the hidden problem with post-conservative welfare policies

Sigrid Betzelt and Ingo Bode

Introduction

According to a widespread reading, Germany, subsequent to the financial crisis of the late 2000s, has seen a stunning comeback as a social model allowing for both a booming economy and generous welfare provision. Compared to other Western European countries, economic growth appears robust, job prospects seem to be good especially for the young, and major public institutions continue to ensure a certain level of social redistribution. In the hegemonic European discourse, this (alleged) success is due to reforms accommodating the population to what globalised markets and financial capitalism (allegedly) require. Indeed, while major institutions of the 'Bismarckian' era (collective bargaining; social insurance; pay-as-you go benefits related to achieved social statuses) persist, scholars studying developments in Germany find evidence for the end of what is often referred to as a conservative welfare state regime (Bosch, 2015; Seeleib-Kaiser, 2016). The *post*-conservative arrangement is located between the traditional legacy and the liberal welfare regime embodied by Anglo-Saxon countries – and, from a distance, it seems that this intermediary position is the 'silver bullet' for reorganising current welfare states.

However, in the recent past Germany has been facing a social crisis that is poorly understood in both the public debate and major contributions to welfare policy analysis. Its epiphenomenon is the hostile reaction of parts of the population to the massive immigration of refugees starting in 2015. Similar to other European countries (albeit belatedly), the related tensions have entailed a formidable electoral success of a xenophobic right-wing party, alongside growing violence against ethnic minorities.

Comments in the press as well as in some quarters of academia state that people are 'worried' by the influx of strangers, anticipating pressures on the welfare state or threats to their jobs. As far as we can see, this is a general pattern in the wider Europe and also in the UK[1] – but in the light of the German 'success story', it may come as a surprise to those who believe in the narrative of post-conservative welfare policies being a 'silver bullet'.

In what follows, we will argue that there should be no surprise here as this narrative is flawed and the aforementioned crisis is indicative of a more deep-seated transformation of Germany's social model, namely its creeping *liberalisation* (see Bridgen and Meyer, 2014). This transformation comes with a *hidden problem*, that is, emotional states of fear – or a new 'German *Angst*'[2] – engendered by both path-breaking welfare reforms and a 'de-securitised' life course. Again, this resembles developments in the UK where commentators have recently observed an 'anxiety epidemic' stemming from pressures to take individual responsibility in ever more areas of life (Hutton, 2016); furthermore, against the backdrop of a redistribution of economic uncertainty (Crouch and Keune, 2012), they echo the international 'moral panic' around immigration as discussed by Bauman (2016). Exploring developments in Germany, we connect these general observations with the analysis of concrete social policies and related living conditions. We show that recent reforms, while sitting uneasily with persisting expectations of the German welfare state, prompt feelings of anxiety that enforce compliance with a recommodified labour market regime as well as with expectations towards greater individual responsibility for income security, including in later life. These feelings are mobilised by a distinctive 'politics of fear' (Furedi, 2005), creating permanent emotional stress from which affected groups can hardly escape. All this entails a nervous configuration in terms of social integration that, in the long run, may also impinge on Germany's economic performance and, more generally, on the frictionless reproduction of the social order and on what Lockwood (1964) has once labelled 'system integration'.

We first describe changes to the German welfare regime in terms of deregulation and recommodification and then review theories on feelings of anxiety and insecurity, including their association with welfare state change. The second section provides two case studies focusing on welfare policies for workers and future pensioners as rolled out since the early 2000s. Drawing on earlier reviews (Bode, 2008; Bothfeld and Betzelt, 2013), these case studies, focusing on the role of anxiety, include a depiction of path-breaking institutional change; an analysis of the accompanying discourse; and summaries of recent research centring on the subjective perceptions and coping strategies of the affected population. We conclude by elaborating on the wider implications of our findings, also in the light of the 'refugee crisis' Germany and other European countries have been experiencing for some time now.

Rising insecurity and anxiety in liberalised welfare capitalism

A core function of modern nation states has always been to 'moderate' social risks associated with capitalist economies, especially via institutions making the commercial use of the labour force more sustainable and allowing for what Esping-Andersen (1990) once termed 'de-commodification'. These institutions have long been cornerstones of a social order referred to as *welfare capitalism*. However, in most European countries, this social order has been reorganised from the 1980s onwards, through a number of reforms that entailed the deregulation of (labour) markets, the privatisation of public goods, shrinking collective risk protection, and various steps towards welfare state retrenchment, all conducive to a *re*-commodification of the life course.

For a conservative welfare regime like the one in Germany, these policies have often been qualified as a *paradigm shift*. They have made the inherited 'Bismarckian' welfare capitalism less inclusive (Bosch, 2015) and diluted the once strongly status-based components of income replacement schemes (Seeleib-Kaiser, 2016). Enacted in a context of changing industrial relations and reduced trade union power (Dingeldey et al, 2015), reforms have resulted in a decreasing collective responsibility for social predicaments and an individualisation of income risks. Consequently, there has been a growing labour market segment of low-paid, temporary, fixed-term and marginal part-time jobs, contributing to increasing wage dispersion as well as to rising income polarisation (OECD, 2015; Herr and Ruoff, 2016). At present, Germany exhibits one of the biggest low-wage sectors across Europe (covering 22% of all employees, see Bosch and Kalina, 2016). On the whole, then, the market and its regulatory mechanisms have become more influential on the allocation of individual welfare, including old age provision (Bridgen and Meyer, 2014).

The overall development – which is referred to in German academic discourse as '*de-securitisation*' ('*Entsicherung*'; Heitmeyer, 2012) – has had *varied consequences for different social classes*. Low-income earners, trapped in precarious jobs and lacking any serious prospect of upward mobility (combined with decent social security standards), find themselves in a critical 'zone of precarious wealth' (Dörre, 2006; own translation), slightly above the poverty line and with low entitlements to unemployment or pension benefits. The middle classes are in a more stable economic situation, but even for them, 'de-securitisation' is an issue. Albeit regular employees in permanent jobs still adhere to inherited norms and expectations of a secure working life, they feel that in today's reality such standards can no longer be taken for granted (Hürtgen and Voswinkel, 2014). The lower middle classes have suffered from downward mobility and income losses since the 1990s (Bosch and Kalina, 2016; Grabka et al, 2016). More generally, and across social classes, volatile (labour and financial) markets have made traditional life-course trajectories appear an exception rather than the rule (Schimank, 2015). Downward mobility becomes a realistic scenario in the case of unemployment or after retirement, since status-protecting insurance schemes have been tightened up and (partly) replaced by means-tested social assistance schemes. The prospect of an uncertain future is now widespread, which is a new experience for a wealthy society accustomed to protective (and in that sense 'conservative') welfare state institutions.

While all this is an international pattern, growing uncertainty in contemporary Germany goes alongside *quite stable (and high) expectations of social security* and, more generally, *de*-commodification. Various opinion polls as well as recent qualitative research show that protection against market risks is what most citizens continue to favour (among others: Heinrich et al, 2016; Hürtgen and Voswinkel, 2014). Public support for both basic safety nets and comprehensive social insurance schemes is high. In *normative* terms, status protection both in the labour market and in later life, organised via collective, solidaristic welfare schemes, is still viewed as being appropriate by a majority of Germans.

Yet despite these expectations being disappointed to a considerable extent, Germany has not witnessed fundamental resistance to the trend of liberalisation and the turn to 'post-conservative' welfare policies. Rather, the large majority of the population shows *compliance* with what the neoliberal narrative regards as unavoidable. It has repeatedly re-elected those political parties that, over the last two or three decades, have defended 're-commodifying' welfare reforms, including labour market deregulation and 'activation'.[3] It remains true that there have recently been massive votes for a new party of the extreme right (*AfD* – Alternative for Germany), which has won numerous mandates in a number of regional parliaments (*Länder*), particularly in the East, with above-average support coming from previous non-voters, low-skilled workers and unemployed citizens (Kroh and Fetz, 2016). While this could be read as a protest against the loss of social security, this issue is completely absent from the party's programme, which focuses on the immigration of refugees since 2015 and, interestingly enough, intends to make further cutbacks to the welfare state. Hence, de-securitisation is hardly challenged politically. Moreover, in their day-to-day life, many low-waged workers adapt to the new behavioural demands (Fehr, 2016). Likewise, large sections of the middle class react to the cutback of public pensions by investing in state-subsidised private saving plans, similar to trends elsewhere (see for instance Fligstein and Goldstein, 2015).

Explanations for the smooth transition towards liberalised welfare capitalism are often based on the assumption of social change being associated with rational processes, be it growing individualisation and related egocentric behaviour, shifts in the distribution of social power, or new government technologies making citizens entrepreneurs of themselves. However, greater attention should be paid to the *emotional* dimension of this transition, as well as to those dynamics that endorse the latter in the mind-sets of citizens. The role of emotions in society has received growing attention in contemporary sociology (for example, Bendelow and Williams, 1998; Hummelsheim et al, 2011). There have also been some studies regarding states of *anxiety* in social change trajectories (Laffan and Weiss, 2012; Plamper and Lazier, 2012) and, more recently, in reactions to immigration (Balch, 2016; Bauman, 2016). Yet while states of social fear are often alluded to in the public debate about challenges to current Western societies, it has not been explored extensively with respect to welfare state change. Exceptions include Hackell (2016), who deals with the management of anxiety in the context of child protection, and Neilson (2015), who examines mental reactions to fears related to inferior class positions in contemporary capitalism. Some scholars have also discussed anxiety with respect to social behaviour related to health care or financial planning (Wilkinson, 1999; van Dalen et al, 2016).

Nonetheless, one has to dig deeper to understand *how anxiety may come into play in a context of welfare state reform*. According to insights from social psychology and philosophy, anxiety is an ontogenetic fact and a human feeling that fulfils important functions as a mental 'warning system' against risks and threats (for what follows, see Vester, 1991 and Dehne, 2017). This feeling emerges as a reaction to undesirable but unavoidable events, especially when individuals experience a loss of control and helplessness, and when they are exposed to diffuse environmental conditions containing ambiguous stimuli. Anxiety remains an acute state if accustomed coping strategies fail and risks appear both inevitable and incalculable. While it is widely assumed that its handling depends on an individual's self-confidence and social integration, fears often relate to mental stress and the feeling of powerlessness. In this context, anxiety can have a *paralysing effect* or lead human beings to *erratic behaviour*, such as aggressive xenophobia.

At the same time, the experience of anxiety and ways of coping with it are highly encultured (Vester, 1991: 148). Modern society brought new uncertainty and worries due to the growing complexity and incomprehensibility of the social world, even as information on, and images of, concrete threats and dangers have become constantly more salient (for example, terrorism, climate change, illnesses and so on). It is safe to posit that *institutional arrangements*, such as welfare state frameworks, were, and still are, highly relevant for the way individuals (manage to) cope with feelings of anxiety. Provisions that reduce uncertainty and risks that are outside individual control are likely to cushion this way of feeling, whereas changes to the institutional arrangements of welfare capitalism can stimulate or increase fears (see also Wilkinson and Pickett, 2009).

From a sociological perspective, the *relational component of anxiety* appears particularly crucial here. According to Neckel (1991), fears can arise due to feelings of shame or guilt when people anticipate or perceive that their social status is (becoming) inferior to that of those belonging to their (accustomed) peer groups, for instance after a longer period of unemployment. In an essay titled 'Society of anxiety', Bude (2014) stresses the importance of social expectations as a key reference point for feelings of anxiety. Likewise, Wilkinson (1999) points out that these feelings can emerge from evaluative comparisons with other people, with a negative impact on human health. In the same vein, Anhut and Heitmeyer (2005), examining the propensity for violent behaviour in contemporary Germany, found that social aggression occurs where people do not feel recognised and respected in their identity. This chimes with theories stressing the role of affects in contemporary social life and the potentiality of the experience of negative emotions being converted into erratic social behaviour (Turner, 2006).

Importantly, feelings of anxiety can also be actively *mobilised* in the political sphere and by the media, especially in a context of precarious life conditions. The respective feelings can be addressed in the public discourse and become activated by 'politics of fear' (Furedi, 2005; see also Massumi, 1993). In his analysis of policies dealing with ecological issues, health promotion and education, Furedi posits that fears are often mediated by the political elites, who tend to 'infantilise' the affected populations. Drawing on this observation, it can be argued that anxiety can also become 'activated' by discourse related to social policy in both the media and political communication, with considerable repercussions for those targeted by this discourse.

As far as *Germany* and *social policy-related developments* are concerned, anxiety has been an issue, at least implicitly, in studies engaging with four broad themes: (a) middle-class fears of status loss and downward mobility; (b) the experience of precarious life conditions in a deregulated labour market; (c) rising worries about one's wellbeing in the future; and (d) concerns related to the recent increase in immigration.

Middle class anxiety. Concerning the first topic, the middle classes[4] have been found to be increasingly concerned about the stability of their social position, in Germany and elsewhere in the world (Besharov et al, 2016). Scholars dealing with this phenomenon place emphasis either on 'objective' socio-structural trends or on subjective sentiments. As for the former, qualitative studies from Germany suggest that the fear of downward mobility is particularly salient among wealthier strata of the population that have something to lose (Dörre, 2006), and among those who have not (yet) been able to establish themselves in a 'zone of normality', for instance younger workers (Weber, 2015: 117ff). In a longitudinal study using representative data, Lübke and Erlinghagen (2014) found that about one third of the population sample experienced constant fears of job insecurity over several years, which could not, however, be explained by objective job characteristics or positions in the labour market. Lengfeld and Hirschle (2009) explain evidence on rising anxiety within the middle classes by the latter becoming aware of the increasingly precarious living conditions of *other,* that is, *lower,* social groups. It seems that states of anxiety do not always correspond with one's objective life situation (see Mau, 2012; Burzan, 2014). This observation resonates with the well-known 'security paradox' identified by Evers and Nowotny (1987), who argued that different levels of objective (in) security might lead to the same level of *subjectively felt* uncertainty. As Lübke and Erlinghagen (2014) suggest, effects of adaptation or 'framing' do matter. Using European Social Survey data, they have shown that subjective job insecurity is influenced by earlier experience of the degree and speed of economic and institutional change. People's (in) security perceptions vary not only with the general economic situation (for example, the recent experience of a crisis) but also with short- and medium-term developments in labour market *policies.*

Precarious life in a deregulated labour market. This brings us to the second approach under which anxiety is currently being studied as a social phenomenon in Germany. Contrary to what is often stated when talking about the situation of the middle classes, empirical findings suggest that social fears diminish with increasing income and are more widespread in poorer sections of the population (for Germany, Heitmeyer, 2012: 24; for Europe, Delanty, 2008). It is at the bottom of the social class structure that worries about how to make ends meet are highly prevalent in people's everyday life, as has been described in qualitative case studies on German low-wage workers (Bude, 2014). It is for this category of citizens that welfare policies geared towards economic liberalisation have been analysed more explicitly, with a focus on how they operate in terms of threats, in Germany and elsewhere (see Fletcher, 2015 or Dickinson, 2016).

Worries about the remote future. There are also studies on worries about an insecure future beyond the working life. In Germany, fears of poverty or income loss in old age have become a major topic in both the public sphere and in academia (Vogel and Motel-Klingebiel, 2013). Recent opinion polls suggest that more than one out of two Germans are afraid of insufficient retirement provision, due to pension reforms we will sketch below.[5] More generally, a recent study bears witness to widespread pessimism with regard to future access to health care and social solidarity in general – despite widely shared views that the reverse prospect would be desirable (*Die Zeit*, 2016).

Anxieties related to immigration. A final strand of research related to issues of anxiety looks at the propensity to use violence in social relations and against migrants or other minorities, on the one hand, and its association with the menace or experience of 'de-securitisation', on the other. A longitudinal study suggests strong correlations between these two trends (Heitmeyer, 2012). This corresponds with research on xenophobic attitudes and support for the extreme right. Sommer's (2010) meta-study has revealed that feelings of insecurity and fears of status loss, together with depressing personal experiences in the recent past, play a strong role in the emergence of such orientations. However, while 'treading on those below' (Hofmann, 2016, for the case of Austria) is a well-known pattern internationally, there does not seem to be a linear correlation between such feelings and xenophobic tendencies, as an enquiry into the so-called 'PEGIDA' movement in Germany has shown (Vorländer et al, 2016).[6] This work suggests that, for those participating in this movement, the feeling of cultural alienation often appears more salient than fears of future job insecurity or enhanced competition on the labour market.

Overall, felt insecurity among the middle classes, as well as the experience of precarious positions on the labour market, are key issues in contemporary Germany. Both connect with more general worries about individual wellbeing in the remote future. In addition, there is some evidence for a diffuse association between these feelings and aggressive xenophobia. Bearing in mind these dimensions, both the rise of (new) fears and their mobilisation should be examined more thoroughly for concrete (social) policy areas and in the context of evolving welfare state frameworks — which is what will be done in the next section.

Two examples: reforms in the labour market and in the pension scheme

In this section, we first analyse major institutional changes in the German welfare state, including their social-structural implications; second, we portray the political and public discourse accompanying (and justifying) the reforms; finally, we shed light on the mental reaction to re-commodifying welfare policies and the potential role anxiety can play here. Our case studies are based on institutional analyses (of reform movements and their implications), a review of available survey data, and some findings from own recent qualitative research on the subjective perceptions and individual strategies of citizens exposed to the liberalisation of welfare capitalism in Germany.

The case of labour market reforms

Between 2003 and 2005, Germany saw the enactment of a large reform package, called 'Agenda 2010' and introduced by a government composed of social democrats and Greens (under Chancellor Gerhard Schröder). It is meanwhile widely acknowledged that this agenda brought a paradigm shift to the German 'conservative' welfare state that, from now on, moved towards the Anglo-Saxon (liberal) welfare regime type, featuring a higher degree of commodification. The core of the agenda, the so-called '*Hartz*-Reforms', was quite comprehensive, reshaping a major social security scheme, labour law and the design of active employment policies (see Knuth, 2014; Betzelt and Bothfeld, 2011).

Thus, access to the status-protecting unemployment benefit scheme (in the social insurance pillar) has been restricted and the payment of the insurance benefit reduced to 12 months (for most workers), which means that today only a quarter of all registered unemployed are entitled to this formerly main pillar. An ancillary benefit scheme, equally based on a wage-replacement mechanism and stepping in after insurance entitlements have expired, was abolished and replaced by the basic Jobseeker's Allowance, which provides a means-tested flat rate benefit on a relatively low level, calculated for the entire household (including stepchildren up to 25 years old) and irrespective of marital status. In the means test, the complete income of all household members and assets above certain thresholds are taken into account (up to a maximum of around 10,000 euros). The threat of losing the social status they have attained (with its wage-related entitlements) has thus become quite real once people lose their job (especially for non-standard workers). The 'Hartz IV' scheme is highly stigmatising and has a bad public image, which is partly due to the strong administrative intervention of jobcentres into the private lives of the unemployed and working poor (who can top up their wages with benefits) when it comes to means-testing, and activation measures that address all household members defined as employable. These deterrent features of the basic Jobseeker's scheme are deemed responsible for a high incidence of non-take-up of benefits.

Importantly, the reforms came with measures intended to further deregulate the German labour market. Among Organisation for Economic Co-operation and Development (OECD) countries, Germany has among the highest proportions of non-standard workers (almost 40%, including self-employment, temporary full-time and part-time jobs). Most of these workers are on low wages, with this feeding into strong income polarisation (OECD, 2015: 140–47). The low-wage sector, measured by the 60% median threshold, steadily increased until 2007 and has stagnated since at a high level of around 22% of total employment. The reforms were intended to foster this sector and to boost the wider economy. As a result, job insecurity and the risk of being low-waged have increased markedly. Of course, these risks are not equally distributed but it is also true that even highly skilled workers, especially younger cohorts, are no longer protected against them.[7] It is obvious that this has a disciplinary effect on the core workforce as well, who face the threat of sliding down into the new social assistance and activation regime.

Besides this reshuffle of the benefit system, a business logic has pervaded public employment services (for example, Hielscher and Ochs, 2012). The focus was on quick (and often dirty) job placements, with high pressure put on the unemployed to take up any job available. Across Western Europe, Germany was exceptional in cutting back major vocational training schemes for the unemployed in the context of 'activation' policies. Moreover, activation policies brought a high level of discretionary power to street-level bureaucrats, whereas the former Public Employment Service administration was based on fixed rules and procedures in terms of what 'users' could expect and were entitled to. The high degree of discretion of administrators in jobcentres is an important source of procedural uncertainty and is prone to mobilise anxiety since the claimants can never be sure what will happen to them.

At a *discursive level*, the main argument for introducing the 'Agenda 2010' was that both a cutback of an overly generous welfare state and the deregulation of the labour market were imperative in an ever more globalised economy. The slogan used by Chancellor Schröder in his parliamentary speech presenting the agenda was 'courage for change' to rescue major elements of the post-war 'social market economy': 'Either we modernise [it] ... or we will get modernised by unbounded market forces, which would push aside the social dimension', he argued (Deutscher Bundestag, 2003: 2481–89, own translation). Hence, the (alleged) risk of massive job losses and a breakdown of the welfare state should traditional institutions remain unchanged was meant to justify the reforms undertaken. This has to be seen in the light of the then hegemonic narrative of the German model as producing comparatively high unemployment and a slackening economy, with the country that was seen as 'the sick man of Europe' – although poverty was lower than today and most Western economies hardly fared any better. With this narrative, however, the threat of a previously successful model falling behind major competitors appeared quite realistic.

In addition, the welfare state was to be defended against those 'free-riders' or 'undeserving poor' allegedly abusing it. 'No right to laziness'[8] was another famous expression used by the then government – it became a key rationale for imposing stricter rules for job take-up and harsh sanctions in the event of non-compliance within a tight monitoring system. This discourse was prone to produce both anxiety *and* compliance among the working population invited to swallow the bitter pills of welfare-state retrenchment and re-commodification. Social rights to protection of a previously attained occupational status, provided through an insurance scheme, were blamed for making benefit claimants welfare dependent, thus undermining their 'self-responsibility'.

Available data suggest that this liberalisation of the conservative model entailed increased fears of job insecurity and losing a previously attained social status in the event of unemployment (see also Lübke and Erlinghagen, 2014). One implication was that fewer people change jobs voluntarily in order to avoid poorer working conditions and the risk of becoming jobless (Knuth, 2014). Moreover, the stigmatising and highly intrusive *Hartz-IV* machinery tends to deter claimants from taking up benefits, as shown by a recent research project on the situation and life-courses of unemployed non-beneficiaries.[9] Interviewees distanced themselves from the stigmatising image of being a '*Hartz-IV* recipient', with some of them not claiming benefits in order to avoid the harsh intervention of jobcentres in their private lives. This was often associated with fears of loss of autonomy and privacy. Thus one respondent living in difficult circumstances together with his spouse was thinking about separating 'officially' from the latter in order to get benefits in a declared single household. Other interviewees revealed considerable emotional strain due to their dependency on their partner in a context of an extremely poor financial situation. They also feared losing their identity as a 'full citizen' and becoming excluded from both the labour market and the social security system. Quantitative studies estimate high numbers of these 'hidden poor' not taking up benefits they are entitled to (Bruckmeier et al, 2013; Frick and Groh-Samberg, 2007). There is also evidence on accrued debts prompting both stress and compliance with the new labour market regime.[10]

Recently, new regulation has brought even harsher sanctions for those deemed to violate the rules of the activation regime, that is, by not accepting or quitting a job classified as acceptable, or by not disclosing all the details required for the means testing (whether intentionally or not). Allowances can now be cut by 30% for up to four years, and even benefits in kind such as food-vouchers can be claimed back by the jobcentre. Moreover, the right to object to the decisions of the latter are going to be markedly restrained, with this being justified under the headline of 'legal simplification'. All this corroborates the image of long-term jobseekers as 'the undeserving poor', and has the potential to increase the fears of those at risk of joining this group.

The case of pension reforms

Pension reforms enacted more than a decade ago have recently become a big issue in Germany. Prominent political leaders have declared that the partial privatisation of the pension system has had important shortcomings, as the public media report on savings plans not delivering what they promised, due to low interest rates and the bad deals made by many contractors. The reforms had brought a marked reduction of wage replacement rates at the point of retirement, and, by extension, a creeping decline of the pay-as-you-go (social insurance based) pillar; in addition, they had introduced direct payments (as well as tax reductions) to those investing in fully funded saving plans (see Bridgen and Meyer, 2014; Schmitz and Friedrich, 2016). This shift in the architecture of the pension system is emblematic for what is called 'incentive-based politics' internationally, leading to *de-secured* retirement provision in most parts of the Western world (Orenstein, 2013; Lawlor, 2016).

In contemporary Germany, social security for (current and) future pensioners may still be more generous than in the UK, yet compared to the past, most retirees will have much less than earlier generations when leaving the labour force. For many, social security will not provide benefits higher than those granted by means-tested social assistance under a regulation similar to the *Hartz*-regime described in the previous section, given that 30% of the population do not have a contracted private pension plan. Even if they did, these plans will yield only small top-ups in most cases. Both poverty in old age and, regarding the middle classes, a marked loss in one's social status after retirement, have become a realistic scenario. Such prospects are alarming for many citizens, as the opinion polls mentioned above indicate.

The liberalisation of the old world of pension provision came with a new hegemonic *discourse* pervading the public sphere. The reforms were strongly endorsed by all political parties (except the far left) and by the financial industry (Wehlau, 2009). Their proponents argued that path-breaking change was imperative, due to a 'demographic trap' and the challenge of globalisation. Given these prospects, collective contributions to the social insurance pillar would no longer provide income security in later life while those not covered by a private saving plan would have little to live on in the future. All this was prone to prompt anxiety among the wider citizenry. Nowadays, there does not seem to be a way out of the pension mess because the alleged solution of privatisation does not deliver its promises since the depression of the financial market. Interest rates are historically low, and a considerable part of payments into pension plans goes into commissions charged by financial institutions. As a result, retirement becomes 'incalculable', and all mechanisms for securing income during old age appear out of control.

Nevertheless, there has been considerable compliance with the new pension regime, if hesitantly and 'against all odds' (Schimank, 2011). Many citizens have embarked on the new (publicly subsidised) 'saving plan business', notwithstanding that becoming involved in that business can be fraught with anxiety too (see van Dalen et al, 2016, with evidence from the Netherlands). Meanwhile, more than 16 million subsidised pension plans have been sold in Germany. Bode and Wilke (2014: 177ff) have shed light on potential ways of reasoning around this stunning compliance by an in-depth analysis of the sense-making of highly educated citizens aged between 20 and 40 years (a group with financial literacy, one would assume). It appears that, for those addressed by the reforms, one option is to take the bull by the horns by adopting the stance that, in this day and age, the onus for securing a decent income package during old age ultimately lies with the individual 'market actor' – despite the discomfort the banking crisis has triggered in the mind-set of those sympathetic to this idea. A second pattern is resignation in a context of inconsistent information and unclear perspectives, with paralysing anxiety as a result. There is also a configuration in which such anxiety does not seem to matter at all, notably when respondents think they are doing well due to a good position on the labour market (whether or not they pay into a private pension scheme). However, there is a fourth pattern, which is of particular interest in our context, that is, a specific combination of internalised pressure to take action on the private pension market, but with a diffuse sense of losing control. Citizens affected by this condition feel a necessity to 'do something' against the prospect of poverty in old age. At the same time, they exhibit strong feelings of uncertainty and lack direction concerning how, and to what extent, to invest in a private pension scheme. This is where financial advisers step in and make people contract a pension plan – although, at the end of the day, existing worries cannot be dispelled.

Importantly, rather than triggering political opposition against the reform movement, the aforementioned coping patterns, particularly the blend of de-securitisation and activation, contribute to the stabilisation of the reform agenda. Many citizens are 'paralysed' by the constraints of the new market and refrain from contracting a pension plan, others have accepted the move towards 'self-made pensions' (Bode, 2007), if without enthusiasm and sometimes desperately. Driven by constant 'propaganda' in the public media (which is an international pattern; see Lawlor, 2016), the population has few clues about what will happen to old age provision as preconditions and contexts are fuzzy.

That said, public expectations regarding social security have remained high in Germany, going beyond what has become 'normal' in the Anglo-Saxon world. Nowadays, politicians seem to perceive the worries of the citizenry, in particular the middle classes. The government in power (as of autumn 2016) has considered taking action to calm these worries. With the exception of better incapacity benefits, envisaged reforms propose 'more of the same': enhanced incentives for contracting private pension plans and measures to extend company-based (funded) schemes, albeit as a pure defined contribution scheme offering no guarantees regarding eventual payoffs. Hence it is very likely that feelings of anxiety and insecurity in later life will persist as an important element of post-conservative pension policies.

Discussion and conclusions

A sociological analysis of the role of anxiety in the process of welfare state transformation helps to better understand both the smoothness and the pitfalls of this transformation. In addition, it sheds a different light on the alleged German 'success story' of a liberalised variety of welfare capitalism. As we argued in this chapter, the mobilisation of anxiety has worked quite well as a 'transmission belt' for realising the neoliberal agenda, at least until recently. Concerning the protection in the labour market, both the prospect of becoming part of a stigmatised social group under the control of welfare bureaucracies and the actual experience of this control are prone to ensure a high level of compliance with 'de-securitised' arrangements. As for pension provision, the expectation of marked income loss at the point of retirement makes many citizens follow the advice to invest in the financial market and accept the related risks. An accompanying pattern is *paralysis* affecting those who feel clueless in the context of activation or marketisation. More generally, such paralysis makes itself felt with regard to political reactions to both pension and labour market reforms as de-securitisation has hardly been contested in the public sphere. Warnings that, because of an increasingly globalised economy and demographic change, things will become worse if 'de-securitisation' is rejected have left their mark.

Importantly, both at the periphery and in the heart of German society, changes to the 'conservative' life course that have been experienced already (whether as a subjective perception or an objective condition) chime together with the reform agenda depicted above. Social change has exposed relevant parts of the population to states or feelings of insecurity, and with this sounding board, the institutional liberalisation of welfare capitalism can develop smoothly. Regarding this new settlement, it seems that the mobilisation of fears has so far been *functional* for '*system integration*', given that it has facilitated the move towards 'de-securitisation' without any substantial political resistance.

However, while mobilised anxiety appears to be one factor for explaining why post-conservative welfare policies were so successful in Germany, the respective emotional states may cause problems for social integration in the long run. They are prone to escalate as the announced payoffs – that is, the promise of a decent and stable income for all and private pension provision for those who have purchased a saving plan – become insecure as well. The psychology of anxiety suggests that such emotional states, arising from a loss of control and perceived helplessness within a diffuse context containing ambiguous stimuli, may provoke *erratic social behaviour*, especially when accustomed coping strategies fail while risks prove incalculable. There are good reasons to assume that, in Germany and elsewhere in the Western world, major social groups are exposed to such emotional stress. In the face of economic liberalisation, coping strategies are insecure for many: it is hard to escape from precarious living conditions at the bottom of the social structure due to low upward mobility; moreover, for wider sections of the population, investment in the financial market to provide for decent retirement conditions appears both unavoidable and extremely risky at this time.

It stands to reason that – particularly if combined with feelings of 'cultural alienation' – structural uncertainty (over one's future) may feed into a dangerous 'cocktail' and trigger outrageous violence against immigrants as well as a deep-seated frustration with politics and the welfare state (among others, see Hofmann, 2016). With growing income polarisation and the menace of social exclusion, this 'cocktail' could eventually prove *fatal* with respect to *social integration*. The aggressive blaming of 'scapegoats' (such as immigrants or refugees) or an extensive orientation towards personal competitiveness at the workplace are likely to bring further fragmentation and conflict to late modern societies (see Penz and Sauer, 2013) – to a point well beyond what proponents of 'de-securitising' welfare policies have intended or desired. In present-day Germany, there might come a moment when the functionality of fears will provoke political disruptions – which at the end of the day would also affect economic growth and, in this sense, become dysfunctional for system integration.

It is important to see that anxiety-driven welfare state change serves the interests of some rather than those of others. Big business and those profiting from a flexible workforce are likely to be winners while those suffering from permanent insecurity, not only mentally but also in material terms, tend to be losers. While distinctive fears (for instance, those of the middle classes) have now become an issue in the public debate, others (for example, those related to poor working conditions and low pay) receive little attention. The 'refugee crisis' mentioned at the outset illustrates what can happen in such a constellation, namely opposition against weak groups, for example, ethnic minorities or homosexuals; and growing support for extreme right-wing parties like the German AfD that – paradoxically – pursues an even more radical liberalisation of welfare capitalism.

More generally, one can infer from our analysis that regarding the future of welfare capitalism it is not only material redistribution but also the emotional 'processing' of social inequality and felt injustice that are at stake. It has been argued elsewhere that the legitimacy of a given social order is strongly related to feelings of social justice and fairness (Nussbaum, 2006; Wilkinson and Pickett, 2009). Likewise, envy and rage against others, fear of status loss, lack of social recognition, or the experience of blocked upward mobility should be understood as providing significant momentum in the 'making' of reform agendas. This is why social policy analysis should pay greater attention to the emotional dimension of welfare state change and those dynamics of social (dis)integration associated with it.

Notes
[1] It has equally been discussed for the case of the US, long before the electoral campaign of Donald Trump (see for instance Bingaman, 2007).
[2] This notion has often been used in historical contexts, alluding, among other things, to the trauma of the Nazi era and related war experiences or to earlier developments in German philosophy. We are drawing on it because of a loose connection with a strong preference for life course security in Germany (which, however, can also be found in other countries of mainland Europe).
[3] With the exception of 'the Left' (*Die Linke*), which became a popular alternative in the light of these reforms.
[4] In what follows, we use the plural form as we are dealing here with a heterogeneous group of citizens that, in some ways, exists only 'on paper' (among others, see Barbehön and Haus, 2015).
[5] This poll was undertaken on behalf of a public TV channel. There are also surveys on anxiety conducted for a big insurance company (www.ruv.de) that display similar results.
[6] This movement, arising after the arrival of large numbers of refugees during 2015 in a couple of (mainly) East German cities, took a clear stance against the admission of these immigrants, expressing its views in weekly demonstrations and blaming major political institutions for no longer representing 'the people'.
[7] This is often overlooked by scholars referring to this configuration as a 'dualisation' of the labour market, arguing that there is little upward

mobility for those working in 'bad jobs' and facing high risks of unemployment (for example, Emmenegger et al, 2012).

[8] Interview for the *'manager magazin'*, 6 April 2001 (on this discourse, see also Kaufmann, 2013).

[9] The qualitative part of the research project is based on a socio-demographically variant sample of 22 in-depth interviews with unemployed respondents who were not taking up benefits or were not entitled to them (see www.boeckler.de/11145.htm?projekt=2014-737-3; Betzelt et al, 2015; Betzelt et al, forthcoming).

[10] According to a recent comparative study (FESSUD), the disciplinary role of debts, making people accept poor(er) working conditions, appears to be particularly strong in Germany (Santos et al, forthcoming).

References

Anhut, R. and Heitmeyer, W. (2005) 'Desintegration, Anerkennungsbilanzen und die Rolle sozialer Vergleichsprozesse', in R. Anhut and W. Heitmeyer (eds) *Integrationspotenziale einer modernen Gesellschaft*, Wiesbaden: Verlag für Sozialwissenschaften, pp 75–100.

Balch, A. (2016) *Immigration and the state: Fear, greed and hospitality*, London: Palgrave Macmillan.

Barbehön, M. and Haus, M. (2015) 'Middle class and welfare state: discursive relations', *Critical Policy Studies*, 9(4): 473–84.

Bauman, Z. (2016) *Strangers at our doors*, Cambridge: Polity Press.

Bendelow, G. and Wiliams, S.J. (eds) (1998) *Emotions in social life: Critical themes and contemporary issues*, London: Routledge.

Besharov, D.J., López Peláez, A. and Sánchez-Cabezudo, S.S. (2016) 'The decline of the middle classes around the world?', *Journal of Policy Analysis and Management*, 35(1): 245–51.

Betzelt, S. (2015) *The myth of more social inclusion through activation reforms. The case of Germany*, IPE Working Paper No. 57/2015, Berlin School of Economics and Law.

Betzelt, S. and Bothfeld, S. (eds) (2011) *Activation and labour market reforms in Europe: Challenges to social citizenship*, Work and Welfare in Europe Series, Houndmills: Palgrave Macmillan.

Betzelt, S., Ebach, M., Schmidt, T. and Kedenburg, O. (forthcoming) 'Autonomiegewinne durch Verlust von Leistungsansprüchen?', *Zeitschrift für Sozialreform*, 62.

Bingaman, K.A. (2007) *Treating the new anxiety: A cognitive-theological Approach,* Lanham, MD: Jason Aronson.

Bode, I. (2007) 'From the citizen's wage to self-made pensions? The changing culture of old age provision in Canada and Germany', *Current Sociology*, 55(5): 696–717.

Bode, I. (2008) 'Social citizenship in post-liberal Britain and post-corporatist Germany: curtailed, fragmented, streamlined, but still on the agenda', in T. Maltby, P. Kennett and K. Rummery (eds) *Social Policy Review 20*, Bristol: Policy Press, pp 191–212.

Bode, I. and Wilke, F. (2014) *Private Vorsorge als Illusion. Rationalitätsprobleme des neuen deutschen Rentenmodells*, Frankfurt/New York: Campus.

Bosch, G. (2015) 'The German welfare state: from an inclusive to an exclusive Bismarckian model', in D. Vaughan-Whitehead (ed.) *The European social model in crisis: Is Europe losing its soul?*, Cheltenham: Edward Elgar, pp 175–229.

Bosch, G. and Kalina, T. (2016) 'Einkommensentstehung als Verteilungsfaktor. Wachsende Ungleichheit in der Primärverteilung gefährdet Mittelschicht', *Wirtschaftsdienst*, 96(1): 24–31.

Bothfeld, S. and Betzelt, S. (2013) 'Activation, social citizenship and autonomy in Europe', *Social Policy Review 25*, Bristol: Policy Press, 249–70.

Bridgen, P. and Meyer, T. (2014) 'The liberalisation of the German social model: public–private pension reform in Germany since 2001', *Journal of Social Policy*, 43(1): 37–68.

Bruckmeier, K., Pauser, J., Walwei, U. and Wiemers, J. (2013) 'Simulationsrechnungen zum Ausmaß der Nicht-Inanspruchnahme von Leistungen der Grundsicherung', *IAB Forschungsbericht* 5/2013, Nürnberg: IAB.

Bude, H. (2014) *Gesellschaft der Angst,* Hamburg: Hamburger Edition.

Burzan, N. (2014) 'Gefühlte Verunsicherung in der Mitte der Gesellschaft', *Aus Politik und Zeitgeschichte* 49: 17–23.

Crouch, C. and Keune, M. (2012) 'The governance of economic uncertainty: beyond the "new social risk" analysis', in G. Bonoli and D. Natali (eds) *The politics of the new welfare state*, Oxford: Oxford University Press, pp 45–67.

Dehne, M. (2017) *Soziologie der Angst. Konzeptuelle Grundlagen, soziale Bedingungen und empirische Analysen,* Wiesbaden: Springer VS.

Delanty, G. (2008) 'Fear of others: social exclusion and the European crisis of solidarity', *Social Policy & Administration*, 42(6): 676–90.

Deutscher Bundestag (2003) *Plenarprotokoll der 32. Sitzung*, 14 March, 15. Wahlperiode, Berlin: Deutscher Bundestag.

Dickinson, M. (2016) 'Working for food stamps: economic citizenship and the post-Fordist welfare state in New York City', *Amercian Ethnologist*, 43(2): 270–81.

Die Zeit (2016) 'Was wollen wir weitergeben. Die große Studie zur Zukunft der Deutschen', Die Zeit, 18 February, pp 13–15.

Dingeldey, I., Holtrup, A. and Warsewa, G. (eds) (2015) *Wandel der Governance der Erwerbsarbeit,* Wiesbaden: Springer VS.

Dörre, K. (2006). 'Prekäre Arbeit und soziale Desintegration', *Aus Politik und Zeitgeschichte*, 40/41: 7–14.

Emmenegger, P., Häusermann, S., Palier, B. and Seeleib-Kaiser, M. (2012) *The age of dualization: The changing face of inequality in deindustrializing societies*, Oxford: Oxford University Press.

Esping-Andersen, G. (1990) *The three worlds of welfare capitalism*, Cambridge: Cambridge University Press.

Evers, A. and Nowotny, H. (1987) *Über den Umgang mit Unsicherheit. Die Entdeckung der Gestaltbarkeit von Gesellschaft ,* Frankfurt am Main: Suhrkamp.

Fehr, S. (2016) 'Gefangen in Arbeitslosigkeit? (Des-)Integrationsprozesse im Zuge der Hartz-Reformen in Deutschland', in W. Aschauer, E. Donat and J. Hofmann (eds) *Solidaritätsbrüche in Europa, Konzeptionelle Überlegungen und empirische Befunde*, Wiesbaden: Springer VS, pp 149–69.

Fletcher, D.R. (2015) 'Workfare – a blast from the past? Contemporary work conditionality for the unemployed in historical perspective', *Social Policy & Society*, 14(3): 329–40.

Fligstein, N. and Goldstein, A. (2015) 'The emergence of a finance culture in American households, 1989–2007', *Socio-Economic Review*, 13(3): 575–601.

Frick, J. and Groh-Samberg, O. (2007) 'To claim or not to claim: estimating non-take-up of social assistance in Germany and the role of measurement error', DIW Discussion Papers 734, Berlin: German Institute for Economic Research.

Furedi, F. (2005) *Politics of fear: Beyond left and right,* London: Continuum International.

Grabka, M., Goebel, J., Schroeder, J. and Schupp, J. (2016) 'Schrumpfender Anteil an BezieherInnen mittlerer Einkommen in den USA und Deutschland', *DIW Wochenbericht*, 18: 391–402.

Hackell, M. (2016) 'Managing anxiety: Neoliberal modes of citizen subjectivity, fantasy and child abuse in New Zealand', *Citizenship Studies*, 20(6–7): 867–82.

Heinrich, R., Jochem, S. and Siegel, N.A. (2016) *Die Zukunft des Wohlfahrtsstaats. Einstellungen zur Reformpolitik in Deutschland,* Bonn: Friedrich-Ebert-Foundation.

Heitmeyer, W. (2012) 'Gruppenbezogene Menschenfeindlichkeit (GMF) in einem entsicherten Jahrzehnt', in W. Heitmeyer (ed.) *Deutsche Zustände,* vol. 10, Berlin: Suhrkamp, pp 15–41.

Herr, H. and Ruoff, B. (2016) 'Labour and financial markets as drivers of inequality', in A. Gallas, H. Herr, F. Hoffer and C. Scherrer (eds) *Combating inequality: the global North and South,* London: Routledge, pp 61–79.

Hielscher, V. and Ochs, P. (2012) 'Das prekäre Dienstleistungsversprechen der öffentlichen Arbeitsverwaltung', in S. Bothfeld, , W. Sesselmeier and C. Bogedan (eds) *Arbeitsmarktpolitik in der sozialen Marktwirtschaft: Vom Arbeitsförderungsgesetz zum Sozialgesetzbuch II und III* (2nd edn), Wiesbaden: VS Verlag, pp 248–59.

Hofmann, J. (2016) 'Fear of decline and treading on those below? The role of social crises and insecurities in the emergence and the reception of prejudices in Austria', in J. Kiess, O. Decker and E. Brähler (eds) *German perspectives on right-wing extremism: Challenges for comparative analysis,* London: Routledge, pp 104–21.

Hummelsheim, D., Hirtenlehner, H., Jackson, J. and Oberwittler, D. (2011) 'Social insecurities and fear of crime: a cross-national study on the impact of welfare state policies on crime-related anxieties', *European Sociological Review,* 27(3): 327–45.

Hürtgen, S. and Voswinkel, S. (2014) *Nichtnormale Normalität. Anspruchslogiken aus der Arbeitnehmermitte,* Berlin: Sigma.

Hutton, W. (2016) Only fundamental social change can defeat the anxiety epidemic, *The Guardian,* 7 May, www.theguardian.com/global/commentisfree/2016/may/07/mental-health-policy-anxiety-natasha-devon-young-people

Kaufmann, M. (2013) *Kein Recht auf Faulheit. Das Bild von Erwerbslosen in der Debatte um die Hartz-Reformen,* Wiesbaden: Springer.

Knuth, M. (2014) 'Labour markets reform and the "jobs miracle" in Germany: the impossible gets done at once, the miraculous takes a little longer', in European Economic and Social Commitee, Extraordinary Workers' Group Meeting, www.researchgate.net/publication/259981455_The_impossible_gets_done_at_once_the_miraculous_takes_a_little_longer_Labour_market_reforms_and_the_jobs_miracle_in_Germany

Kroh, M. and Fetz, K. (2016) 'Das Profil der AfD-AnhängerInnen hat sich seit der Gründung der Partei deutlich verändert', *DIW Wochenbericht*, 34: 711–19.

Laffan, M. and Weiss, M. (eds) (2012) *Facing fear: The history of an emotion in global perspective*, Princeton, NJ: Princeton University Press.

Lawlor, A. (2016 'Getting citizens to save: media influence and incentive-based politics', *Journal of Social Policy*, 45(2): 181–200.

Lengfeld, H. and Hirschle, J. (2009) 'Die Angst der Mittelschichten vor dem Abstieg. Eine Längsschnittanalyse 1984–2007', *Zeitschrift für Soziologie* 38(5): 379–98.

Lockwood, D. (1964) 'Social integration and system integration', in G. Zollschan and W. Hirsch (eds) *Explorations in social change*, Boston, MA: Houghton Mifflin, pp 244–57.

Lübke, C. and Erlinghagen, M. (2014) 'Self-perceived job insecurity across Europe over time: does changing context matter?', *Journal of European Social Policy*, 24(49): 319–36.

Massumi, B. (ed.) (1993) *The politics of everyday fear*, Minneapolis, MN: University of Minnesota Press.

Mau, S. (2012) *Lebenschancen. Wohin driftet die Mittelschicht?*, Frankfurt/Main: Suhrkamp.

Neckel, S. (1991) *Status und Scham. Zur symbolischen Reproduktion sozialer Ungleichheit*, Frankfurt: Campus.

Neilson, D. (2015) 'Class, precarity, and anxiety under neoliberal global capitalism: from denial to resistance', *Theory & Psychology*, 25(2): 184–201.

Nussbaum, M. (2006) *Frontiers of justice: Disability, nationality, species membership*, Cambridge, MA: Belknap.

OECD (2015) *In it together: Why less inequality benefits all*, Paris: OECD.

Orenstein, M. (2013) 'Pension privatization: evolution of a paradigm', *Governance*, 26(2): 259–81.

Penz, O. and Sauer, B. (2013) *Affektives Kapital. Die Ökonomisierung der Gefühle im Arbeitsleben*, Frankfurt: Campus.

Plamper, J. and Lazier, B. (eds) (2012) *Fear: Across the disciplines,* Pittsburgh, PA: University of Pittsburgh Press.

Santos, A.C., Lopes, C. and Betzelt, S. (forthcoming) 'Financialisation and work: inequality, debt and labour market segmentation', *World Economy Journal (REM Revista de Economía Mundial)*, 17.

Schimank, U. (2011) 'Against all odds: the "loyalty" of small investors', *Socio-economic Review*, 9(1): 107–35.

Schimank, U. (2015) 'Lebensplanung!? Biografische Entscheidungspraktiken irritierter Mittelschichten', *Berliner Journal für Soziologie*, 25(1): 7–31.

Schmitz, J. and Friedrich, J. (2016) 'Legitimationsfragen der gesetzlichen Rentenversicherung', in M. Lemke, O. Schwarz, R. Stark and K. Weissenbach (eds) *Legitimitätspraxis. Politikwissenschaft und soziologische Perspektiven*, Wiesbaden: Springer VS, pp 175–206.

Seeleib-Kaiser, M. (2016) 'The end of the conservative German welfare state model', *Social Policy & Administration*, 50(2): 219–40.

Sommer, B. (2010) *Prekarisierung und Ressentiments. Soziale Unsicherheit und rechtsextreme Einstellungen in Deutschland*, Wiesbaden: Springer VS.

Turner, J.H. (2006) 'Psychoanalytical theories of emotion', in J.E. Stets and J.H. Turner (eds) *Handbook of sociology of emotions*, New York: Springer, pp 276–94.

van Dalen, H., Henkens, K. and Hershley, D.A. (2016) 'Why do older adults avoid seeking financial advice? Adviser anxiety in the Netherlands', *Ageing & Society* doi10.1017/S0144686/X16000222.

Vester, H.-G. (1991) *Emotion, Gesellschaft und Kultur. Grundzüge einer soziologischen Theorie der Emotionen,* Opladen: Westdeutscher Verlag.

Vogel, C. and Motel-Klingebiel, A. (eds) (2013) *Altern im sozialen Wandel: Die Rückkehr der Altersarmut,* Wiesbaden: Springer VS.

Vorländer, H., Herold, M. and Schäller, S. (2016) *PEGIDA: Entwicklung, Zusammensetzung und Deutung einer Empörungsbewegung,* Wiesbaden: Springer VS.

Weber, C. (2015) *Erwerbsorientierungen und Problemlagen junger Erwerbstätiger. Eine soziologische Zeitdiagnose,* Wiesbaden: Springer VS.

Wehlau, D. (2009) *Lobbyismus und Rentenreform. Der Einfluss der Finanzdienstleistungsbranche auf die Teil-Privatisierung der Alterssicherung,* Wiesbaden: Verlag für Sozialwissenschaften.

Wilkinson, R.G. (1999) 'Health, hierarchy and social anxiety', in N.E. Adler, M. Marmot, B.S. McEwen and J. Stewart (eds) *Annals of the New York Academy of Sciences*, 896: 48–63.

Wilkinson, R. and Pickett, K. (2009) *The spirit level: Why more equal societies almost always do better,* London: Allen Lane.

EIGHT

Beyond 'evidence-based policy' in a 'post-truth' world: the role of ideas in public health policy

Katherine E. Smith

Introduction: the crisis of 'evidence-based policy'

The past two decades witnessed the international re-emergence, following the disappointment of earlier US and UK efforts (Rein, 1980), of an extremely persuasive idea – the notion that policy decisions should be 'evidence-based'. From early official government commitments to 'evidence-based policy' (EBP) in the UK (Cabinet Office, 1999), the emergence of 'boundary organisations' spanning research and policy in the Netherlands (for example, Bekker et al, 2010; Van Egmond et al, 2011), and the creation of a new position of Chief Scientific Adviser by the European Commission President (Barroso, 2009) – examples of efforts to achieve a better relationship between science and policy are ubiquitous. These efforts have stimulated a wealth of studies explicitly concerned with better understanding the relationship between research, knowledge and policy, as evidenced in the pages of journals such as *Evidence & Policy* and *Implementation Science*. Despite this, there are very few successful examples of EBP (Smith, 2013). For many observers, this failure simply reflects the primacy of politics in policy making (for example, Bambra, 2013; Pawson, 2006). Yet, as Geoff Mulgan (previously adviser to then UK Prime Minister Tony Blair) argues, in democratically elected countries, 'the people, and the politicians who represent them, have every right to ignore evidence' (Mulgan, 2005: 224). There are, in short, crucial tensions between the desire to use the best available evidence in policy and the need for sufficient citizen engagement in or, at the very least, support for policies.

The weaknesses of EBP are currently being magnified by rising public disillusionment with traditional elites, as epitomised in a recent declaration from a British politician that people have 'had enough of experts' (Gove, quoted in Mance, 2016; Pisani-Ferry, 2016). Such assertions, combined with the rise of populist political parties across Europe, suggest that efforts to enhance the consideration given to scientific evidence in decision making (which have been particularly strong in public health, as discussed below) are now facing serious challenges. For Saltelli and Giampietro, the solution is radical and 'implies abandoning dreams of prediction, control and optimization' associated with EBP 'and moving instead to an open exploration of a broader set of plausible and relevant stories' (2015: 1). This chapter takes a somewhat less radical perspective. After critiquing the persistence of the flawed EBP ideal, it briefly presents two empirical public health case studies (research and policy debates relating to tobacco control and health inequalities in the UK). This analysis is used to argue, first, that it makes more sense to consider the role of *ideas*, than *evidence*, in public health policy. This claim then informs a second argument, developed in the concluding discussion, that we now urgently, in the context of claims of a 'post-truth' era (see McCartney, 2016), need to explore mechanisms for overcoming perceived tensions between 'expert' and 'public' opinions. We need, in short, to develop mechanisms for better supporting a democratically legitimate role for evidence in policymaking.

The struggle to move beyond 'science vs politics'

Over the past decade, there have been regular media stories in which scientists are either depicted as embattled critics of politicians or as out-of-touch individuals, whom politicians might be well advised to ignore. A classic example of this, encapsulating both characterisations, was the media coverage of the UK government's decision to sack a scientist, Professor David Nutt, from its Advisory Council on the Misuse of Drugs (ACMD). This decision followed the publication of an article by Nutt in *The Guardian* newspaper, in which he challenged the government's decision to reclassify cannabis to a higher (more harmful) category (for more a more detailed account of the affair, see Henderson, 2012; Monaghan, 2011). A media storm quickly ensued with a *Guardian* editorial accusing the responsible minister, Alan Johnson, of lacking 'the strength of character to listen to people who tell him difficult truths' (*The Guardian*, 2009), while a subsequent *Daily Mail* commentary dismissed Nutt as 'barmy' and 'dangerous' (Glover, 2010).

The existence of conflicts between evidence-based and ideological (or populist) approaches to politically contentious issues, such as illicit drugs, is widely recognised (again, see Monaghan, 2011). However, for policy issues in which there seems to be rather more of a consensus about the overarching objectives, it seems less obvious how or why 'politics' might obstruct the use of evidence within policy making. Public health is precisely such a policy area and, indeed, the majority of civil servants and politicians in a post-1997 UK context have (rhetorically, at least) signed up to taking an evidence-based approach to improving population health and reducing health inequalities, an agenda which is strongly supported by many leading public health researchers (for example, Macintyre, 2011). The existence of such a cross-sector consensus suggests that public heath might be one area in which evidence-based (or at least evidence-informed) policy and practice are feasible. Yet, disappointingly, most assessments of public health policies continue to conclude that they are not evidence-based (for example, Bartley, 1994; Hunter, 2009; Katikireddi et al, 2011; Macintyre et al, 2001; Smith, 2007).

A popular explanation for this disjuncture is that it results from communicative, institutional and cultural gaps between researchers and policy makers. In other words, the gaps between research and policy are perceived to reflect divisions between those involved in *producing research* evidence and those involved in *constructing policies* (see, for example, Innvær et al, 2002; Mitton et al, 2007). Concern about these 'knowledge to action gaps', as they are commonly conceived (Wehrens et al, 2011), has been particularly acute in countries where the evidence-based movement has been most active, such as Australia, Canada, the Netherlands and the UK. Such concerns have stimulated efforts to develop 'bridges' that might help connect the 'two communities', including the creation of 'knowledge broker' posts and organisations, and a growing support for the 'co-production' of research, in which decision makers are involved from an early stage (see Smith and Joyce, 2012; Wehrens et al, 2011).

Yet, if we turn instead to the available literature concerning policy change within the political sciences, sociology and policy studies, the question becomes not, 'Why is public health policy not evidence-based?' But, 'Why would we ever assume it could (or even should) be?' This is because the literature within these disciplines tends to highlight the normative, democratic and interest-driven aspects of politics and policy making (see Smith and Katikireddi, 2013). Sociological studies of science go further, demonstrating that research itself is also a value-laden activity (for example, Bartley, 1992; Knorr-Cetina, 1981; Latour and Woolgar, 1986). Yet, despite periodic acknowledgement of these issues within the public health community, there appears to be a reluctance to let go of the possibility that we might someday achieve rational, 'evidence-based' public health policies (for example, Lavis et al, 2004; Macintyre et al, 2001; Orton et al, 2011).

The case for focusing on the role of ideas in policy

Arguing that the concept of EBP is flawed is, of course, not the same as arguing that evidence cannot, or should not, play an important role in policy, for it may well be ideas emerging from research that inform policy debate. This may seem like rather a simple distinction but it is also essential to acknowledge because, once decoupled from specific research findings, ideas are more easily amenable to differing interpretations and uses by various actors. The result is that a range of factors unrelated to the nature of the evidence shape the ways in which these ideas are able to influence policy. Consequently, those promoted by charismatic individuals or marketed by lobbyists, those perceived to be attractive to the electorate, and those which easily fit within dominant ideologies, may all have more appeal than anything based upon 'evidence' alone. In this context, it makes sense to examine how ideas are constructed and promoted by academics and what happens to these ideas once they move beyond academia.

Yet, although ideas were clearly 'an important variable' in many of the analyses developed by political scientists in the 1970s and 1980s, this literature said 'very little about the specific role that ideas play in the policy process or about the characteristics that tend to give some ideas more influence than others over policy' (Hall, 1990: 57). It is only over the past 15 years that ideational theories have attracted significant attention within political science and policy studies (for example, Béland, 2005; Béland and Cox, 2011; Blyth, 1997; Campbell, 2002) and ideational scholars still need to undertake further work to explain why some ideas, and not others persist (Berman, 2013).

Before moving on to outline the empirical case studies, it is necessary to consider how to define ideas. This is not an easy task; existing definitions are often vague, prompting Blyth (1997) to warn that 'ideas' may be employed as 'catch-all concepts' that do little to advance current theoretical understandings (see also Berman, 2013). However, it is possible to identify three distinct levels of idea that are regularly referred to within policy analyses

First, there are overarching paradigms (or ideologies) involving 'organized principles and causal beliefs', such as neoliberalism or Keynesianism (Béland, 2005). At this level, ideas represent organising frameworks for understanding the world which provide policy makers 'with a relatively coherent set of assumptions about the functioning of economic, political and social institutions' (Béland, 2005, 8). From the perspective of understanding how policy change (or stasis) occurs, this way of thinking about ideas, which highlights the importance of values and causal beliefs, shares similarities with Hall's (1990, 1993) concept of 'policy paradigms' and Jobert and Muller's (1987) notion of 'the *référential*'. Second, literature focusing on agenda setting emphasises the importance of understanding how particular policy problems are constructed and promoted in ways which inform actors' perceptions of potential solutions and determine who is (and who is not) involved in the policy process (for example, Edelman, 1988; Schattschneider, 1960). From this perspective, ideas might be understood as 'policy frames' which, when successfully applied by particular actors/interests, play a crucial role in shaping policy processes and outcomes (Riker, 1986). Finally, ideas are also often presented as specific policy initiatives or solutions to recognised policy problems (see Béland, 2005; Kingdon, 1995 [1984]). This three-level division, which to some extent reflects both Kingdon's (1995 [1984]) notion of three policy 'streams' (politics, problems and policies) and the three levels of 'belief' outlined in Sabatier and Jenkins-Smith's (1999) 'advocacy-coalition framework' (deep core, policy core and secondary beliefs), is inevitably simplified (see, for example, Berman, 2013) but it is hopefully not a caricature in so far as it reflects the varying ways in which ideas are commonly referred to in political studies.

While it is heuristically useful to distinguish between these three levels, what the above summary quickly illustrates is how different levels of ideas are often closely intertwined. This means it is not always easy to disentangle the elements of complex ideas. Mehta (2011: 33) advises that separating out 'the battle over problem definition from the battle over policy solutions' can be a critical step to advancing our understanding of policy development and the role of ideas within this. Yet, ideas are often constructed, or reinterpreted, in ways which promote, or perhaps even depend on, this kind of conflation. Moreover, as Béland and Cox (2011: 5) note, ideas 'are constantly in flux, being reconsidered and redefined as actors communicate and debate with one another'. This can make it difficult to trace the influence of ideas which, as Hall (1993: 290) reflects, 'do not leave much of a trail when they shift'. Without being witness to each of the moments in which ideas are translated between actors, it becomes difficult to know whether what appears to be a 'trace' of a particular idea is merely another idea with some similar characteristics.

This is especially so given that, as Keynes (1936) once observed, actors may be relatively unconscious of the ideas shaping their thinking.

Two empirical case studies from public health

This chapter draws on data from two empirical case studies from the UK, health inequalities and tobacco control, to outline an alternative way of distinguishing between idea types; one which aims to respond to Cox and Béland's (2013: 308) observation that, 'we still know very little about why some ideas acquire paradigmatic status (Hall, 1993), while other seemingly good ideas fail to gain traction'. Health inequalities are an archetypal 'wicked issue' in which evidence remains contested (Blackman et al, 2006), while tobacco control is often hailed as a (rare) public health success story (for example, Petticrew et al, 2004). In this sense, the two case studies provide a useful contrast. There are also, however, some important similarities. For both issues, there have been strong commitments to promoting EBP responses (Smith, 2013). Yet research evidence often lags (necessarily) behind policy decisions, because researchers are only able to empirically assess the effectiveness of policy changes after they occur. Both case studies also involve policy issues for which evidence-informed ideas tend to be intertwined with normative assumptions and ethical frames (Smith, 2013).

The primary data source for both case studies is 146 interviews, undertaken in three batches between 2004 and 2013 (reflecting three, linked projects), with researchers, campaigners/lobbyists and other policy actors, as summarised in Table 8.1. All those selected for interview were chosen on the basis of their interest in public health research and/or policies, with some topic-expertise variation across the three projects (the first set of interviews focused on individuals interested in health inequalities, the second on tobacco control and the third expanded the focus to public health generally). Interviews were digitally recorded and transcribed verbatim, before being anonymised and thematically coded (initially in the qualitative data analysis programme *Atlas.ti* and subsequently with *NVivo10*) using a coding framework that was developed iteratively, via analysis and reanalysis of the transcripts. This was supplemented by an analysis of relevant policy documents and statements, existing research evidence and publicly available internal tobacco industry documents concerning tobacco policy developments in a wide range of countries, including the UK (released through a series of litigation cases in the US and available online at http://legacy.library.ucsf.edu/).

Table 8.1: A breakdown of interviewees' professional positions

Interviewees' primary professional position	Number of inter-viewees 2004–07	Number of inter-viewees 2009–10	Number of inter-viewees 2011–13	Total number of inter-viewees
Academic researchers	30	0	20 (2*)	48
Individuals working in policy settings (largely civil servants)	10	7	15 (2*)	30
Researchers working in independent/private research organisation (e.g. think tanks)	5	2	1	8
Public sector researchers / policy advisers	5	0	3	8
Journalists or media communications staff	5	0	0	5
Politicians (including ministers)	4	1	4	9
Research funders	3	0	4	7
Public health 'knowledge brokers'	0	0	3	3
Senior staff in third sector / advocacy organisations	0	5	16	21
Staff working for business interests (consultancies etc.)	0	7	0	7
Total	62	22	66 (4*)	146

Note: (N*) indicates the number of interviewees in 2011–13 who had been interviewed in 2004 and 2007.

Despite strong rhetorical commitments to EBP in the UK (for example, Cabinet Office, 1999), both the documentary analysis and the interview data support the suggestion that it is research-informed ideas, rather than evidence itself, which are influential in policy settings. As one interviewee reflected, the culture of UK policy making often involves searching for new or persuasive ideas, rather than systematically reviewing available evidence.

Introducing case 1: health inequalities in the UK

Health differences between geographical areas and social groups have been identifiable in the UK for over 200 years (Davey Smith et al, 2001), remaining remarkably persistent over time (Marmot, 2010). One of the most shocking statistics in the World Health Organization

(WHO, 2008) Commission on Social Determinants of Health report was that men living in the Calton area of Glasgow (Scotland) live, on average, 28 years less than men living in Lenzie, just a few kilometres away. The evidence as to why this is so is growing on a weekly basis. The current consensus is that unequal quality, and use of, health services (which are tax-funded and free at the point of delivery in the UK) play only a minimal role in health inequalities (Marmot, 2010). Similarly, social mobility (that is, the impact of health status on people's ability to move up the social hierarchy) is thought to play only a small role in the UK's health inequalities (Blane et al, 1993). It is accepted that lifestyle-behavioural differences, notably smoking, play an important role, but these are understood by most health inequalities researchers to be symptoms of broader inequalities (Marmot, 2010). Overall, several decades of research largely suggests that it is the unequal distribution of 'upstream' social and economic factors, such as income, education, housing and employment, that are key to explaining the UK's health inequalities (see Marmot, 2010 for an overview). Within this broad consensus, however, there are diverging ideas about what exactly policy makers ought to be doing to reduce health inequalities. While some researchers focus on the potential for lifestyle-behavioural or health service interventions to ameliorate health inequalities (for example, Buck and Frosini, 2012), others are actively calling on policy makers to address upstream, structural dimensions of inequalities (for example, Scott et al, 2013).

In policy terms, when the 'New' Labour Party won the UK general election in 1997, there was widespread optimism among health inequalities researchers. Not only did the new government officially commit itself to reducing health inequalities (in contrast to the previous Conservative government) but it also claimed that policy decisions were going to be evidence based. Yet, despite two government-commissioned reviews of the available evidence, and much other policy activity, health inequalities have not significantly reduced (Marmot, 2010). Some commentators have suggested that this is due to a failure to improve the links between research and policy (for example, Hunter, 2009). However, the data on which this chapter draws indicate that civil servants and ministers generally had a good understanding of the available research (see Smith, 2013). Consequently, the question is not, 'Why did health inequalities research fail to influence policy under governments that were officially committed to reducing these inequalities?' but 'Why did research-informed theories about health inequalities travel into policy circles without stimulating the kinds of policy changes that researchers might have anticipated?'

Introducing case 2: tobacco control in the UK

Having been a luxury pursuit in the Victorian era, by 1948, 82% of British men smoked some form of tobacco and 65% were cigarette smokers (Wald and Nicolaides-Bouman, 1991). In the context of emerging evidence about the harms caused by smoking, rates among men fell rapidly from the 1960s until the mid-1990s and have since continued to decline, albeit at a slower rate (Wald and Nicolaides-Bouman, 1991). The rates for women were never as high but rose to just under 50% in the late 1960s (Wald and Nicolaides-Bouman, 1991) and have subsequently been slower to decline. Smoking rates are now strongly socially patterned, with rates being significantly higher in socially deprived groups in all four jurisdictions (Department of Health, 2010). The societal economic costs estimated to be associated with tobacco use in the UK are high, particularly for the NHS (Twigg et al, 2004), so there is a recognised economic (as well as social) rationale for government intervention to reduce tobacco use.

Evidence concerning the health damaging consequences of tobacco first emerged in 1947 and, as evidence mounted in the 1950s and 1960s, calls for policy interventions grew louder (Berridge, 2006). In the UK, the (government-funded) charity Action on Smoking and Health (ASH) was established in 1971 (Berridge and Loughlin, 2005) and subsequently played a high-profile part in advocacy efforts to encourage policy interventions to address the 'tobacco epidemic' (Lopez et al, 1994). By the 1990s, a consensus had emerged that passive smoking was also carcinogenic (Scientific Committee on Tobacco and Health, 1998). A series of UK public policy efforts to reduce tobacco use and/or the harms associated with smoking ensued, including health warnings on packs, bans on tobacco advertising, tax-funded smoking cessation services and, more recently, bans on smoking in indoor public places (Cairney, 2007). These UK-level efforts have been reinforced by policy developments at European Union and international levels (Gilmore and McKee, 2004). In 2013, the UK was identified as having the most advanced tobacco control policies in Europe, with further interventions, including product display restrictions (now implemented) and standardised (plain) packaging (due to be enforced from May 2017), being pursued (Joossens and Raw, 2014).

All this has occurred despite the well-resourced efforts of the tobacco industry (Cairney, 2007). As such, tobacco is increasingly being positioned as a successful case study of evidence-informed policy, from which other public health areas might learn (for example, Freudenberg, 2005; Douglas et al, 2011). Yet, while evidence clearly played a role in the UK's policy responses to tobacco, it would be difficult to argue that the raft of recent policy initiatives in this area can be *explained* by evidence, given the long time-lag between evidence of the harms caused by tobacco and policy responses (Berridge, 2006). Indeed, available evidence has rarely provided clear 'solutions' to the problem of tobacco and, as Chapman (2007) points out, tobacco control advances have often involved a degree of willingness to pursue plausible policy interventions *in advance* of a fully fledged evidence base.

How an ideational focuses helps explain the contrasting fates of these two case studies

One key finding to emerge from the data was that certain ideas appeared to have become embedded in the policy world, either in terms of the organisation of policy institutions (Schmidt, 2010) or in terms of the language with which policy actors communicate. These ideas were then able, through their continual and effective circulation within networks of actors, to exhibit the characteristics of 'facts'. Two such 'ideas' are clearly visible within the empirical data, each of which has been institutionalised in a different sense. The first involves an understanding of health that is based upon a medical model (that is, a highly individualised way of thinking about health which focuses attention on medical interventions and intervening to reduce 'risky' health behaviours). In policy terms, the very decision to locate responsibility for health inequalities and tobacco control solely within departments/directorates of health (across the UK) reflects the tendency to think about these issues through a medical-health lens. The data indicate that the institutional structuring of these departments, which represent the institutionalisation of a medical model of health, is likely to have significantly shaped the construction and circulation of research-based ideas for both case studies. As Table 8.2 summarises, policy-based interviewees' accounts suggested there were limited possibilities for ideas which did not fit within this medical model of health to travel into policy; civil servants' organisational location and specific responsibilities encouraged them to focus on highly restricted areas of policy, working within the confines of this broader medical model. The process functions to encourage ideas that involve

Table 8.2: How the organisational institutionalisation of a medical model of health within policy functions as an ideational filter

Organisational feature	Illustrative interview extracts	Consequences for case studies
Links with other departments are limited, despite official commitments to 'joined-up government'.	Policy adviser (England): "They [the Department of Health] treat health as purely about the health issues of the individual, not about the wider social issues that the individual may be having problems with [...] The nature of government at the top is that ministers have their patches and they look out for their patches, that's what they see as their responsibility but also where their careers and ... development lie. Solving somebody else's problem is ... it's not zero value but it's very much second order."	Research-informed ideas which fit within the boundaries of the responsibilities of departments of health, such as tobacco, have a clear policy audience which vertically connects to relevant ministers. Research-informed ideas which do not fit neatly within the responsibilities of departments of health, such as health inequalities, are likely to fall between departmental divisions.
Within health departments, most people work in sub-units and are charged with responsibility for particular health conditions, risks or services.	Civil servant (Scotland): "We have got divisions ... which look after specific topics, so, for example [...] alcohol, smoking .... So, you will have very specific interests ..."	Divisions work well for ideas about tobacco control, which have a clear vertical route via which they can influence policy. Departmental divisions often 'block' more complex, crosscutting ideas about health inequalities.
Individuals within sub-units focus on looking for/assessing ideas and evidence relating to their specific area of responsibility (and less on broader issues, even when they are on official government agendas).	Civil servant (Scotland), in response to a question about how civil servants identify emerging evidence: "You ... have specialists within the department ... So, for example, on diet and physical activity, there is a Diet Coordinator and there is a Physical Activity Coordinator [...] many of whom do actually spend a bit of time with the ... journals."	Civil servants are likely to encounter new research relating to specific, institutionalised divisions, including tobacco. They are less likely to encounter new research relating to broader, crosscutting ideas about health policy, including research and ideas concerning health inequalities and the social determinants of health.
Policy actors commission and/or undertake research which is likely to help them address the specific policy issues for which they are responsible; they are less likely to do so for broader health issues.	Senior academic: "[T]he Department of Health, in England or Scotland, hasn't paid sufficient attention to the health consequences of non-health policies [...] The research commissioning is very silo-based and although ... they claim to have these crosscutting social justice policies, there's not much evidence of crosscutting research ..."	Policy bodies are likely to commission and/or undertake research relating to tobacco. They are less likely to commission and/or undertake research relating to broader, crosscutting ideas about health policy, including research and ideas concerning health inequalities and the social determinants of health.

thinking about particular lifestyle behaviours, such as smoking, while *filtering out* ideas concerning more complex, crosscutting determinants. Interviewees' accounts reveal the self-perpetuating qualities of ideas once they have been institutionalised (for example, research supporting this way of thinking is commissioned and undertaken by policy actors, while research on alternative approaches is not).

In our two cases, the institutionalisation of a medical model of health has worked well for tobacco in the UK; indeed, it is notable that some of the research-informed ideas about tobacco that seem to have been particularly successful in the UK, such as the provision of subsidised nicotine replacement therapy and smoking cessation clinics, fit particularly well with a medical model of health. In contrast, as one civil servant in Scotland reflected, even though the whole health department might be aware of the overarching policy commitment to reducing health inequalities, everyone ended up thinking about it as 'it applies to their own areas of interest'. This inevitably restricts the kinds of ideas about health inequalities that are likely to successfully travel into policy discussions, given many of these ideas cut across departmental divisions.

The second 'institutionalised idea' evident within the data is the notion that economic growth takes primacy over all other policy goals. Here, while the data suggest that policy actors based in departments not primarily responsible for economic policy did not feel able to influence these policies (in line with the siloed approach to policy work described above), the goal of national economic growth seemed to be a rare example of a policy position that had cross-government buy-in. Reflecting this, civil servants working on health policy development consistently suggested that they felt it was necessary to account for how their proposals would contribute to (or at least not undermine) the overarching goal of national economic growth. This idea had been institutionalised in a more discursive sense, appearing to be so deeply embedded in policy actors' language that it seemed difficult to imagine a policy space in which it would be possible to critique this idea. It was evident, for example, in the way health policy statements and civil servants regularly referred to the necessity of economic arguments for justifying health policy action:

> The Confederation of British Industry has estimated that 187 million working days are lost each year because of sickness. That's a £12 billion social tax on business every year, damaging to competitiveness and a brake on prosperity. (Secretary of State for Health, 1998: pt 1.16)

'The Communities Minister has a part to play, the Education Minister, the Justice Minister – they all have a part to play in health [...] So what I need to do [...] is show them [...] that by delivering the agenda they want to deliver – safer streets, better educated children – they're actually delivering the agenda that I want and, by doing that, the next link in the chain I make is that, by delivering a healthier Scotland, we're ultimately delivering a *wealthier* Scotland [...] So, my argument is, yes, I want better educated children because I know that they will be healthier children and I want them there because I want them to pay my pension, because this will create a wealthier economy, a more sustainable economy, one ... that fits well with everybody else.' (Senior civil servant, Scotland)

In the above interview extract, there is a clear assumption that it is somehow obvious and indisputable that securing economic wealth at the national level constitutes a key motivating factor underlying every aspect of policy making. The interviewee claims that the argument most likely to persuade both himself and his policy making colleagues to tackle health concerns is that there are *economic* advantages to doing so (as opposed to, say, ethical or human rights-based imperatives).

The institutionalisation of an overarching, economic frame was also evident within the broader interview data, with interviewees working in a wide variety of sectors all employing economic terms such as 'marketing' and 'selling' to explain what their day-to-day work involved. It is clear, for example, that interviewees working in academia, the civil service and the mass media all perceived themselves to be in competition with other sources as 'ideational vendors'. Indeed, economic discourses appeared to have been so successfully translated across a range of contexts that they were employed even by interviewees who directly challenged the domination of economic ideals over others. The fact that it appears logical to employ economic terms when trying to communicate ideas which are not directly related to economics highlights the extent to which an orientation towards the importance of the economy has become embedded in the language that we use and, therefore, in the ways in which we think. This had important consequences for the two case studies. While health inequalities research has been critiqued by policy makers for failing to frame either the problem or potential solutions in economic terms (Petticrew et al, 2004), from the 1970s onwards, tobacco control researchers and activists began successfully bolstering health oriented arguments with economic ones (Seligman,

1978). A 1999 World Bank report, which concluded that tobacco was economically damaging to all but a handful of tobacco-dependent agricultural economies, reinforced the credibility of this economic framing, which is now frequently evident in UK tobacco control advocacy material (for example, ASH, 2011) and helps explain the eventual policy success of many ideas concerning tobacco control in the UK.

Achieving the level of change that has been possible in tobacco control in the UK over the past two decades also required positive ideas to be put forward about what might be possible. Here, it seems useful to consider Weber's notion that the potential for dramatic change often rests with 'charisma', a force that works in precisely the opposite manner to institutionalisation, by first changing people's values and mentality, which then function to produce new conditions (Samier, 2005). Most commonly, Weber attributes the quality of charisma to individual 'leaders' who are able to convince others that their vision of the future will 'come to pass' (Spencer, 1973: 347). In other words, 'charisma' involves the ability of an individual to persuade others that the future will develop in a particular manner. If actors are sufficiently persuaded of this vision, they will then make decisions and take action based on this belief (or understanding), much as social constructivists describe processes of 'enactment', where actors come to enact what they perceive to be the reality, thereby (potentially unconsciously) constructing such a reality (for example, Law and Urry, 2004).

If we understand 'charisma' in this sense, we can see that it might also be applied to ideas. Indeed, Weber explicitly states that charisma is a 'de-personalised' trait (for example, Weber, 1992 [1968]), being inherently *relational*. Hence, in the same way that Spencer describes the persuasion of others by an individual, it seems plausible that it may equally be the qualities of a particular idea that succeed in persuading others to believe that a particular vision will 'come to pass', encouraging them to act accordingly. Developing the notion of charisma in an ideational sense has some important implications for how we might think about the role of ideas in public policy because it suggests that ideas themselves can have a degree of agency. This is not necessarily making a great leap from Weber's own writings, many of which reveal an underlying interest in the agency of ideas (see, for example, Collins, 2005; Weber, 1995 [1906]).

'Charismatic ideas', then, are those imbued with a creative, transformative power. They are revolutionary in their nature, providing a truly alternative way of thinking that challenges ideas that have become institutionalised. As 'institutionalised ideas' are often elevated to the status of 'facts', 'charismatic ideas' are likely to seem irrational to many (at least initially) because they challenge accepted ways of thinking. Indeed, Weber describes 'charismatic authority' as being 'specifically irrational in the sense of being foreign to all rules' (Weber, 1992 [1968]: 244). In other words, they are ideas which seek to influence perceptions of reality, replacing what is believed to be the legitimate vision of the world with something quite different. Their emergence depends on the ability of individuals to think outside the current boundaries of rationality and acceptability, and, given the effects of institutionalisation on individuals, it is clear that Weber believed that the potential for such ideas to develop within bureaucratic societies was slim (Weber, 1968a).

Such ideas are also, necessarily, short-lived, disappearing for one of two reasons: either they succeed in replacing previously 'institutionalised ideas' but, as a result, themselves become institutionalised (and can, therefore, no longer be described as charismatic); or they fail to successfully challenge 'institutionalised ideas', eventually causing followers to lose faith and, consequently, the charismatic qualities associated with the idea to evaporate. Hence, as Weber (1968b: 54) reflects, 'in its pure form, charismatic authority may be said to exist only in the process of originating'.

Within the empirical case studies, there is a noticeable absence of ideas about health inequalities with 'charismatic' qualities. Indeed, health inequalities researchers frequently stated that they did not believe that health inequalities were likely to substantially reduce in their lifetime and often seemed reluctant to advocate any specific policy solutions or scenarios, beyond some broad sense that wider social and economic inequalities needed to be addressed:

> 'Well, obviously reducing income differences [is what is needed to reduce health inequalities]. I often shy away from saying how to do it [...] So I always say, when people ask me about policy implications, that I think we need to redistribute income but I don't know whether you do that through education policies, through taxes and benefits, through minimum wages ... all sorts of things. And I still ... take that line because, as I say, it's a technically difficult problem – to know what is the best policy to redistribute...' (Senior academic)

In contrast, the package of ideas developed and promoted by the tobacco control community over the past two decades exhibits many of the characteristics of 'charismatic ideas'. This has included: (1) developing and collectively promoting clear 'policy solutions' (that is, an alternative vision), as well as calling attention to the 'policy problem' of the harms caused by tobacco; (2) employing an economic frame, as well as various health frames for these policy changes (thereby extending the support-base); (3) using evidence concerning the addictive qualities of nicotine, the (early) age at which smokers tend to start and the impacts of passive smoking to challenge arguments regarding the 'free will' of smokers; and (4) making a case for the exclusion of tobacco industry interests from policy debates. The latter was perhaps particularly radical and has now been institutionalised via Article 5.3 of the WHO Framework Convention on Tobacco Control (Conference of the Parties to the FCTC, 2008). Although the implementation of this idea still needs to be explored, by the time the second two batches of interviews were undertaken (see Table 1), the exclusion of the tobacco industry from policy debates appeared to seem entirely rational to most interviewees, having been deemed entirely irrational when first mooted (for example, Berridge, 2007). This achievement occurred relatively quickly in policy terms, between the mid-1990s and 2008, decades after evidence emerged of the health harms caused by smoking.

Health inequalities, of course, is a rather more complex, crosscutting policy issue. Nonetheless, although the data suggest there have been few, if any, ideas about health inequalities that have exhibited 'charismatic qualities' (potentially reflecting the more complex nature of this issue), a range of research-informed ideas about health inequalities, which appear to challenge the 'institutionalised ideas' described above, were identifiable in policy statements and interviews. However, these ideas fell into two main groups. The first set appeared to provide critical alternatives to institutionalised ideas but without a clear vision of the kinds of policy scenarios they required. I labelled these 'critical ideas', reflecting the fact they provided valuable critiques of ideas currently dominating policy without the persuasive qualities of 'charismatic ideas'. The second group was ideas that seemed to have altered during their journey into policy to such an extent that, despite radical research beginnings, they appeared able to fit within the boundaries of the 'institutionalised ideas' within policy settings. Such ideas do not fit within any of the three ideational types (institutionalised, critical and charismatic) outlined above. Rather, these are ideas which had been enabled to move between actors and across boundaries due to their elasticity, fuzziness and transformability, exhibiting characteristics similar to the 'vehicular' ideas that McLennan (2004) describes (see also Fischer, 2003, in relation to the malleability of policy narratives and Eisenberg (1984), on 'strategic ambiguity' in organisational communication). These, then, some interviewees suggested, might be understood as 'chameleonic ideas': ideas that were deliberately constructed in ways that would enable them to be framed in very different ways to contrasting audiences.

Within health inequalities, 'psychosocial' theories about health inequalities (which emphasise the importance of people's subjective sense of control, status, confidence and so on) were frequently evident in policy documents and in interviews with policy-based individuals. Indeed, several policy-based interviewees specifically linked these ideas to academics associated with these theories, Richard Wilkinson and/ or Michael Marmot. However, while Wilkinson (2005) and Marmot (2004) argue that psychosocial determinants reflect underlying material and social inequalities, notably income inequalities, policy-based interviewees who mentioned these ideas in positive terms tended to frame psychosocial ideas about health inequalities in ways which ignored or denied this link. This happened to the extent that one very senior civil servant in Scotland, who had a copy of a book by Wilkinson in his office and who spoke very enthusiastically about this work, stated that Wilkinson's research supported the idea that income inequalities do *not* explain health inequalities. In contrast, as readers of *The Spirit Level* (Wilkinson and Pickett, 2009) will be aware, much of Wilkinson's work explicitly focuses on arguing that income inequalities not only explain health inequalities but a raft of other social inequalities. Despite this interviewee specifically associating the ideas he was discussing with Wilkinson's work, the interpretation he offered (mirroring that of other interviewees) suggests that, while aspects of psychosocial ideas about health inequalities travelled into policy (for example, elements emphasising the importance of social capital, confidence and perceptions of status and control), the link between these factors and income inequalities was somehow lost (or discarded) along the way.

Various aspects of the data in which individuals describe 'selling' ideas to policy audiences help explain how this could have occurred. Academic interviewees, policy advisers and civil servants *all* described a process of carefully judging how to frame particular ideas for senior policy colleagues so they did not appear too 'radical' (or 'irrational'). Both a desire to influence policy and a concern with their personal and professional interests (prospects for funding, career progression and so on) seemed to inform interviewees' accounts of having moulded ideas in ways that they felt were likely to enhance their credibility among policy audiences. Hence, with the psychosocial example, the findings suggest that, in marketing Wilkinson's ideas to a policy audience, the emphasis was placed (by at least some of the actors promoting these ideas) on psychosocial pathways rather than income inequalities, with the consequence that psychosocial ideas became less challenging to 'institutionalised ideas'. This idea (or set of ideas) was therefore able to travel into policy because it was translated in chameleonic ways. However, it did not, in so doing, lead to substantive changes in the policy approach to health inequalities.

Conclusion

This chapter employed qualitative data relating to two public health case studies in the UK to argue that it may be both more accurate, and more useful, to consider the role of ideas in policy than to focus on the role of evidence. This shift, which involves considering how the ideas emerging from research are constructed, promoted and translated by multiple actors, may help explain: (1) how and why some ideas are so persistent over time; (2) how ideas can appear to travel from research into policy without effecting substantive change; and (3) why, occasionally, ideas (including those informed by research) can inform radical policy change. While such an approach helps explain the 'crisis' of EBP outlined at the start of the chapter, it does little to redress it. For Saltelli and Giampietro, the solution is radical and 'implies abandoning dreams of prediction, control and optimization' associated with EBP 'and moving instead to an open exploration of a broader set of plausible and relevant stories' (Saltelli and Giampietro, 2015: 1). However, in the context of claims that we are entering a 'post-truth era' (McCartney, 2016), there is an understandable desire to work to retain (and explain) the value of evidence for policy. Perhaps, as Carmen and colleagues (2016) argue (see also Fischer, 2003), forms of deliberative engagement offer a more promising way forward. The suggestion here is that creating spaces and mechanisms that enable increased public understanding of evidence will, in turn, enable members of the public to engage more meaningfully in policy debates about particular ideas/ proposals. All this requires more consideration of how best to combine existing knowledge concerning specific public health research with expertise in scientific communication, democratic engagement and deliberative forums and facilitation. How such approaches would fare in terms of supporting (or not) the use of public health evidence in policy is a question open to empirical testing. It seems clear, however, that post-1997 efforts to develop evidence-based policies to tackle the

UK's health inequalities were, in contrast to longer-standing efforts to reduce smoking, insufficiently engaged with the political and democratic dimensions of policy making to succeed.

References

ASH (2011) *Tobacconomics: How big tobacco uses dodgy data to 'throw sand in the gears' of global health policy.* London: ASH.

Bambra, C. (2013) 'The primacy of politics: the rise and fall of evidence-based public health policy?', *Journal of Public Health*, 35(4): 486–7.

Bartley, M. (1992) *Authorities and partisans: Debate on unemployment and health*, Edinburgh: Edinburgh University Press.

Bartley, M. (1994) 'The relationship between research and policy: the case of unemployment and health', in A. Oakley and A.S. Williams (eds), *The politics of the welfare state*, London: UCL Press.

Bekker, M., van Egmond, S., Wehrens, R., Putters, K., and Bal, R. (2010) 'Linking research and policy in dutch healthcare: infrastructure, innovations and impacts', *Evidence & Policy*, 6(2): 237–53.

Béland, D. (2005) Ideas and social policy: an institutionalist perspective. *Social Policy and Administration*, 39(1): 1–18.

Béland, D. and Cox, R.H. (eds) (2011) *Ideas and politics in social science research*, New York: Oxford University Press.

Berman, S. (2013) 'Ideational theorizing in the social sciences since "Policy paradigms, social learning, and the state"', *Governance*, 26(2): 217–37.

Berridge, V. (2006) 'The policy response to the smoking and lung cancer connection in the 1950s and 1960s', *Historical Journal*, 49(4): 1185–209.

Berridge, V. (2007) *Marketing health: Smoking and the discourse of public health in Britain, 1945–2000.* Oxford: Oxford University Press.

Berridge, V. and Loughlin, K. (2005) 'Smoking and the new health education in Britain 1950s–1970s', *American Journal of Public Health*, 95(6): 956–64.

Blackman, T., Greene, A., Hunter, D. J., McKee, L., Elliott, E., Harrington, M. et al (2006) 'Performance assessment and wicked problems: the case of health inequalities', *Public Policy and Administration*, 21(2): 66–80.

Blane, D., Davey Smith, G. and Bartley, M. (1993) 'Social selection: what does it contribute to social class differences in health?', *Sociology of Health & Illness* 15(1): 1–15.

Blyth, M. (1997) '"Any more bright ideas?" The ideational turn of comparative political economy', *Comparative Politics*, 29(2): 229–50.

Barroso, J.M. (2009) 'Passion and responsibility: strengthening Europe in a time of change', European Commission Press Release (SPEECH/09/391), http://europa.eu/rapid/press-release_SPEECH-09-391_en.htm

Buck, D. and Frosini, F. (2012) *Clustering of unhealthy behaviours over time: Implications for policy and practice*, London: The King's Fund.

Cabinet Office (1999) *Modernising government*. London: The Stationary Office.

Cairney, P. (2007) 'A "multiple lenses" approach to policy change: the case of tobacco policy in the UK', *British Politics*, 2: 45–68.

Campbell, J.L. (2002) 'Ideas, politics, and public policy', *Annual Review of Sociology*, 28: 21–38.

Carmen, K.L., Maurer, M., Mangrum, R., Yang, M., Ginsburg, M., Sofaer, S. et al (2016) 'Understanding an informed public's views on the role of evidence in making health care decisions', *Health Affairs*, 35(4): 566–74.

Chapman, S. (2007) *Public health advocacy and tobacco control: Making smoking history*. Oxford: Blackwell.

Collins, R. (2005) 'Weber and the sociology of revolution', in C. Camic, P.S. Gorski and D.M. Trubek (eds) *Max Weber's 'Economy and Society': A critical companion*, Stanford, CA: Stanford University Press, pp 297–321.

Conference of the Parties to the FCTC (2008) Guidelines for implementation of Article 5.3 of the WHO Framework Convention on Tobacco Control on the protection of public health policies with respect to tobacco control from commercial and other vested interests of the tobacco industry. www.who.int/fctc/guidelines/article_5_3.pdf

Cox, R.H. and Béland, D. (2013) 'Valence, policy ideas, and the rise of sustainability', *Governance*, 6(2): 307–28.

Davey Smith, G., Dorling, D. and Shaw, M. (eds) (2001) *Poverty, inequality and health in Britain: 1800–2000 – A Reader*. Bristol: Policy Press.

Department of Health (2010) *A smokefree future: A comprehensive tobacco control strategy for England*. London: Department of Health.

Douglas, M.J., Watkins, S.J., Gorman, D.R. and Higgins, M. (2011) 'Are cars the new tobacco?', *Journal of Public Health*, 33(2): 160–69.

Edelman, M. (1988) *Constructing the political spectacle* (2nd edn). Chicago: University of Chicago Press.

Eisenberg, E. (1984) 'Ambiguity as strategy in organizational communication', *Communication Monographs*, 51: 227–42.

Fischer, F. (2003) *Reframing public policy: Discursive politics and deliberative practices*, Oxford: Oxford University Press.

Freudenberg, N. (2005) 'Public health advocacy to change corporate practices: implications for health education practice and research', *Health Education & Behavior*, 32(3): 298–319.

Gilmore, A. and McKee, M. (2004) 'Tobacco-control policy in the European Union', in E. Feldman and R. Bayer (eds) *Unfiltered: Conflicts over tobacco policy and public health*, Cambridge, MA: Harvard University Press.

Glover, S. (2010) 'Why doesn't this dangerous man come clean and admit he wants to legalise drugs?' *The Daily Mail*, 3 November, www.dailymail.co.uk/debate/article-1325788/Why-doesnt-Prof-David-Nutt-come-clean-admit-wants-legalise-drugs.html

Hall, P.A. (1990) 'Policy paradigms, experts and the state: The case of macro-economic policy making in Britain', in S. Brooks and A.-G. Gagnon (eds) *Social scientists, policy and the state*, New York: Praeger.

Hall, P.A. (1993) 'Policy paradigms, social learning, and the state: The case of economic policymaking in Britain. *Comparative Politics*, 25(3): 275–96.

Henderson, M. (2012) *The geek manifesto: Why science matters*, London: Bantam Press.

Hunter, D.J. (2009) 'Relationship between evidence and policy: A case of evidence-based policy or policy-based evidence?', *Public Health*, 123(9): 583–86.

Innvær, S., Vist, G., Trommald, M. and Oxman, A. (2002) 'Health policy-makers' perceptions of their use of evidence: a systematic review', *Journal of Health Services Research & Policy*, 7(4): 239–44.

Jobert, B. and Muller, P. (1987) *L'Etat en action: Politiques publiques et corporatismes*, Paris: Presses Universitaires de France.

Joossens, L. and Raw, M. (2014) *The tobacco control scale 2013 in Europe*, Belgium: Association of European Cancer Leagues, www.europeancancerleagues.org/images/TobaccoControl/TCS_2013_in_Europe_13-03-14_final_1.pdf

Katikireddi, S.V., Higgins, M., Bond, L. Bonell, C. and Macintyre, S. (2011) 'How evidence based is English public health policy?' *BMJ*, 343(d7310).

Keynes, J.M. (1936) *The general theory of employment, interest and money*, London: Macmillan.

Kingdon, J.W. (1995 [1984]) *Agendas, alternatives, and public policies* (2nd edn), New York: HarperCollins College Publishers.

Knorr-Cetina, K. (1981) *The manufacture of knowledge: An essay in the constructivist and contextual nature of science*, Oxford: Permagon.

Latour, B. and Woolgar, S. (1986) *Laboratory life – the construction of scientific facts*, Princeton, NJ: Princeton University Press.

Lavis, J.N., Posada, F.B., Haines, A. and Osei, E. (2004) 'Use of research to inform public policymaking', *Lancet*, 364: 1615–21.

Law, J. and Urry, J. (2004) 'Enacting the social', *Economy and Society*, 33(3): 390–410.

Lopez, A.D., Collinshaw, N.E. and Tiha, P. (1994) 'A descriptive model of the cigarette epidemic in developed countries', *Tobacco Control* 3: 242–47.

Macintyre, S. (2011) 'Good intentions and received wisdom are not good enough: the need for controlled trials in public health', *Journal of Epidemiology and Community Health*, 65: 564–67.

Macintyre, S., Chalmers, I., Horton, R. and Smith, R. (2001) 'Using evidence to inform health policy: case study', *BMJ*, 322(7280): 222–25.

Mance, H. (2016) 'Britain has had enough of experts, says Gove', *Financial Times*, 3 June, www.ft.com/content/3be49734-29cb-11e6-83e4-abc22d5d108c

Marmot, M. (2004) *The status syndrome: How social standing affects our health and longevity*, New York: Times Books.

Marmot, M. (2010) *Strategic review of health inequalities in England post-2010*, Marmot review final report, London: University College London.

McCartney, M. (2016) 'Evidence in a post-truth world', *British Medical Journal*, 355: i6363.

McLennan, G. (2004) 'Travelling with vehicular ideas: the case of the Third Way', *Economy and Society*, 33(4): 484–99.

Mehta, J. (2011) 'The varied roles of ideas in politics: from "whether" to "how"', in D. Béland and R.H. Cox (eds) *Ideas and politics in social science research*, New York: Oxford University Press, pp 23–46.

Mitton, C., Adair, C.E. McKenzie, E., Patten, S.B. and Waye Perry, B. (2007) 'Knowledge transfer and exchange: review and synthesis of the literature', *The Milbank Quarterly*, 85(4): 729–68.

Monaghan, M. (2011) *Evidence versus politics: Exploiting research in UK drug policy making*, Bristol: Policy Press.

Mulgan, G. (2005) 'Government, knowledge and the business of policy making: the potential and limits of evidence-based policy', *Evidence & Policy*, 1(2): 215–26.

Orton, L., Lloyd-Williams, F., Taylor-Robinson, D. O'Flaherty, M. and Capewell, S. (2011) 'The use of research evidence in public health decision making processes: systematic review', *PLoS ONE*, 6(7): e21704.

Pawson, R. (2006) *Evidence-based policy: A realist perspective*, London: SAGE Publications.

Petticrew, M., Whitehead, M., Macintyre, S., Graham, H. and Egan, M. (2004) 'Evidence for public health policy on inequalities: 1 The reality according to policymakers', *Journal of Epidemiology and Community Health*, 58: 811–16.

Pisani-Ferry, J. (2016) 'Pourquoi les citoyens rejettent-ils les experts? Project Syndicate', 1 July, www.project-syndicate.org/commentary/brexit-voters-ignoring-experts-by-jean-pisani-ferry-2016-07?version=french&barrier=true 4-abc22d5d108c

Rein, M. (1980) 'Methodology for the study of the interplay between social science and social policy', *International Social Science Journal*, 22(2): 361–68.

Riker, W.H. (1986) *The art of political manipulation*, New Haven, CT: Yale University Press.

Sabatier, P.A. and Jenkins-Smith, H.C. (1999) 'The advocacy coalition framework: an assessment', in P.A. Sabatier (ed.) *Theories of the policy process*, Oxford: Westview Press, pp 117–66.

Saltelli, A. and Giampietro, M. (2015) 'What is wrong with evidence based policy?', paper submitted for a special issue on *FUTURES*, www.andreasaltelli.eu/file/repository/FUTURES_Saltelli_Giampietro_3.pdf

Samier, E. (2005) 'Toward a Weberian public administration: the infinite web of history, values, and authority in administrative mentalities', *Halduskultuur*, 6: 60–94.

Schattschneider, E.E. (1960) *The semisovereign people: A realist's view of democracy in America*, New York: Holt, Rinehart & Winston.

Schmidt, V. (2010) 'Taking ideas and discourse seriously: explaining change through discursive institutionalism as the fourth "new institutionalism"', *European Political Science Review*, 21(1): 1–25.

Scientific Committee on Tobacco and Health (SCoTH) (1998) *Report of the Scientific Committee on Tobacco and Health*, London: The Stationery Office.

Scott, S., Curnock, E., Mitchell, R., Robinson, M., Taulbut, M., Tod, E. et al (2013) *What would it take to eradicate health inequalities? Testing the fundamental causes theory of health inequalities in Scotland.* Glasgow: NHS Health Scotland.

Secretary of State for Health (1998) *Our healthier nation: A contract for health* (Green Paper), London: The Stationery Office.

Seligman, R.B. (1978) Meeting in New York. Source: Philip Morris. Exact date: 20 November. Bates number(s): 2074827747, http://legacy.library.ucsf.edu/tid/uvi05a00

Smith, K.E. (2007) 'Health inequalities in Scotland and England: the contrasting journeys of ideas from research into policy', *Social Science & Medicine*, 64(7): 1438–49.

Smith, K.E. (2013) *Beyond evidence based policy in public health: The interplay of ideas*, Basingstoke: Palgrave Macmillan.

Smith, K.E. and Joyce, K.E. (2012) 'Capturing complex realities – understanding efforts to achieve evidence-based policy and practice in public health', *Evidence & Policy*, 8(1): 59–80.

Smith, K.E. and Katikireddi, S.V. (2013) 'A glossary of theories for understanding policymaking', *Journal of Epidemiology and Community Health*, 67(2): 198–202.

Smith, K.E., Fooks, G., Gilmore, A.B., Collin, J. and Weishaar, H. (2015) 'Corporate coalitions and policymaking in the European Union: how and why British American Tobacco promoted "better regulation"', *Journal of Health Politics, Policy and Law*, 40(2): 325–72.

Spencer, M.E. (1973) 'What is charisma?', *British Journal of Sociology*, 24(3): 341–54.

The Guardian (2009) 'Drugs policy: shooting up the messenger', *The Guardian*, 31 October, www.guardian.co.uk/commentisfree/2009/oct/31/david-nutt-sacking-alan-johnson

Twigg, L., Moon, G. and Walker, S. (2004) *The smoking epidemic in England*, London: Health Development Agency.

Van Egmond, S., Bekker, M., Bal, R., and van der Grinten, T. (2011) 'Connecting evidence and policy: bringing researchers and policy makers together for effective evidence-based health policy in the Netherlands: a case study', *Evidence & Policy*, 7(1): 25–39.

Wald, N. and Nicolaides-Bouman, A. (1991) *UK smoking statistics* (2nd edn), Oxford: Oxford University Press.

Weber, M. (1968a) 'Meaning of discipline', in S.N. Eisenstadt (ed.) *Max Weber: On charisma and institution building*. Chicago: University of Chicago Press.

Weber, M. (1968b) 'Charismatic authority and its routinization', in S.N. Eisenstadt (ed.) *Max Weber: On charisma and institution building*, Chicago: University of Chicago Press, pp 48–65.

Weber, M. (1968 [1922]) *Economy and society: An outline of interpretive sociology*, trans. E. Fischoff et al, New York: Bedminster Press.

Weber, M. (1992 [1968]) *Economy and society*, edited by G. Roth and C. Wittich, London: University of California Press.

Weber, M. (1995 [1906]) *The Russian revolutions*, trans. G.C. Wells and P. Baehr, Ithaca, NY: Cornell University Press.

Wehrens, R., Bekker, M. and Bal, R. (2011) 'Coordination of research, policy and practice: a case study of collaboration in the field of public health', *Science and Public Policy*, 38: 755–66.

WHO Commission on the Social Determinants of Health (2008) *Closing the gap in a generation: Health equity through action on the social determinants of health. Final report of the Commission on Social Determinants of Health*, Geneva: World Health Organization, www.who.int/ social_determinants/final_report/en/index.ht

Wilkinson, R. (2005) *The impact of inequality: How to make sick societies healthier*, New York: The New Press.

Wilkinson, R. and Pickett, K. (2009) *The spirit level: Why more equal societies almost always do better*, London: Penguin.

World Bank (1999) *Curbing the epidemic: Governments and the economics of tobacco control*, Washington, DC: The World Bank.

Part Three

'Benefit tourism'? EU migrant citizens and the British welfare state

Elke Heins

The UK's vote to leave the European Union (EU) in the referendum of 23 June 2016 was to a considerable extent influenced by concerns about immigration. These concerns have been expressed in various forms, such as fears of cultural alienation or worries about downward pressure on wages exerted by cheap migrant workers. Notable from a social policy perspective is the fear that the EU's free movement policy places a financial strain on public services such as housing, schools and the National Health Service (NHS). For example, a poll of 1,002 British adults in March 2016, commissioned by the Chartered Institute of Public Finance and Accounting (CIPFA), found that 78% of respondents believed that EU membership puts pressure on UK public services (CIPFA, 2016). Particular worries about 'health tourism' arose in relation to the free-at-the-point-of-use NHS. Social policy related concerns were also expressed in other forms in the run-up to the referendum; claims by the Vote Leave campaign that the contributions made by the UK to the EU budget could be spent instead on the NHS became particularly notorious in this respect.

A final important facet of the social policy related immigration debate has been subsumed under the controversial heading of 'benefit tourism', that is, the allegation that migrants do not come to the UK for work reasons, but due to the availability of social benefits and services. The debate on so-called 'benefit tourism' had already gained prominence long before the referendum in the context of EU Eastern enlargement in 2004 and the full opening of EU-15 labour markets to accession countries thereafter. As a consequence, a range of political parties took on board apparently widespread concerns about the exploitation of the welfare system by migrants and suggested policy measures to stop any alleged 'benefit tourism'. It is also in this context that the UK's renegotiation with the EU in February 2016 had to be understood.

The deal achieved by then Prime Minister David Cameron included concessions to phase in immigrants' in-work benefits and to limit the amount of child benefit for children living in other EU countries depending on the standard of living abroad.

It is thus not surprising that issues around immigration and the welfare state have also raised notable academic interest. On the one hand, questions of EU migration and welfare have traditionally been analysed from a more legal angle to establish which rights and responsibilities exist under free movement of people, or how the EU regulates in the case of cross-border public service provision such as in health care. On the other hand, a number of recent studies, partly motivated by the pre-referendum debates, have focused on calculating net contributions rates of migrants (see, for example, Dustmann and Frattini, 2014). While such findings, based on quantitative analysis or econometric modelling, typically demonstrate a positive overall fiscal and economic contribution made by EU immigrants, myths about 'benefit tourism' stubbornly persist in some parts of the media and political debate.

This themed section recognises the importance of investigating some of the identified issues around EU migration and the British welfare state from an explicit social policy perspective. We therefore invited contributions to the 'benefit tourism' debate using diverse perspectives and bringing in various specialist policy areas. We especially deemed valuable research on EU migration and the British welfare state that closes some of the gaps in the existing literature.

Notable is the scarcity of research that qualitatively explores migrants' views on and experiences with the British welfare state. Both the contributions by Rebecca Etaha and Martin Seeleib-Kaiser on the one hand, and by Philip Martin, Lisa Scullion and Philip Brown on the other, address this important gap. Ehata and Seeleib-Kaiser examine the 'real-world experiences' with the British welfare system of EU migrants from a number of older and newer EU member states. In their chapter, Martin, Scullion and Brown challenge mainstream narratives regarding a particular EU migrant group in the UK, namely Roma from the Central and Eastern European EU member states, a group that has been particularly strongly associated with 'benefit tourism' due to a number of enduring negative stereotypes. Based on substantial qualitative research evidence, both chapters dismantle any 'benefit tourism' myths and highlight interesting parallels between diverse EU migrant groups. Respondents in both studies stated that they had little to no knowledge of the benefit system prior to arrival in the UK and indeed often did not make use of their rights to welfare benefits or services either due to ignorance of their entitlement or scepticism about the quality of services in Britain (particularly in relation to the NHS, a finding confirmed by the study of Horsfall and Pagan in this volume). Respondents also highlighted the importance of work as the main reason to migrate to the UK (the de facto exclusion of Roma from the labour market in Central and Eastern European countries constitutes an important difference between them and other EU migrant groups).

Based on the International Passenger Survey, Daniel Horsfall and Ricardo Pagan present an explorative, yet nuanced analysis of 'health tourism' as a specific form of alleged benefit fraud. Developing a typology of patient mobility rather than assuming one homogeneous health traveller, they consider how the EU Directive on Cross-Border Care is (under) utilised, and how the NHS is inappropriately utilised – but not necessarily by the archetypal 'health tourists'. Contrasting the case of Polish nationals living in the UK who return to Poland for medical care with UK expats returning from Spain, they find evidence that some forms of patient mobility reflect patterns of migration rather than rational consumer behaviour and do not support claims of fraudulent use of the NHS by EU citizens.

Finally, in her chapter, Isabel Shutes approaches the debate on migration and so-called benefits tourism from an explicit gender perspective, an often overlooked aspect in the debate. She examines how the aim of controlling migration led to the introduction of work-related conditions for benefit receipt that have restricted migrants' access to rights of residence and entitlement to social benefits in the UK. Specifically, she argues that the emphasis on a particular relationship of migrants to the labour market privileges the high-income and continuously employed migrant worker, thus reinforcing women's risk of exclusion from access to social rights. She concludes that debates on so-called 'benefit tourism' are thus not only misplaced, since access to income-related benefits is highly restricted in relation to work, but that the restrictions on migrants' access to rights and resources have strong gendered effects as regards who is excluded.

All four chapters enhance our understanding of issues of citizenship and migration alongside the existing regulatory frameworks guiding access to social benefits and public welfare services within the EU, some of which are likely to change in the wake of the UK's decision to leave the EU. In doing so, they bring much needed clarity to a debate that has been conducted in a cloud of myths and misconceptions.

References

CIPFA (2016) *CIPFA Warns that People Unaware of EU Impact on Public Services*, www.cipfa.org/about-cipfa/press-office/latest-press-releases/cipfa-warns-that-people-unaware-of-eu-impact-on-public-services

Dustmann, C. and Frattini, T. (2014) 'The fiscal effect of immigration to the UK', *Economic Journal*, 124(580): F593–F643.

NINE

Benefit tourism and EU migrant citizens: real-world experiences

Rebecca Ehata and Martin Seeleib-Kaiser

Introduction

According to the 'welfare magnet theory', generous welfare states are said to be negatively affected by immigration, as migrants may be attracted by high welfare benefits or services. In a nutshell: the higher the benefits are, *ceteris paribus*, the higher the number of (unskilled) immigrants entering the country (Borjas, 1999). In fact the dominant interpretative pattern within the political discourse leading up to the Brexit referendum was that European Union (EU) migrant citizens were attracted to the UK by its relatively generous welfare benefits and services. Prime Minister David Cameron in 2014 claimed:

> 'Someone coming to the UK from elsewhere in Europe, who's employed on the medium wage and who has 2 children back in their home country, they today will receive around £700 per month in benefits in the UK. That is more than twice what they'd receive in Germany, and 3 times more than they would receive in France. No wonder so many people want to come to Britain.' (Cameron, 2014)[1]

However, empirical evidence on the impact of welfare state generosity on migration flows within the EU is rather mixed. De Giorgi and Pellizzari (2009) find weak evidence for welfare magnets, while others reject the magnet hypothesis and argue that labour market opportunities and networks largely determine migration flows (Giulietti and Wahba 2012; Zimmermann et al, 2012; Giulietti et al, 2013; Skupnik 2014). The suggestion that EU migrant citizens will create a smaller net benefit (or larger net cost) in countries with tax-financed benefits, such as the UK, than in countries with predominantly insurance-based welfare states (Ruhs 2015) is also far from clear, as the financing structure is not necessarily a robust indicator for the ease of access and the level of social rights available to EU migrant citizens (Bruzelius et al, 2016). Benefits important to working-age EU migrant citizens, such as Child Benefit, Housing Allowance and in-work benefits, are largely tax financed independently of the overall financing structure of the welfare state. Research by Dustmann and Frattini (2014) found that the migration of EU citizens to the UK provides a clear economic benefit, as the average fiscal contribution of EU migrant citizens is higher than among British nationals. Spreckelsen and Seeleib-Kaiser (2016) emphasise the high employment rate among young EU migrant citizens in the UK as well as the low probability of them receiving Jobseeker's Allowance when unemployed.

Studies investigating the welfare magnet theory are often based on macro indicators, such as social expenditure in relation to GDP, spending on unemployment benefits or replacement rates as measures for welfare state generosity, or on quantitative analyses of micro data, neglecting the de facto knowledge and experiences of EU migrant citizens with the welfare state in destination countries. In other words, research so far has paid little attention to the real-world experiences of EU migrant citizens that can provide us with hard evidence relating to the mechanisms associated with the welfare magnet theory (but cf. Spencer et al, 2007; Kremer, 2016). Do migrants actually know which benefits are available? Do they migrate because of available benefits and services or are work opportunities the more likely reason to move? Can EU migrant citizens actually access benefits, or are they denied access due to discrimination? To answer these questions we employed a qualitative research approach based on semi-structured interviews with EU migrant citizens. It was our aim to obtain insights into participants' own understanding of their social rights and their perceptions of the impact of having (or being denied) access to such rights in the UK.

We studied the experiences of EU migrant citizens from Germany, Poland, Romania and Spain living in Britain with regard to their knowledge of social rights in Britain and their history of accessing them in the domains of education, health care, benefits and housing. The countries of origin were chosen based on the largest groups of EU migrant citizens living in Oxfordshire. Since we also wanted to account for possible differences in the location of destination in the UK, we selected Oxford and Manchester. Oxford is an affluent city with very low unemployment rates, a world-class university and a large automotive industry. In contrast, Manchester is a de-industrialised city in northwest England with some of the most deprived wards in the UK. A total of 56 EU migrant citizens from Germany (13 interviews), Poland (17 interviews), Romania (9 interviews) and Spain (17 interviews) took part in the research (see Table 9.1 for an overview of participant profiles). Participants were recruited using snowballing, with starting points established through personal contacts, work with migrant support and advice organisations and informal approaches to likely employers of EU workers. As suggested by Triandafyllidou and Maroufof (2013), knowledge about EU citizenship rights may be associated with demographic factors such as age, educational level and nationality. Thus, the interview schedule sought to probe the impact of factors such as country of origin, level of skills and qualification, employment status, presence of dependent children and reasons for coming to the UK. Interviews were conducted between January 2015 and May 2016, in the run-up to the UK's 'Brexit' referendum. Almost all participants acknowledged an awareness of the hostility towards EU migrant citizens that characterised much of the Brexit debate, and its impact on newer arrivals in particular and their willingness to exercise their social rights should be taken into account.[2] All interviews were recorded, coded and subsequently thematically analysed using NVivo.

Table 9.1: Overview of interview participants' profiles

Location	Age	German		Polish		Romanian*		Spanish	
		M	F	M	F	M	F	M	F
Manchester	18–24								
	25–34	2	3		2				1
	35–44	1		3	2		2	2	1
	45–54		1	1			2	1	1
	55–64								1
Oxford	18–24		1						1
	25–34		1	1	3		2	4	3
	35–44	1	3	2	2		2	1	1
	45–54				1		1		
	55–64								
Total		4	9	7	10		9	8	9

Note: * Recruiting Romanian participants proved extremely difficult, with many people distrustful of any interest in their community following sustained hostile media attention in the months leading up to and following the lifting of transitional restrictions on Romanian and Bulgarian citizens at the end of 2013 (see Vicol and Allen, 2014).

Coming for work purposes

Contrary to popular discourse in the UK, EU citizens who move to the UK do not have an unconditional right to claim social benefits or services. Rather, their rights largely depend upon their status as an economically active 'worker', self-employed person, or as an unemployed worker with retained worker status. EU citizens who are economically inactive have very few social rights outside the member state of origin.[3] Thus, it is not surprising that a large majority of the predominantly young EU migrant citizens who come to Britain do so to work, and are employed in a range of economic sectors (Spreckelsen and Seeleib-Kaiser, 2016). Although our sample of participants was not statistically representative of EU migrant citizens in the UK, the overwhelming majority of participants in our research were engaged in work, in occupations ranging from au-pairs, cleaners, construction workers and various professionals to academics. Twelve participants were out of work at the time of the interview; 10 of these were actively seeking work, while the remaining two were undertaking childcare responsibilities. Participants possessed varying English language abilities and academic qualifications. Only a small number of our sample were in receipt of social benefits at the time of participation, with the exception of Child Benefit, which was being claimed by 21 out of 27 participants with dependent children. Three of the 56 participants were in receipt of Jobseeker's Allowance and three were claiming tax credits. Five people were receiving Housing Benefit, while four gave their housing type as 'council house'. Three participants were homeless and not in receipt of any benefits (for an overview see Table 9.2). The duration of residence in the UK varied widely; 8 participants had been in the UK for a year or less; 17 had arrived between two and five years ago; the remaining 31 participants had lived in the UK for between 6 and 15 years.

Table 9.2: Benefit receipt at the time of interview by length of time in UK

Time in UK	Child Benefit	Tax credits	Jobseeker's Allowance	Housing Benefit
<12 months (total = 8)	1	0	0	0
12 mths–5 yrs (total = 17)	5	2	1	3
>5 years (total = 31)	15	1	2	2
Total	21	3	3	5

Participants were keen to stress that they had been motivated to move to the UK primarily because of work; moreover, most of the people we interviewed strongly rejected the notion of EU citizens as benefit tourists by emphasising their work contributions, their lack of knowledge regarding their potential entitlement to social rights and their cultural conditioning of self-reliance. A group of Polish and Romanian participants stressed that many benefits do not (did not) exist in their country of origin (eumc18, eumc27, eumc42, eumc47) as a result of which they took it as given that they would have to work to support themselves: "In Poland we don't have benefits: we need to work. You don't have a choice, or you will die on the street, and no-one will care" (eumc18). Spanish citizens who participated in our research underlined their work motivation with reference to high levels of unemployment in Spain, and (for the young in particular) noted that they had not expected to be eligible for anything in the UK since financial support for jobseekers in Spain is only available to people with a previous employment record (eumc06, eumc08, eumc21, eumc22).

Lack of knowledge about EU migrant citizens' social rights

The pure availability or generosity of social benefits and services is insufficient to substantiate the welfare magnet theory, as EU migrant citizens would also need to have detailed knowledge of what would be available to them to establish the causal mechanism and causal relationship. Following the thesis to its logical conclusion, they would also need to have made a comparative evaluation of the benefits and services they would receive in the UK against what they might receive in other member states.

However, our findings strongly indicate that knowledge of benefits is minimal, in terms of its extent and its importance in the decision making of intra-EU migrants coming to the UK (also see Hudson et al, 2011: 14; Dagilyte and Greenfields, 2015). Very few of our participants (6 out of 56) had undertaken *any* research to find out which specific rights would be available to them, and under what circumstances, prior to coming to the UK. Only two participants claimed to have had a more in-depth knowledge of rights before arriving in the UK: one had acquired the knowledge through previously studying EU law (eumc09), and the other (eumc47) explained that knowing she would be eligible for some benefits if she could not find well-paid work was critical for her decision to come to the UK as a single parent.

The majority of participants explained that they did not investigate rights to welfare benefits prior to their arrival in the UK because they came to work, and that they had only looked into such rights as the need arose (eumc17). Others told us that they had not had time to look into their entitlements before moving (a few participants told us that they only had two or three weeks' notice between receiving a job offer and moving to the UK), that they were not planning to stay long term and/or only came to study, or cited youth as their reason for not finding out more (for example, eumc10, eumc48). Lack of comparable welfare rights at home was another reason given for not researching entitlements prior to arrival in the UK (eumc35). A very small number of participants from Poland and Romania did not expect to have *any* rights at all as migrants, beyond the right to work. When asked what she had known about her rights prior to arriving in the UK, one Romanian participant stated that, "I had no idea and I honestly didn't expect to be entitled to something!" (eumc44). Another (Polish) participant stated that, "I wasn't really expecting anything, any help: I thought I would go to work, earn the money, get a house and buy stuff" (eumc56).[4] Some participants suggested that they simply expected the UK "as a civilised country" to have accessible health care and to provide school places for children (for example, eumc01).

Health care was the one area that had been checked by some participants. Two German participants confirmed that they had struggled to believe that they would be able to use the NHS "for free", as they were required to enrol in statutory health insurance schemes in Germany (eumc25, eumc26). Others acknowledged that friends and relatives already living in the UK had told them about access to the NHS (eumc35, eumc47). Since participants did not mention prior knowledge in relation to other areas of social rights, this may indicate the relative importance of health.

Finally, some of our Spanish (eumc21, eumc22) and German (eumc17, eumc52) participants, who were knowledgeable about the basics of the different welfare systems, pointed out that for those people who are eligible for unemployment and certain other benefits in their countries of origin, coming to the UK to claim benefits would not make sense, since the levels of support available are so much *lower* than in their countries of origin (eumc52).

With the exception of the particularly acute lack of knowledge among a group of citizens from Poland and Romania, the broad similarity in responses to questions about prior knowledge suggests that the factors of location, skill level, employment status and reasons for coming to the UK appear to have little bearing on the extent to which individuals were aware of, or made an effort to inform themselves regarding the nature and extent of their social rights in the UK. One participant (eumc07), who is employed in a postdoctoral capacity and has lived in the UK for 10 years, was representative of many when she told us that "still now I'm not quite sure whether I'm entitled to all the benefits, like a UK national, or whether there are differences for EU citizens". She had no knowledge of the right of permanent residence that is automatically acquired after five years of legal residence in the member state in which the EU citizen lives, and which entitles an EU migrant citizen, irrespective of economic status, to the same rights enjoyed by British citizens.[5]

Ignorance or discrimination?

The role of 'street-level bureaucrats' (Lipsky, 1980) in determining eligibility and access to social benefits and services should not be underestimated, as frontline workers are the ones that interpret and implement the formal rules governing social policies. Based on the complexity of EU regulation and the complex transposition of EU law into national law, it is not surprising that frontline staff may struggle to keep up to date with the intricacies of who is eligible for which kind of support or service (Oliver and Jayaweera, 2013). Such uncertainty may increase the likelihood of making mistakes, as some staff admit (Rightsnet, 2011). One Romanian participant told us that: "When I came here [in 2007] I found that a lot of agencies didn't have a lot of information about Romanians and their entitlements, so – it wasn't in my case but friends were refused at the beginning, yes, so there were lots of issues like that" (eumc42).[6] The problem may be exacerbated in areas which have fewer migrants and thus less opportunity for staff in service provider agencies to recall and reinvigorate their knowledge of migrant entitlements. Additional pressure comes from the fact that staff working for statutory organisations have a legal duty to ensure that all recipients of resources are eligible for them, and conversely not to allocate to ineligible individuals. In a political environment of cost cutting and retrenchment, as well as widespread allegations of 'welfare tourism', uncertainty is likely to lead to rejections of applications by staff unsure of entitlements.

Although many of our participants praised the efforts of individual frontline workers, a significant number had experienced difficulties accessing, or had been denied, their social rights as a consequence of outright discrimination. Others spoke of negative experiences by friends or other members of their networks. One Polish participant, who now undertakes both paid and voluntary work assisting her compatriots to exercise their social rights in the UK, explained that one of her clients "received a letter telling her she wasn't eligible for child benefit because Poland is not in the EU" (eumc56), while another client, who was to receive an allocated social housing tenancy, had her Polish ID card incorrectly refused as an identity document; after calling various government agencies and eventually persuading the official of the validity of that ID the client "was then asked to provide proof that Poland is part of the EU". In another case, a Polish family was directly discriminated against when they applied for social housing at their local council (described here by an interpreter):

"They tried and were applying twice for a council house. They had one kind of conversation with the council worker, and she wasn't very nice, and she said that because she's a teacher and her husband has a higher education degree, they are not entitled to council housing, because they can go back to Poland. Because there are English people who are kind of in greater need, they don't have any work, they don't have any education. But they complained about this lady! So then the application went to another worker and he said yes, you're entitled to this." (eumc29)

A single parent (eumc47) found herself fighting to keep benefits to which she was entitled after being made redundant from her agency job. She explained that it had taken months of correspondence and the intervention of the Citizens Advice Bureau to get official recognition of the validity of her claim. Discrimination and/or ignorance of rights extend beyond nationality: a participant of Romanian origin who had acquired British citizenship a few years previously, went to apply for Universal Credit when she recently lost her job, but was told that she could not apply because "you're not born here; Universal Credit is only for people who were born British citizens, born in the UK" (eumc42).

Some of these cases that we came across were the result of individual ignorance or discrimination by frontline workers, but some of the evidence suggests organisational ignorance and instances of institutional discrimination. How widespread these discriminatory practices are is unclear. Our data seems to suggest that participants with sufficient educational attainment and language proficiency are at times able to effectively challenge the wrongful decision of a local authority or public employee, whereas participants with very limited English language skills are less likely to challenge decisions without additional assistance. However, the necessary assistance to support claimants in effectively gaining access to their rights was largely cut by the Conservative–Liberal government's Legal Aid, Sentencing and Punishment of Offenders Act 2012, which the Ministry of Justice itself estimated would reduce the legal aid funding available to advice charities which help individuals to appeal negative welfare decisions by more than 90% (Morris and Barr, 2013: 81). Clearly, there is an urgent need for frontline staff in British service provider organisations to receive better training and clearer operational guidance on the eligibility criteria governing EU migrant citizens' social rights, though this is unlikely to be prioritised as the UK government moves towards negotiating the country's exit from the EU, and as yet no clear policy intentions regarding the rights of EU citizens currently resident in the UK have been set.

Going private or going 'home'

In contrast to the notion of the welfare magnet theory or 'benefit tourism', a group of EU migrant citizens seems to be opting out of obtaining social rights from the state by sourcing private provision or by returning to their country of origin to access provision there (eumc01, eumc18, eumc23, eumc40, eumc42, eumc47, eumc53). While a few participants had acquired access to private health care through their employers (such as eumc44), some of our Polish participants had accessed the growing number of Polish private clinics that have been established in the UK since the 2004. For example, a low-waged Polish participant was paying for private dental care at a private Polish clinic in Manchester because of her concern about the poor standard of NHS dental care (eumc47). More frequently, however, our interviewees revealed practices of returning to the country of origin for partial or full medical treatment. Among our interviewees, reasons for deciding to go 'home' for treatment varied. In some instances it was about the impracticality of accessing care in the UK vs. the ease of access in the country of origin. For example:

'In the UK, it's quite difficult to take time off work and go and do those things. It is very hard sometimes to get to an appointment, and so I need to wait several months. But when I go to Romania on holiday, I just go straight to the doctor, pay for everything and have the treatment done, so it's very quick.' (eumc42)

An EU migrant citizen from Spain (eumc23) who has been in the UK for five years, continues to use a dentist in Spain, having had difficulty getting onto the list of an NHS dentist in the UK; lack of trust in the competence of the local GPs prompted an EU migrant citizen from Poland (eumc01) to return to her country of origin to see a doctor for non-urgent medical complaints. In addition to negative opinions of the available care and competence of practitioners in the UK, a further reason given for returning to the country of origin for medical assistance concerns the importance of familiarity with the system and with individual health care professionals (as is the case with eumc40, who returns to Germany twice a year to use the dentist who has treated him since he was a child). Our findings are in line with Migge and Gilmartin's (2011) research in the Republic of Ireland, which identifies a number of reasons why migrants might travel back to their country of origin to access health care, including affordability, the perceived quality of care, bad prior experience of health care including excessive waiting times, as well as issues of (lack of) familiarity in terms of 'feelings of unease about local care provision due to (perceived) social, cultural, religious and linguistic differences' (Migge and Gilmartin, 2011: 1148).[7]

One German family experienced disruption due to the differences between the education systems in their previous country of residence (Austria) and the UK, where they were shocked to find that applying for a school place is not a matter of turning up in person on the first day of school, but rather requires a sometimes lengthy procedure with an uncertain outcome. The resolution to a missed school place for this family has been to send the child to a private school. Others did mention the possibility of opting for private education for their children based on their perception of the poor standards of state education in the UK (eumc40, eumc53).

These experiences suggest that a group of EU migrant citizens explicitly opt out of health and social services or procedures and go private or access services in their country of origin. Partly this seems to be a coping strategy by those who perceive the services and competency provided by the British welfare state to be of comparatively low quality.

Public discourse and access to social rights

In recent years, the public and media debate in the UK has been dominated by a political discourse which characterises EU migrant citizens as benefit tourists who come to Britain to exploit or defraud the system (e.g. Balabanova and Balch, 2010; Bruzelius et al, 2014).

In our interviews, participants felt an obligation to reject or downplay the use of benefits as a response to the highly politicised role that the exercise of such rights plays in current media discourse. Many people stressed that they did not know anyone in their social networks who had come to rely on benefits, that all of their contacts came with the intention of working and are contributing to the system. The spectre of EU migrant citizens living on benefits was largely dismissed as the fanciful creation of the media rather than being based on reality. There was very limited acceptance of the idea that some EU citizens might in fact be exploiting free movement rights in order to access British benefits, but even in this case, the speaker emphasised such behaviour to be exceptional and not representative of EU migrant citizens in general: "Those people are ruining the reputation for those people who want to stay here. We're not like that: keep your benefits, we don't want them!" (eumc18).

Some people voiced opinions which seem to chime with the rhetoric of earned rights, the need for migrants to 'pay in' before they 'take out', and proposals for deferred access to social provisions which were put forward by former Prime Minister David Cameron (2014). One participant stated:

> 'I don't think people should access social welfare easily in a different country. I know we are all in Europe, but each country has its own budget and system, people to look after, so I think yes that migrants should actually take employment, and then after a period of paying taxes and working and settling, they could access welfare.' (eumc42)

This finding corresponds with Kremer's (2016) research in the Netherlands, which found that some migrants also favour 'earned citizenship' rather than immediate access to social rights.

Though our participants did not come to the UK expressly to access welfare rights, some found themselves in the position of needing to apply for various types of assistance as a result of the birth of children, involuntary unemployment, ill-health or other unanticipated circumstances. Given their collective rejection of the discursive stereotype of EU migrant citizens as benefit tourists and several identifications with the negative portrayal of welfare recipients, it is unsurprising that a number of our participants, and in particular from those of Polish or Romanian nationality, intimated the conviction that they needed to justify their access to welfare. One participant who was currently in receipt of benefits as she could only work part time explained that "I didn't want to get them ... if you get them, then you inform people that you cannot count on yourself ... this situation is very uncomfortable for me" (eumc47). A mother who had given up work to care for her daughter, who had a serious health condition, felt the need to justify (through an interpreter) her recent application for Housing Benefit with this qualifier: "But she's not planning to stay on it for long, she is planning to go back to work in September" (eumc29). Another participant declared that, "This is a bit embarrassing for me, because I wanted to live my life never having to be on support, but I was unemployed for a few months, so that's when I [claimed JSA]" (eumc50).

In contrast, this was not a theme that arose automatically with our German and Spanish participants, although almost all of them were aware of the growing public discourse around EU migrants, and, when probed about the effects of events such as media stories about migrants having undeserved access to welfare payments, there was a general consensus that this discourse damaged the image of all EU migrant citizens in the UK. Most of the EU migrant citizens we interviewed were at pains to point out the distance between their own behaviour and that of the discursive stereotype of an EU national living in the UK solely to claim benefits. For some participants this distance was linked to the stigma of dependence on welfare in general, while for others it came from an assertion of difference to the stereotype.[8] As a consequence of the political discourse and the introduction of restrictions, it seems plausible that EU migrant citizens 'underclaim' benefits, as participants emphasised that they only claim benefits when it is *absolutely necessary* (for example, eumc01, eumc 23 and eumc47).

Conclusion

From a methodological perspective, our research has shown how important it is not solely to rely on quantitative macro and micro analyses in assessing the welfare magnet theory, as these approaches often operate with very abstract concepts and are unable to capture the complexities of experiences and knowledge required to effectively access social rights. Research based on local implementation (for example, see Bruzelius, 2016) and individual experiences can also complement socio-legal research, which is often limited to assessing statutory entitlements and neglecting substantive access to social rights (cf. Pennings, 2015). Although our research project was conducted on a relatively small scale in Oxfordshire and Manchester, we were able to identify various experiences of accessing social rights among EU migrant citizens, which are very likely to be found across the United Kingdom as well as other member states.

Overall, we were unable to empirically identify the causal mechanisms necessary for the welfare magnet theory to be plausible. Our findings clearly show that EU migrant citizens are largely unaware of their social rights when they move to the UK. Even after living in the UK for a number of years, a relatively high degree of uncertainty with regard to social rights can be found, which might be partly the result of the complexity of the regulatory framework or of the highly salient negative political discourse in Britain. While we cannot ascertain the extent of ignorance and deliberate discrimination among government officials regarding access to social rights by EU migrant citizens, we were able to document a number of instances of such treatment. Although those with sufficient language skills and educational attainment seemed able to effectively challenge and appeal decisions, those who did not possess sufficient language skills were less likely to overcome the discriminatory practices. This is of particular significance in an environment in which central government has cut legal aid and other support which might help people to overcome discrimination. In contrast, we also came across a group of EU migrant citizens who had deliberately opted out of public provision by choosing private education and health care provision, or health services in their country of origin, due to the perceived low level and quality of social and health care services in the United Kingdom. Finally, the potential consequences of the hostile public discourse towards EU migrant citizens should not be underestimated, as it is very likely to have contributed to feelings of shame and stigma as well as undeservingness among this group, and may result in EU migrant citizens not claiming benefits or services despite being legally entitled. To conclude: contrary to the welfare magnet thesis, our research clearly points towards a situation whereby various groups of EU migrant citizens underutilise the British welfare state.

Acknowledgements
We thank all participants of our research for their input, without their time and trust we would not have been able to conduct this research. We want to especially thank Suzie Drohan and Michal Gogut for their advice and overall great support for our project as well as for assistance in recruiting participants in Oxfordshire, and Amanda Jones-Said, Amanda Croome, Beth Plant and Claudia Paraschivescu for similar assistance in Manchester. We thank Elaine Chase, whose input was crucial in the

initial stages of the research project, and Cecilia Bruzelius for her research assistance. Last, but not least, we are grateful for the generous funding received from the John Fell OUP Research Fund. Martin Seeleib-Kaiser thanks the WZB Berlin Social Science Centre for the generous support during his sabbatical in academic year 2016/17.

Notes

[1] It is unclear to the authors what the basis of this calculation was.

[2] Ethical approval for the fieldwork was given by the University of Oxford's Central University Research Ethics Committee, and informed written consent was obtained from all participants prior to interviews taking place. Given the politically contentious nature of EU migrant citizens' social rights in the UK, which was especially severe in the months leading up to the Brexit referendum, questions inevitably arise regarding the extent to which our participants' responses were shaped by social desirability bias. While bias may never be eliminated completely, efforts were made in the research design to minimise such effects and to destigmatise access to social rights, so that participants didn't feel obliged to under-report knowledge and use. The project introduction sheet, which was given to all prospective participants, framed education, housing, health care and social protection rights as positive aspects of EU citizenship, and the interview normalised access to those rights by focusing on the experience of applying. Questions relating to knowledge of benefits were raised after discussions about main motivations for moving to the UK. The consistency of the responses across the entire cohort, including all levels of education and national background, together with frequent explanations of finding out what support was available as situations arose, suggests that participants' stated lack of knowledge about benefits prior to arriving was reliable. Interestingly, though there has been disagreement on whether higher levels of education increase or reduce social desirability bias (Heerwig and McCabe, 2009), the lowest-educated participants were as likely as any other group to report a lack of knowledge of UK benefits before living in the UK.

[3] The precise regulations on eligibility for social rights are, however, highly complex and subject to frequent change: for more information see Pennings (2015).

[4] Kremer (2016) identified a similar disbelief of entitlement to welfare provisions among low-skilled Polish workers in the Netherlands.

[5] Article 15, the Immigration (European Economic Area) Regulations 2006, SI 2006 1003.

[6] The welfare rights of working Romanian and Bulgarian ('A2') citizens arriving in the UK between January 2007 and December 2013 were nominally the same as those of other EU migrant citizens working in the country. However, it was much more difficult for A2 citizens to qualify as 'workers'. For example, while they were permitted to work in a self-employed capacity, most Romanian and Bulgarian ('A2') citizens (with the exception of highly skilled workers or those in a shortage occupation) were unable to take paid employment in the UK or were required to obtain worker authorisation prior to arrival. Unlike those arriving from the 2004 Central and Eastern European accession states, most A2 citizens were not permitted to enter the UK as jobseekers, a category which at that time gave access to welfare rights such as Jobseeker's Allowance. An A2 worker who was given permission to work but lost her job involuntarily would not retain worker status and would then lose the right to in-work benefits. Full 'worker' status was only achieved on completion of 12 months' continuous employment. See AIRE Centre (2014) for more details.

[7] Differences between the national health care systems include, for example, access to specialists (in the UK, this is usually obtained through a GP referral, whereas in Germany the patient makes direct contact with the specialist), or the willingness of medical practitioners to prescribe certain kinds of medication (all of our Polish participants complained that British GPs are reluctant to prescribe antibiotics, which they would expect to get readily from a Polish GP).

[8] The stigma of accessing benefits is not exclusive to migrants. An extensive literature documents the prevalence of stigma and shame among the claimants of welfare benefits (e.g. Spicker, 2011; Walker, 2014; Chase and Bantebya-Kyomuhendo, 2015).

References

AIRE Centre (2014) 'Frequently asked questions about the rights of EEA nationals to access benefits and the changes for A2 nationals from 1 January 2014', www.airecentre.org/data/files/TFL_Training_Materials_Feb_2014/A2_Nationals_Information_Note.pdf.

Balabanova, E. and Balch, A. (2010) 'Sending and receiving: the ethical framing of intra-EU migration in the European press', *European Journal of Communication*, 25(4): 382–97.

Borjas, G.J. (1999) 'Immigration and welfare magnets', *Journal of Labor Economics*, 17(4): 607–37.

Bruzelius, C. (2016) 'Facilitating and restricting European social citizenship at the domestic level', paper presented at the 23rd International Conference of Europeanists, Philadelphia, PA, 14–16 April.

Bruzelius, C., Chase, E., Hueser, C. and Seeleib-Kaiser, M. (2014) *The social construction of European citizenship and associated social rights*, Barnett Papers in Social Research 14-01, Oxford: University of Oxford.

Bruzelius, C., Chase, E. and Seeleib-Kaiser, M. (2016) 'Social rights of EU migrant citizens: Britain and Germany compared', *Social Policy and Society*, 15(3): 403–16.

Cameron, D. (2014) 'Prime Minister's speech', delivered at JCB Staffordshire, 28 November, transcript of the speech as delivered, www.gov.uk/government/speeches/jcb-staffordshire-prime-ministers-speech

Chase, E. and Bantebya-Kyomuhendo, G. (2015) Poverty and shame: Global experiences, Oxford: Oxford University Press.

Dagilyte, E. and Greenfields, M. (2015) 'United Kingdom welfare benefit reforms in 2013–2014: Roma between the pillory, the precipice and the slippery slope', *Journal of Social Welfare and Family Law*, 37(4): 476–95.

De Giorgi, G. and Pellizzari, M. (2009) 'Welfare migration in Europe', *Labour Economics*, 16(4): 353–63.

Dustmann, C. and Frattini, T. (2014) 'The fiscal effect of immigration to the UK', *The Economic Journal*, 124(November): F593–F643.

Giulietti, C., Guzi, M., Kahanec, M. and Zimmermann, K.F. (2013) 'Unemployment benefits and immigration: evidence from the EU', *International Journal of Manpower*, 34(1): 24–38.

Giulietti, C. and Wahba, J. (2012) *Welfare migration*, IZA Discussion Paper 6450, Bonn: Forschungsinstitut zur Zukunft der Arbeit.

Heerwig, J. and McCabe, B. (2009) 'Education and social desirability bias: the case of a black presidential candidate', *Social Science Quarterly*, 90(3): 674–86.

Hudson, M., Radu, D. and Phillips, J. (2011) *European migrant workers' understanding and experience of the Tax Credits system*, HM Revenue & Customs Research Report 114, Bristol: Policy Studies Institute.

Kremer, M. (2016) 'Earned citizenship: labour migrants' views on the welfare state', *Journal of Social Policy*, 45(3): 395–415.

Lipsky, M. (1980) *Street level bureaucracy: Dilemmas of the individual in public service*, New York: Russell Sage Foundation.

Migge, B. and Gilmartin, M. (2011) 'Migrants and healthcare: investigating patient mobility among migrants in Ireland', *Health and Place*, 17: 1144–49.

Morris, D. and Barr, W. (2013) 'The impact of cuts in legal aid funding on charities', *Journal of Social Welfare and Family Law*, 35(1): 79–94.

Oliver, C. and Jayaweera, H. (2013) *Country case study on the impacts of restrictions and entitlements on the integration of family migrants: Qualitative findings*. Oxford, COMPAS, University of Oxford.

Pennings, F. (2015) *European social security law*, Antwerp: Intersentia.

Rightsnet (2011) 'EU migrant serious case review. Discussion forum', www.rightsnet.org.uk/Forums/viewthread/1598/

Ruhs, M. (2015) *Is unrestricted immigration compatible with inclusive welfare states? The (un)sustainability of EU exceptionalism*, COMPAS Working Paper, Oxford.

Skupnik, C. (2014) 'EU enlargement and the race to the bottom of welfare states', *IZA Journal of Migration,* 3(15).

Spencer, S., Ruhs, M., Anderson, B. and Rogaly, B. (2007) *Migrants' lives beyond the workplace: The experiences of Central and East Europeans in the UK,* York: Joseph Rowntree Foundation.

Spicker, P. (2011) *Stigma and social welfare*, http://openair.rgu.ac.uk.

Spreckelsen, T. and Seeleib-Kaiser, M. (2016) 'Dimensions of labour market integration among young EU migrant citizens in the UK', Barnett Papers in Social Research 11, Oxford: Department for Social Policy and Intervention, University of Oxford.

Triandafyllidou, A. and Maroufof, M. (2013) 'EU citizenship and intra EU mobility: a virtuous circle even in times of crisis', in B. De Witte, A. Héritier and A.H. Trechsel (eds) *The Euro crisis and the state of European democracy*, Luxembourg: Office des Publications de la Commission Européenne, pp 370–92.

Vicol, Dora-Olivia and Allen, W. (2014) *Bulgarians and Romanians in the British National Press: 1 Dec 2012 – 1 Dec 2013*, Migration Observatory report, COMPAS, University of Oxford, August.

Walker, R. (2014) *The shame of poverty: Global perspectives*, Oxford: Oxford University Press.

Zimmermann, K.F., Kahanec, M., Giulietti, C., Guzi, M., Barrett, A. and Maître, B. (2012) *Study on active inclusion of migrants*, Bonn and Dublin: IZA and ESRI.

TEN

"We don't rely on benefits": challenging mainstream narratives towards Roma migrants in the UK

Philip Martin, Lisa Scullion and Philip Brown

Introduction

The expansion of the European Union (EU) in 2004 and 2007 brought ten Central and Eastern European (CEE) nations into what had primarily been a Western European bloc.[1] Several of these new member states contained large Roma minorities, and members of this community were among those exercising their new found rights of freedom of movement, settling in many countries across the EU.

The portrayal of Roma populations as 'benefit tourists' has become common within popular media over the last decade, both in the UK and the wider EU, evident in headlines such as 'The Roma gipsy who sparked a crackdown on benefit tourism' (*Daily Mail*, 2014) and 'German economist denounces Roma "benefits tourism"' (EurActiv, 2013). Indeed, the prominent use of the term 'Roma' in such contexts has been referred to as the 'ethnicisation of the topic' (Benedik, 2010: 160). However, such narratives need to be seen within a particular social and political context, specifically, the increasing problematisation of immigration since 2000 (Blinder, 2015) coupled with increasingly Eurosceptic attitudes (Ormston and Curtice, 2015). 'Benefit tourism' is one of a number of themes which recur in British media reporting on migrants in general, along with competition for state resources, criminality, anti-social behaviour and, more recently, purported links to terrorism (Garner et al, 2009; Gerard, 2016).

As Allen and Blinder's (2013) analysis of UK newspaper stories demonstrates, accusations of 'benefit tourism' are not exclusively directed at any single migrant group. Based on the British Social Attitudes survey, Curtice (2016: 8) reported that reducing the ability of migrants from other EU countries to claim welfare benefits in Britain was the most popular reform respondents wished to see. However, despite this homogenisation of migrants, as Luhman suggests: 'One of the implications of the benefits tourism case is to show how a focus on the perceived problems of fraud and abuse can lead to the identification of certain groups of migrants as problematic' (2015: 39).

Roma are especially vulnerable to such characterisation, as this group has been confronted with majority populations' perceptions and media portrayal of criminality, 'work-shyness' and deceitfulness for many years all across the European continent (see for example McGarry, 2013). Furthermore, it is also clear that the content of popular narratives about migrant Roma and 'benefit tourism' is not a uniquely British phenomenon. Indeed, there are prevalent discourses on Roma and welfare not only among established communities in Central and Eastern Europe but also in other locations which have experienced large-scale migration of Roma (for example, Italy, France and Belgium) (see, for example, FRA, 2009).

There is a general consensus that media narratives play an important role in shaping popular opinion towards migrants in general, and Roma in particular (Richardson, 2010, 2014; Okely, 2014; Kroon et al, 2016) and a number of researchers have attempted to counter these representations by presenting detailed statistical rebuttals (for example, Finney and Simpson, 2009; Dustmann and Frattini, 2013; Pompova, 2015). While recognising the importance of these contributions to counter-narratives, a surprising amount of the research that challenges representations of Roma migrants has not included the voice of the community itself. The aim of this chapter is therefore to provide new and unique insights into the perspectives of Roma in relation to employment and welfare in the UK, drawing on qualitative research undertaken in five locations in England and Scotland during 2014 and 2015. Grounded in the narratives of Roma themselves, our analysis provides a more in-depth understanding of people's motivations for migration and experiences within the UK, but also where the welfare system features within their stories.

'Benefit tourism' and migrant Roma: exploring dominant narratives

It is evident that intra-EU migration has reinforced a range of pre-existing and widespread prejudices towards settled Roma communities – what has been referred to as 'delinquent subjectivities' (Parker and

López Catalán, 2014). These stereotype Roma as inherently work-shy, uneducated, socially backward, predisposed to criminality and persistently reliant on 'handouts'. The prevalence of such attitudes among the general public has been amply documented at both the EU (FRA, 2009; Brown et al, 2013a) and national levels (see Brown et al, 2015). Indeed, as Kroon et al (2016: 15) demonstrate, these views are not restricted to one part of Europe. Using content analysis to examine 825 published articles which made reference in some way to Roma across five EU countries (the UK, Slovakia, the Netherlands, Germany and the Czech Republic), they concluded that 'representations of Roma as threats to society were salient'. One indication of the pervasiveness of such views appears in the booklet *Debunking myths and revealing truths about the Roma* (ENAR/ERIO, n.d.). This highlighted seven common stereotypes applied to Roma across the EU, including 'The Roma are criminals', 'The Roma don't want to work' as well as 'All Roma from Eastern Europe come to Western Europe to beg'.

With reference to the UK specifically, a number of researchers have explored media discourse towards Roma migrants (for example, Clark and Campbell, 2000; Richardson and O'Neill, 2010; Tremlett, 2012), highlighting that, as early as the 1990s, negative associations of Roma and 'benefit tourism' were appearing. Since then, the concept has become central to mainstream media narratives about migrant Roma in the UK. Over the past decade, the majority of UK press articles relating to migrant Roma make explicit their ethnicity, their status as migrants, and their access to different forms of social welfare (potential or actual). For example, in an analysis of 89 national and local news stories which included reference to the Roma community of Sheffield, Richardson (2014) demonstrated that the word 'benefits' appeared on 81 separate occasions in six months, second in popularity only to the terms 'migrants/immigrants'. Perhaps unsurprisingly, the overwhelming majority of the examples which discussed Roma and the benefit system were unfavourable towards the community.

In addition to print media, there are also notable examples of negative visual representations, such as television and advertising. One specific instance which unequivocally linked migrant Roma to 'benefit tourism' was the series *Gypsies on benefits and proud*, first screened on Channel 5 in 2014. The accompanying information described it as: 'An insight into how easily Gypsies can get their hands on benefits' (Channel 5, 2016). This achieved viewing figures of 1.87 million (BARB, 2016). In fact, the series had been foreshadowed in a storyline in Channel 4's controversial series *Benefits Street*, which had featured a Roma family, although without specifically identifying them as such. However, demonstrating how different forms of media interact with and reinforce each other, many national newspapers ran articles from the programme with headlines such as: 'I know it's easy to take benefits in England'; 'Gipsies who move to Britain reveal how they claim thousands of pounds every month as part of their bundle of benefits even though they do not work' (Reilly, 2014).

Several authors have highlighted that the narratives concerning Roma and 'benefit tourism' are often qualitatively different from debates involving other communities, nationalities or ethnic groups because they perpetuate much older representations of Gypsies and Travellers (Clark and Campbell, 2000; Okely, 2014). In the UK, for example, the arrival of migrant Roma simply added new impetus to long-standing prejudices, bearing a strong resemblance to historic prejudices towards indigenous Gypsy and Irish Traveller communities (Okely, 2014). As such, 'benefit tourism' could be regarded as 'supercharging' existing anti-Gypsy beliefs: 'The Roma frame is particularly effective because it taps into and fleshes out a long history of both local and imported anti-Roma prejudices ... in other words, they stepped right into home-grown narratives about Gypsies and Travellers' (Fox et al, 2012: 688)

The reach of these stories goes far beyond the daily readership, not least because the content is often replicated online, which then remains live for months, if not years. As Richardson highlighted (2014: 60), they also evolve as 'below the line' comments from readers pick up and amplify the themes raised in the stories. These are then often circulated on social media platforms and reach new audiences. The impact of such negative media attention has 'resulted in the authorities frequently regarding arriving Roma as "fraudulent" when they approach the public authority for legitimate entitlements, including social welfare assistance' (Cahn and Guild, 2010: 15).

However, this discourse is not just a feature of media debate; the discourse is also evident among some members of the political elite, with the expansion of the EU prompting an increased visibility of such allegations. Indeed, in 2013, the European Commission published a report investigating the uptake of the variety of social welfare and assistance schemes available in each member state. Describing the rationale for the research, the authors explained that it had been commissioned because: 'it is feared that the entitlement which EU law gives to non-active EU migrants to claim access to healthcare and special non-contributory benefits in cash can lead to "welfare tourism" and threaten the sustainability of European welfare states' (Juravle et al, 2013: 2).

While focusing on migration more broadly, the dense statistical analysis included one brief, but significant, reference to Roma and 'benefit tourism', citing a French source: 'The EU enlargement process in 2004 and 2007 raised concerns among public opinion about possible waves of Roma people migrating to France and accessing benefits' (Juravle et al, 2013: 113).

While the report concluded that there was little evidence to substantiate fears that 'benefit tourism' was a problem in the EU, this discourse remains a pervasive feature of debate in relation to Roma migration. Indeed, in 2013 Romanian Prime Minister Victor Ponta was moved to remark to the British Broadcasting Corporation (BBC) that 'benefit tourism' was a 'specific situation of the Roma community' (BBC, 2013). Within the UK, in response to concerns around increasing migration more broadly, the government introduced a series of new measures aimed at restricting access to benefits for European migrants. Within these measures was a clear discourse around 'benefit tourism', as demonstrated by the then Prime Minister David Cameron (2014): 'Over the past 4 years we have clamped down on abuses, making sure the right people are coming for the right reason.'

While the government may not have focused specifically on Roma, it is suggested that this broader agenda 'trickles down from the political elite to administrative bodies assessing welfare benefits claims', impacting on Roma as a 'particularly vulnerable' group (Dagilyte and Greenfields, 2015: 476). In their exploratory study with Roma migrants in the UK and workers in both governmental agencies and organisations providing advice and guidance, Dagilyte and Greenfields indicated that access to benefits was not a primary driver for migration, suggesting very low levels of awareness of the UK's welfare system. Furthermore, they comment that, despite the plethora of media reports associating migrant Roma with 'benefit tourism', research on the extent and nature of benefit claims by the community remains 'exceptionally limited' (2015: 1). Despite this, the dominant narrative of Roma and 'benefit tourism' appears to prevail.

As a counter to this narrative, the remaining sections of this chapter will focus on analysis of substantive primary research carried out with migrant Roma. The data was collected as part of a participatory research and community development project called Supporting Roma Voice, which was co-designed and led by trained community researchers from the Roma communities. The research element of the project consisted of 19 focus groups with Roma in six locations across England and Scotland: Glasgow, Leicester, Oldham, Salford, Sheffield and London. These locations were chosen because earlier work (Brown et al, 2013b) suggested sizeable populations of migrant Roma living in these respective areas. A total of 159 Roma participated in the focus groups, 74 male and 85 female, with a spread of ages from 18 to 60 years of age. Collectively the participants represented six nationalities: Slovakia, the Czech Republic, Romania, Lithuania, Poland and Hungary. All focus groups were co-facilitated by Roma and delivered in the preferred language of participants. In recognition of the fact that some homogeneity within groups can increase the comfort of participants (Knodel, 1993), separate men's and women's groups were preferred, with the exception of a small number of mixed gender groups which were carried out pragmatically due to participants' limited availability. All focus group discussions were audio recorded and subsequently transcribed verbatim and, where required, translated into English. To ensure that the research was ethically robust, it was formally reviewed by the Research Ethics Panel within the School of Nursing, Midwifery, Social Work and Social Sciences at the University of Salford, UK.

When conducting research with excluded populations, it can sometimes be the case that the most excluded individuals are not reached. Indeed, the very nature of their social exclusion and isolation can make people difficult to access. To overcome some of these issues and widen participation, recruitment was undertaken by Roma community advocates working in partnership with local voluntary sector organisations. However, the focus groups were routinely made up of individuals who were members of existing networks and could, therefore, be considered to be relatively privileged when compared to others within the wider diverse communities of migrant Roma resident in the UK. Nonetheless, the sample represents one of the largest in qualitative research carried out with migrant Roma in the UK to date. As a result, a significant archive of information was obtained across a range of issues relevant to the wider integration experiences of Roma.

Given that the focus groups were part of the wider Supporting Roma Voice project, they were guided by the issues of relevance to that project. More specifically, the focus groups were convened to explore experiences of integration, covering key themes including motivations for migration; initial arrival and settlement experiences; specific experiences of employment, benefits, housing, education and health care in the UK; and future aspirations. The data was analysed according to these key themes to produce a full research report, using

NVivo software to aid storage and retrieval of data. However, for our discussions here, we revisited the data to explore the discussions around motivations for migration, and employment and benefit experiences, in order to position these narratives within the wider literature and debates highlighted above focusing on 'benefit tourism' and migrant Roma populations.

The primacy of work

The 'benefit tourism' narrative places an emphasis on welfare systems as a pull factor. As such, exploring people's push/pull factors in migration is vital. Across our sample, it was evident that endemic discrimination and racism was a fundamental reason for leaving countries of origin and coming to the UK. Reiterating findings from earlier studies which observed employment opportunities as a driver for Roma migration (for example, Brown et al, 2013a; Cherkezova and Tomova, 2013), many participants referred to being persistently unemployed in their countries of origin, framed in terms of a constant battle to find work. Indeed, there was no sense that work had been actively avoided; conversely, many Roma spoke of trying to obtain work but being continuously denied access to the labour market, with the 'visibility' of their ethnicity being highlighted in many cases, as illustrated here:

> My husband works here [the UK], but in Slovakia he was unable to work because they were racist and nobody would have employed him. They could not stand Roma men. (Sheffield, women's focus group)

> Here, at least you know that you can work, even if it's a factory job; it is a job and you can get paid. Back home, you don't even have the opportunity to have a job; especially if they hear or see that you are a Roma, you will not get a job. (Oldham, women's focus group)

The denial of access to the labour market was linked by some participants to the high proportion of Roma receiving welfare benefits in some countries of origin. One participant, for example, after stating that she had left Slovakia because of racism, compared the chances of Roma and non-Roma at a job interview, suggesting that even if the former was better educated their prospects were slim. The consequence of this ostracism was that Roma were often forced to fall back on the limited state welfare available in order to survive: 'That's why people [in Slovakia], why Roma people take the benefits.... If we don't have a chance to go and show we can work. That's why' (Leicester, mixed focus group).

In some countries of origin, work and welfare were interdependent, with social welfare payments contingent on participation in specific labour programmes (Brown et al, 2015). However, the payments were usually insufficient even to put food on the table. As such, it was the realistic prospect of finally securing work that had primarily prompted people's migration to the UK and not the opportunity to swap one benefit system for another. Indeed, far from the widespread stereotype of indolence, the majority of research participants were currently working now that they were in the UK. In fact many commented that it had been relatively easy to secure work here: "I don't have any problems with finding a job here in the UK. It might not be my dream job, but it's much easier" (London, mixed focus group).

This was common experience; for example, in Glasgow, of the 12 men attending one group, 8 were working across a diversity of jobs, including potato and chicken factories and restaurants. In Salford, 9 of the 12 participants were in work, of whom 6 held full time positions.

There were also numerous examples where individuals had jobs arranged for them prior to arrival. For instance, one participant in Glasgow stated that the reason he came to the city was because his friends were already there and had arranged two jobs for him. Likewise, a respondent in Leicester explained the process of 'chain migration', whereby one family member at a time was able to join the first arrivals: 'So [the] first came [to] get a job, then help[ed] another one and then basically one after another. The whole family managed to come ... so that's how the community grows' (Leicester mixed focus group).

However, while participants were positive about their ability to access the labour market in the UK, there were concerns about the precarity of the work, but also the conditions under which some were employed. For example, many talked about harsh and exploitative conditions, where long hours and tough physical labour were the norm: "They don't give us a break, only to work, work, work, work, work" (Leicester, mixed focus group).

Several respondents in Glasgow talked about working for very low pay, often below the national minimum wage, and without any formal contract. Indeed, it was evident that some were receiving far less for working than they could expect from the benefit system. It was also evident that many participants had been working constantly since arrival, and, while acknowledging the negative aspects of the labour market, some participants felt that in the UK they were judged on their work ethic as opposed to their ethnicity. For example, one participant in Leicester explained that her husband had started off as a supervisor at a factory with a group of other Roma and collectively they had progressed to team leaders, supervisors and managers: 'So that's a result because Roma they want to work and they work hard and the people here they recognise it, so that's why they have a better position after a while.'

However, it is important to note that these discourses of hard work, but also exploitation, are not unique to research on Roma migrants, with such debates observed in multiple studies of migrant workers, including other CEE migrants (see for example, Scullion and Pemberton, 2010; Scott et al, 2012; Lewis et al, 2013). Nonetheless, these examples are important on two fronts. First, they challenge the notion that Roma are inherently unwilling to work. Second, they challenge the narrative that the UK benefit system is the primary reason for migration. Indeed, if that were the case we would have expected to see far less effort to find work and far fewer people in employment. Furthermore, given the length of time some participants had been employed, and the consequent contributions they would have made (if formally employed), many of the Roma we interviewed were entitled to welfare support. Even among those unemployed at the time of the research, most had worked at some point during their time in the UK.

Where do benefits feature?

As highlighted previously, the 'benefit tourism' narrative places an emphasis on welfare as a pull factor in migration. As such, for those accused of 'benefit tourism', one would expect some pre-arrival knowledge of the benefits system and entitlements therein. However, among our research participants, levels of awareness of the benefits system on arrival appeared to be relatively poor, suggesting that prior understanding of any potential financial advantage was not a significant incentive for migration. None of our participants referred to receiving information on welfare entitlements *before* migration, unlike intelligence on employment opportunities, which was routinely mentioned, as highlighted above. This is consonant with the reality for many migrants who 'contrary to the popular conception of "benefit tourists" coming to the UK to take advantage [...] had very limited knowledge of the support available' (Dwyer et al, 2016: 5). There was evidence in our research that this lack of awareness of entitlement could be detrimental to those who were in dire circumstances. For example, one research participant in London – a single woman with children – was currently homeless but had been 'turned down' for housing, and was unclear as to why this had happened or what to do to access support.

It was apparent that a number of those who had applied for benefits had to rely on the assistance of friends and family for information and for making their claims. As Paterson et al (2011) indicate, accessing in- or out-of-work benefits is extremely challenging for Roma and the conditions have since become much more restrictive for EU migrants more broadly, with suggestions that such restrictions may have disproportionately impacted on Roma (see Dagilyte and Greenfields, 2015). With the introduction of a three-month moratorium on claiming Jobseeker's Allowance (JSA) in 2014, the prohibition on Housing Benefit for new income-based JSA claims, plus a halving of the maximum claim period and a requirement to 'prove' a 'genuine prospect of work' (Kennedy, 2015), it was hardly surprising that many recent arrivals stated that they didn't receive any benefits. Only a small number of participants were claiming JSA at the time of the research, but they were only able to do so because they had passed the 'genuine prospect of work' test. Indeed, the onerous 'burden of proof' to demonstrate eligibility was evident: "In order to have or keep my benefits, I almost, I have to spend a lot of time for administration and sending different documents" (Oldham men's focus group).

Furthermore, those participants who indicated they were (or had been) claiming JSA all stated they had worked previously, often for considerable lengths of time, during which they would have contributed to the system via tax and national insurance. As such, they were demonstrating their 'entitlement' to make claims on the welfare system during a period of need. Indeed, this narrative of 'entitlement' features across a number of focus group discussions, and while our sample included a significant proportion of longer term residents who were making claims on the UK welfare system, it was evident that many of the benefits that were being accessed were actually supplements to low-paid employment (that is, in work benefits), with 'entitlement' a feature of the discussions when talking about such claims: "Yes. I applied for it [Working Tax Credit] because I worked, so I requested those benefits that I'm entitled to. Because if you don't work you cannot have them" (Oldham men's focus group).

As such, it was evident within our sample that understandings of the welfare system appeared to develop over a period of time of living and working in the UK and interactions with the benefit system occurred when people had gained an understanding of their eligibility, for example, through their length of time in the UK or their employment contributions. The main non-contributory welfare payment regularly mentioned across all focus groups was child benefit, supporting the findings of a recent study, which suggested that child benefit and tax credits were by far the most common benefits taken up by CEE migrants more broadly (Pemberton et al, 2014).

For those who had managed to navigate our complex welfare system, and subsequently access financial support, there was acknowledgement that such benefits were actually insufficient to rely upon as a sole source of income and that finding work was still essential: "That money doesn't cover everything so we still need a job" (Sheffield, men's focus group); "Waiting for [the] Job Centre every two weeks, there's nothing for you and £121.40 is nothing" (Glasgow, men's focus group).

Interestingly, however, some participants highlighted opportunities beyond income that could arise from the benefit system. For example, one of the few opportunities to access free English language courses was through the courses provided for individuals claiming JSA and in Glasgow, Leicester and Sheffield male respondents stated that they had improved their English language skills through this support. Significantly, such references were always made in the context of enhancing their job prospects, although it is also worth noting that attendance on such courses can be mandatory if poor English is regarded as an obstacle to work and sanctions applied for refusal (Dwyer et al, 2016).

For some of our participants, the benefit system featured due to experiences of ill health, whether their own or that of a family member. Indeed, there were many examples of people who had given up work to care for spouses or relatives. In these instances, individuals or their family members were often in receipt of disability benefits or carer's allowance. However, as above, there was a recognition that such allowances were sometimes insufficient and participants talked about the need to secure employment to supplement this support. A Roma woman in Oldham, for example, commented that after organising her husband's care: "Then I prepare lunch and try to look for a job because our income doesn't cover our needs and the expenses" (Oldham, women's focus group).

Finally, there was little evidence in our research of a desire to remain on benefits in the longer term. A number of participants indicated that, although they had been claiming out-of-work benefits they had now stopped; some had secured work while others had simply decided to cease their claims, the following excerpt is indicative of such occasions:

'I used to be on Employment Support Allowance, but I feel okay now here. I want to work now. I used to claim Disability Living Allowance, but I stopped everything and I want to go to work now, because I have a baby in my house.' (Glasgow, men's focus group)

This statement is important, implying as it does that work was fundamental to supporting the family, but also that work is desirable in of itself, with work often seen as the gateway to achieving a sense of belonging. However, it was evident that some participants were aware of the wider discourse around Roma and 'benefit tourism'. Indeed, some felt that such narratives sometimes impacted on how they were treated, particularly by staff at employment agencies:

'A few times they ask me if I'm Polish or a Roma from Poland. Why did they ask me that? They think that all of us came here and we're like on benefits so they make it as difficult for us as possible.' (London, mixed focus group)

On the whole, however, many felt that the difficulties Roma faced in navigating the UK welfare system were no worse than any other migrant population who had to contend with language barriers and limited knowledge of their rights.

Discussion and conclusions

Within academic research on Roma, the subject of 'benefit tourism' has often been subsumed within general discussions of hate speech, discriminatory discourse or anti-Gypsy prejudice. One problem with this approach is that it risks obscuring the particular contexts of employment and poverty within larger questions of ethnicity, human rights and citizenship. In addition, anti-Gypsy discourse has many overlapping faces which complement and reinforce each other, and change form according to the context. As such, a lack of examination with regard to the issue of 'benefit tourism' may impact on understandings in relation to other areas of discrimination. It also risks separating Roma from the wider 'migration debate', which includes many different types of migrants, from the EU and beyond, some of whom share similar motives for migration and experiences within host countries.

The experiences of exclusion from work in Central and Eastern Europe have played a role in shaping a range of pejorative stereotypes applied to Roma, including accusations of laziness, welfare dependency and inherent dishonesty (McGarry, 2013). But this exclusion is also fundamental to understanding why work is so important to Roma and our research suggests that the movement of Roma to the UK is primarily linked to a lack of work in countries of origin and the relative ease of finding employment in the UK. Informal family and community networks of information were vital in building awareness of employment opportunities, even prior to arrival.

However, as noted earlier, the primacy of work for Roma in the UK is not simply a British phenomenon and other studies across the EU have shown similar findings. For example, Cherkezova and Tomova (2013), with reference to Bulgarian Roma in Belgium, concluded that unemployment in their country of origin and the search for work was the primary motivation for migration. Similarly, Vlase and Preotesa (2012), who studied Roma in Italy and Spain, found 'job searching' was the main driver, within a context of improving overall quality of life. Indeed, many of these studies – ours included - highlight that while Roma could be described as 'working poor' in host countries, 'even irregular remunerations exceed many times the ones they would receive in their native country, if they could find any job there' (Cherkezova and Tomova, 2013: 155).

So, where do benefits feature? The 'benefit tourism' discourse would have us believe that access to the welfare system in the UK is the primary motivating factor in Roma migration. However, for many of our participants pre-arrival knowledge of the system appeared low, and, for some, knowledge of the benefits system remained relatively poor, as low levels of literacy and limited English language skills made access problematic. This is not to suggest that benefit take-up rates were low within our sample and, indeed, many participants were in receipt of various forms of financial support; rather, our study suggests that benefits feature in people's narratives once they are established in the UK, often within a discourse of 'entitlement' through contributions they have made while in employment. Furthermore, in many cases, the benefits that people were receiving were supplements to low wages rather than the sole source of financial income. In this sense, benefits were being accessed in much the same way as many British citizens in low-paid employment. For the few who were seeking to access out-of-work benefits such as JSA, it was apparent that – like other EU migrants – they now faced additional administrative barriers, such as the three-month initial exclusion, the habitual residence test and the genuine prospect of work test, all of which restricted access and placed a greater 'burden of proof' on migrants in terms of demonstrating eligibility (Dwyer et al, 2016).

We of course need to acknowledge the potential 'social desirability bias' within our research. Indeed, as highlighted above, it was apparent that some of our participants were aware of this discourse in relation to Roma, and it is possible that participants – like those in most research – may have been apprehensive about the interviewer's evaluation of them (Collins et al, 2005). However, such concerns were mitigated to a certain extent for two key reasons. First, as a project co-led by Roma community members, participants were being interviewed by members of their own community, rather than members of the 'host' population. Such participatory approaches have long been advocated as a means of addressing the power relations between the 'researcher' and the 'researched' and building trust in research (Maguire, 1987; Fals-Borda and Anishur Rahman, 1991), including research with Gypsy, Roma and Traveller populations (Greenfields and Home, 2006; Brown and Scullion, 2010). Second, as referred to previously, the focus groups explored a number of integration issues. As such, discussions around the benefit system formed part of a wider discussion around experiences of a range of services in the UK and were not the central focus of the research, which could have potentially elicited more apprehensive responses, given the dominance of the 'benefit tourism' narrative.

As highlighted earlier, the European Commission examination on social welfare in member states found little evidence to substantiate fears that 'benefit tourism' was a significant issue (Juravle et al, 2013). Nevertheless, across Europe, Roma remain consistently maligned as the worst offenders with regard to such activity. However, our findings provide a counter to this narrative, providing unique insights from Roma themselves which challenge such normative stereotypes. Indeed, the opportunity to work and the aspiration for a better future for the whole family were the driving force for migration, and this remains the central feature of people's lives in the UK. As such, there is a need to ensure that such counter-narratives feature within media and political debates around migration more broadly, but regarding Roma migration specifically, offering a balance to the 'hysterical' approach that appears to dominate reporting in relation to migrant and minority populations (Greenslade, 2005).

Note
[1] The ten were colloquially known as the A8 (Slovakia, Slovenia, the Czech Republic, Hungary, Estonia, Latvia, Lithuania, Poland and the A2 (Bulgaria and Romania).

References
Allen, W. and Blinder, S. (2013) *Migration in the news: Portrayals of immigrants, migrants, asylum seekers and refugees in national British newspapers, 2010 to 2012*, Migration Observatory report, COMPAS, University of Oxford.

BARB (Broadcasters Audience Research Board) (2016) 'Viewing data for weekly top 30 programmes 2014', www.barb.co.uk/viewing-data/weekly-top-30/

BBC (2013) 'Romanian PM: benefit tourism is "Roma problem"', BBC, 19 March, www.bbc.co.uk/news/world-europe-21842317

Benedik, S. (2010) 'Define the migrant, imagine the menace: remarks on narratives of recent Romani migrations to Graz', in H. Konrad and S. Benedik (eds) *Mapping contemporary history, II*, Vienna: Böhlau Verlag, pp 159–76.

Blinder, S. (2015) *UK public opinion toward immigration: Overall attitudes and level of concern*, Migration Observatory Briefing, COMPAS, University of Oxford.

Brown, P. and Scullion, L. (2010) '"Doing research" with Gypsy-Travellers in England: reflections on experience and practice', *Community Development Journal*, 45(2): 169–85.

Brown, P., Dwyer, P. and Scullion, L. (2013a) *The limits of inclusion? Exploring the views of Roma and non-Roma in six European Union Member States*, Salford: University of Salford: Salford.

Brown, P., Scullion, L. and Martin, P. (2013b) *Migrant Roma in the UK: Population size and experiences of local authorities and partners*, Salford: Sustainable Housing & Urban Studies Unit, University of Salford.

Brown, P., Dwyer, P., Martin, P., Scullion, L. and Turley, H. (2015) *Rights, responsibilities and redress? Research on policy and practices for Roma inclusion in ten Member States*, Salford: University of Salford.

Cahn, C. and Guild, E. (2010) *Recent migration of Roma in Europe* (2nd edn), Vienna: OSCE/Council of Europe.

Cameron, D. (2014) 'New measures to tighten up the immigration system', Press release from the Prime Minister's Office, www.gov.uk/government/news/new-measures-to-tighten-up-the-immigration-system

Channel 5 (2016) *Gypsies on benefits and proud*, tv series, www.channel5.com/show/gypsies-on-benefits-proud

Cherkezova, S. and Tomova, I. (2013) *An option of last resort? Migration of Roma and non-Roma from CEE Countries*, Bratislava: UNDP.

Clark, C. and Campbell, E. (2000) '"Gypsy invasion": a critical analysis of newspaper reaction to Czech and Slovak Romani asylum-seekers in Britain', *Romani Studies* 10(1).

Collins, M., Shattell, M. and Thomas, S.P. (2005) 'Problematic Interviewee behaviors in qualitative research', *Western Journal of Nursing Research,* 27(2): 188–99.

Curtice, J. (2016) *How deeply does Britain's Euroscepticism run?* London: NatCen Social Research.

Dagilyte, E. and Greenfields, M. (2015) 'United Kingdom welfare benefit reforms in 2013–2014: Roma between the pillory, the precipice and the slippery slope', *Journal of Social Welfare and Family Law*, 37(4): 476–95.

Daily Mail (2014) 'The Roma gipsy who sparked a crackdown on benefit tourism: Elisabeta Dano, 25, tracked down to German city after finding herself at centre of landmark welfare case', 15 November, www.dailymail.co.uk/news/article-2835442/The-Roma-gipsy-sparked-crackdown-benefit-tourism-Elisabeta-Dano-25-tracked-German-city-finding-centre-landmark-welfare-case.html#ixzz4KPuBcVrq

Dustmann, C. and Frattini, T. (2013) *The fiscal effects of immigration to the UK*, CReAM Discussion Paper 22-13, London: Centre for Research and Analysis of Migration.

Dwyer, P., Jones, K., Scullion, L. and Stewart B.R. (2016) *First wave findings: Migrants and conditionality*, First Wave Findings from Welfare Conditionality: Sanctions, Support and Behaviour Change, York: University of York.

ENAR/ERIO (European Network Against Racism and European Roma Information Office) (n.d.) *Debunking myths and revealing truths about the Roma*, Brussels: ENAR/ERIO.

EurActiv (2013) 'German economist denounces Roma "benefits tourism"', 6 May, www.euractiv.com/section/social-europe-jobs/news/german-economist-denounces-roma-benefits-tourism/

Fals-Borda, O. and Anishur Rahman, M. (1991) *Action and knowledge breaking the monopoly with participatory action research*, New York: Apex Press.

Finney, N. and Simpson, L. (2009) *Sleepwalking to segregation? Challenging myths about race and migration*, Bristol: Policy Press.

Fox, J., Morasanu, L. and Szilassy, E. (2012) 'The racialization of the new European migration to the UK', *Sociology* 46(4): 680–95.

FRA (EU Agency for Fundamental Rights) (2009) *EU-MIDIS – European Union Minorities and Discrimination Survey – Data in Focus Report 1: The Roma*, http://fra.europa.eu/en/publication/2009/eu-midis-data-focus-report-1-roma

Garner, S., Cowles, J., Lung B. and Stott, M. (2009) *Sources of resentment, and perceptions of ethnic minorities among poor white people in England*, report compiled for the National Community Forum, Department for Communities and Local Government.

Gerard, L. (2016) 'The press and immigration: reporting the news or fanning the flames of hatred?' *Sub-scribe*, 3 September, www.sub-scribe.co.uk/2016/09/the-press-and-immigration-reporting.html

Greenfields, M. and Home, R. (2006) 'Assessing Gypsies' and Travellers' needs: partnership working and "The Cambridgeshire Project"', *Romani Studies*, 16(2): 105–31.

Greenslade, R. (2005) *Seeking scapegoats: The coverage of asylum in the UK press*, Asylum and Migration Working Paper 5, London: Institute for Public Policy Research (IPPR).

Juravle, C., Weber, T., Canetta, E., Fries Tersch, E. and Kadunc, M. (2013) *A fact finding analysis on the impact on the Member States' social security systems of the entitlements of non-active intra-EU migrants to special non-contributory cash benefits and healthcare granted on the basis of residence*, DG Employment, Social Affairs and Inclusion via DG Justice Framework Contract, http://ec.europa.eu/social/main.jsp?langId=en&catId=89&newsId=1980&furtherNews=yes

Kennedy, S. (2015) *Measures to limit migrants' access to benefits*, House of Commons Library Briefing Paper 06889, 17 June, file:///C:/Users/Sophie/Downloads/SN06889.pdf

Knodel, J. (1993) 'The design and analysis of focus groups: a practical guide', in D.L. Morgan (ed.) *Successful focus groups, advancing the state of the art,* London: Sage.

Kroon, A., Kluknavská, A., Vliegenthart, R. and Boomgaarden, H. (2016) 'Victims or perpetrators? Explaining media framing of Roma across Europe', *European Journal of Communication* 31(4): 1–18.

Lewis, H., Dwyer, P., Hodkinson and Waite, L. (2013) *Precarious lives: Experiences of forced labour among refugees and asylum seekers in England,* Leeds: University of Leeds.

Luhman, M. (2015) 'Benefit tourism and migration policy in the UK: the construction of policy narratives', paper prepared for EUSA Conference 5–7 March, Boston, MA: Johns Hopkins University.

Maguire, P. (1987) *Doing participatory research: A feminist approach*, Amherst, MA: Center for International Education, University of Massachusetts.

McGarry, A. (2013) 'Romaphobia: the last acceptable form of racism', 13 November, www.opendemocracy.net/can-europe-make-it/aidan-mcgarry/romaphobia-last-acceptable-form-of-racism

Okely, J. (2014) 'Recycled misrepresentations: Gypsies, Travellers or Roma treated as objects, rarely subjects', *People, Place and Policy*, 8(1): 65–85.

Ormston, R. and Curtice, J. (eds) (2015) *British social attitudes: the 32nd report*, London: NatCen Social Research.

Parker, O. and López Catalán, O. (2014) 'Free movement for whom, where, when? Roma EU citizens in France and Spain', *International Political Sociology*, 8(4): 379–95.

Paterson, L., Simpson, L., Barrie, L. and Perinova, J. (2011) *Unequal and unlawful treatment: Barriers faced by the Roma community in Govanhill when accessing welfare benefits and the implications of section 149 of the Equality Act 2010*, Glasgow: Oxfam Law into Practice Project / Govanhill Law Centre Report.

Pemberton, S., Phillimore, J. and Robinson, D. (2014) *Causes and experiences of poverty among economic migrants in the UK*, IRIS Working Paper Series 4/2014, Birmingham: University of Birmingham.

Pompova, I. (2015) 'European migrants: burden or benefit for the British economy? The depiction of EU migrants in the UK and its consequences', Migrants & Society 814F8, University of Nottingham Student Conference, online at: www.nottingham.ac.uk/hrlc/documents/student-conference-2015/izabela-pompova-paper.pdf

Reilly, J. (2014) '"I know it's easy to take benefits in England": Gipsies who move to Britain reveal how they claim thousands of pounds every month as part of their bundle of benefits even though they do not work', *Daily Mail*, 3 April, www.dailymail.co.uk/news/article-2595815/I-know-s-easy-benefits-England-Gipsies-Britain-reveal-claim-thousands-pounds-month-bundle-benefits-not-workxxx.html

Richardson, J. (2010) 'Discourse dissonance: an examination of media, political and public discourse and its impact on policy implementation for Roma, Gypsies and Travellers at a local level', in Conference Proceedings, *Romani mobilities in Europe: Multidisciplinary perspectives*, 14–15 January, University of Oxford, pp 166–97.

Richardson, J. (2014) 'Roma in the news: an examination of media and political discourse and what needs to change', *People, Place and Policy*, 8(1): 51–64.

Richardson, J. and O'Neill, R. (2010) 'Stamp on the camps: the social construction of Gypsies and Travellers in media and political debate', in J. Richardson and A. Ryder (eds) *Gypsies and Travellers: Empowerment and inclusion in British society*, Bristol: Policy Press, pp 169–86.

Scott, S., Craig, G. and Geddes, A. (2012) *Experiences of forced labour in the UK food industry*, York: Joseph Rowntree Foundation.

Scullion, L. and Pemberton, S. (2010) *Exploring migrant workers motivations for migration and their perceived contributions to the UK: A case study of Liverpool*, Salford: University of Salford.

Tremlett, A. (2012) '"Here are the Gypsies!" The importance of self-representations and how to question prominent images of Gypsy minorities', *Ethnic and Racial Studies*, 36(11): 1–20.

Vlase, I. and Preotesa, A.M. (2012) 'Roma migrants from Bulgaria and Romania: migration patterns and integration in Italy and Spain', in D. Tarnovschi (ed.) *Roma from Romania, Bulgaria, Italy and Spain between social inclusion and migration: Comparative study*, Bucharest: Soros Foundation Romania, pp 65–87.

ELEVEN

Jumping the queue? How a focus on health tourism as benefit fraud misses much of the medical tourism story

Daniel Horsfall and Ricardo Pagan

Introduction

Medical tourism is a multi-billion pound industry that has seen substantial growth over the last 15 years (Horsfall and Lunt, 2015a). As a process it has been the focus of wide-ranging, business, political, academic and, intermittently, media interest. Early media references to medical tourism were often either to highlight the novelty of travel as an option for those seeking care (BBC, 2004; *The Independent*, 2008; Francis, 2011), decry the state of a National Health Service (NHS) so stretched that people felt the need to travel (Gregory, 2013; Buckland, 2015; Burman, 2015), inform readers of the risks associated with travelling for health through tales of 'medical tourism gone wrong' (Lakhani, 2010; Topham, 2013; BBC, 2014; Pietras, 2014), or highlight how these risks ultimately fell on the NHS when corrective procedures were needed (Smith, 2008; Triggle, 2008). More recently, media coverage of medical tourism has adopted the narrative of benefit fraud or exploitation, with tourists either purposely or unwittingly accessing care they are not entitled to or not paying for that which they are required to pay (Doughty, 2011; Adams, 2012; DoH, 2013; Kovacevic, 2016; McDermott and Wooller, 2016). This issue has proven particularly incendiary, prompting formal responses from the government, including the establishment of an NHS visitor and migrant cost recovery programme (DoH, 2014), an NHS levy on non-European Economic Area (EEA) migrants who enter the UK (NAO, 2016; *The Telegraph*, 2016) and a requirement for those seeking treatment to produce their passports (Syal and Campbell, 2016). In the lead-up to and aftermath of the UK's European Union (EU) referendum the issue played a central role in wider discussions around migration and the free movement of individuals across Europe (see Kovacevic, 2016).

For those with an interest in medical tourism, especially from a social or public policy perspective, this medical tourism as a form of benefit fraud discourse is both strange and frustrating. Medical tourism researchers are likely to find this perspective strange as it is one that is almost completely lacking from the literature on medical tourism. This is of course not to say that it is not happening, rather that it has garnered no real attention. This lack of coverage may reflect academic interest, but as we will see later, given the size of the medical tourism 'market' and the complexities involved, it is unlikely to account for a noticeable portion of the estimated medical tourism activity. Cohen (2012a, 2012b, 2015) and others (Krishnan et al, 2010; Rhodes and Schiano, 2010; Yakupoglu et al, 2010; Gilmartin and White, 2011; Van Hoof and Pennings, 2011; He, 2015) have discussed medical tourism from the perspective of those attempting to circumvent legal or regulatory frameworks, though this has often been limited to transplant, fertility or abortion services.

The conflation of medical or health tourism with health fraud is likely to also be rather frustrating as, being at best a niche issue, it has the potential to distract from other pressing matters related to the process of travelling for care. A wide body of literature can be identified exploring issues of ethics related to medical tourism, as well as the risks involved, to individuals, source countries and destination or treatment countries (for a useful introduction see Lunt et al, 2015a). In particular, one concern relates to the impact that accommodating, and indeed tailoring a health service towards, rich 'Western' medical tourists, might have in undermining already precarious health systems in developing or less economically developed countries (MacReady, 2007; Chen and Flood, 2013; Cohen, 2012a). The (poor and often misleading) quality of information and lack of avenues through which to seek legal redress in what is an alarmingly under-regulated industry available to medical tourists is another area that has fostered close scrutiny and is particularly worrying. Likewise, how patient records are used (or not) and whether principles of confidentiality and informed consent are meticulously upheld is a cause for concern (Crooks and Snyder 2010; Lunt et al, 2011, 2014a; Horsfall and Lunt, 2015b). At the most extreme is the body of work that has attempted to illuminate the exploitative practices that take place as part of the medical tourism process, with the most notable being those who have questioned how legitimately organs have been harvested for so-called 'transplant tourists' (Krishnan et al, 2010). It is not the place to explore these issues here (see Lunt et al, 2015a), however it is worth highlighting that a considerable body of work focused on medical tourism exists and has burgeoned rapidly over the past ten to fifteen years, primarily concerned with the many and often substantial risks involved. During this time very little mention of medical tourism as benefit fraud has been seen.

But this is getting ahead of ourselves. At this juncture it is worth exploring what exactly is understood by the term 'medical tourism' within current research. For Lunt et al, medical tourism can be defined as the process by which patients travel to another country to pay 'out-of-pocket' for medical treatment (Lunt et al, 2011). As such it can be thought of as a type of patient or 'consumer' mobility in which individuals travel outside their country of residence for the consumption of health care services. Medical tourism takes place when individuals opt to travel overseas with the primary intention of receiving medical (usually elective surgery) treatment. These journeys may be long distance and intercontinental, for example from Europe and North America to Asia, and cover a range of treatments including dental care, cosmetic surgery, bariatric surgery and fertility treatment.

While that all seems straightforward, it isn't, and the very term 'medical (or health) tourism' is a controversial one. There are many objections to the very fusion of 'medical' or 'health' with 'tourism', with a number of scholars arguing that the notion of often major procedures being somehow conceptualised as tourism, with connotations of enjoyment, is at best crass (Connell, 2015). The much more neutral term 'health (or medical) travellers' is thus preferred by some. However, the most vehement rejections of the terms 'health' or 'medical tourism' come from those who have researched the great hardships faced by those who have had to travel for life-saving treatment. Here we see labels such as 'healthcare migrants' (Horton and Cole, 2011; Inhorn, 2011), 'medical refugees' (Inhorn, 2011; Cohen, 2012b), 'medical exiles' (Inhorn and Patrizio, 2009; Kangas, 2010), or even 'biotech pilgrims' (Song, 2010) being suggested. Others have dedicated substantial effort to arguing the finer detail of what should be considered 'health', 'wellness' or 'medical' (see Connell, 2015; Lunt et al, 2015b), while considerable debate has been had around whether we should be concerned only with those who pay out-of-pocket, those whose primary purpose of travel is for health reasons, and even what kinds of treatment should be considered genuinely health or medical rather than simply restorative. As a context to the 'health tourism' debate from a social policy perspective, it is important to note that these debates exist and indeed two bodies of work exploring what appears to be the same concept might have different conceptualisations of the processes, starting with the very definitions they adopt.

In this chapter we would like to keep matters simple; we will consider any form of travel across national borders with an expressed intention of accessing medical care during the visit as being a form of medical tourism. How long a person stays, whether they are expected to pay (either out-of- pocket or by other means), whether the medical treatment was the primary purpose of travel, and what form of care they access will not be used to determine whether a person is considered a medical tourist. In this sense, 'medical tourism' is being used as an umbrella term to cover all forms of medical travel. Other terms, such as 'health tourism' or 'medical/health travel' may be used, but these will be kept to a minimum and should all be considered as sitting underneath this umbrella of 'medical tourism'.

Given the focus of both this themed section of the *Social Policy Review* and the aforementioned media attention, it is worth reflecting on the fact that, for most involved in both the academic pursuit of medical tourism research, as well as those within the medical tourism industry, the process is often seen as involving the movement of patients from more developed countries in the 'global north' travelling for medical care to less developed countries in the 'global south' (Connell, 2015). The medical 'fraudsters' who generate so much press attention represent a largely unmeasurable, yet almost certainly tiny proportion of only one direction of travel – a direction that is actually actively encouraged by the UK government (and many others) and has been demonstrated to be of financial benefit to both the NHS and the wider UK economy (Hanefeld et al, 2013). We say this because while the umbrella term 'medical tourist' would clearly also include such perpetrators of fraud or exploitation, they would represent only a tiny proportion of those covered by the term.

Measuring medical tourism

Given the difficulties associated with defining medical tourism, it is hardly surprising that measuring it is also problematic. Added to issues of definition is the fact that most of the records related to medical tourism flows are held in the hands of private organisations, many of which have a vested interest in depicting a robust industry, which has led to many suggesting that most numbers in the public domain have been subjected to industry 'boosterism' (Connell, 2013, 2015). That said, the past 15 years have seen the popularity of this form of consumer expenditure increase substantially, at a time, it is worth noting, that many health systems are under immense financial pressure. While there is little agreement on the size of the medical tourism market, a conservative estimate suggests that globally at least 5 million people travel to another country and pay out-of-pocket for medical treatment each year (Horsfall and Lunt, 2015a). This number is derived through a series of assumptions, none of which are infallible and have a number of caveats. Chief among these is that any number really depends on the definitions being used and the often commercial interests of those generating the data. As such, providing accurate and reliable figures with regard to the flows of medical tourists and the size of the industry is in reality impossible.

At the heart of the estimate produced by Horsfall and Lunt (2015a) is data taken from the International Passenger Survey (IPS), collected and published by the Office for National Statistics (ONS). According to the IPS, across the period 2000 to 2010, the number of UK residents travelling outside the UK for medical treatment increased from 8,500 in 2000 to 63,000 in 2010 (an increase of roughly 750%) while the number of people not resident in the UK travelling for treatment in the UK rose from near 35,000 to 53,000 in the same period (Lunt et al, 2011; ONS, 2016). Two caveats must be outlined here. First, the IPS only samples 0.2% of all travellers and then uses a weighting variable to produce total numbers. This weighting procedure may skew total medical traveller numbers; second, medical travellers are only recorded as such if they state that their primary purpose of travel is medical. The second issue is particularly problematic as it undoubtedly underestimates the number of people who access medical care while visiting or leaving the UK for other reasons – an important issue we will return to later. The most recent IPS data depicts a slowdown in the growth of non-UK residents recorded as travelling to the UK for primarily medical reasons over the past couple of years, and in fact since 2012 the numbers have been in decline, falling from 63,000 to 54,000 in 2014. Similarly, the number of outbound travellers, having seen modest increases until 2012, declined relatively sharply to the extent that, by 2014, the figure of just over 48,000 was in fact lower than it had been in 2010. It had been assumed that the EU directive on cross-border health care might pave the way for increased medical tourism activity. The directive grants patients – under certain conditions (European Parliament and the Council of Europe, 2011; Lunt et al, 2014a: 143) – the right to access health care across borders. While it certainly helps to normalise the process, uptake has been slow, with just over 1,000 UK residents being reimbursed for treatment outside the UK in 2015 under the scheme (European Commission, 2016).

Numbers taken from the IPS are incredibly important given the problems identified with nearly all other reported measures; notwithstanding the possible issue related to how the samples are weighted, however, even if we are incredibly confident that the IPS has accurately recorded 54,000 inbound and 48,000 outbound medical travellers in 2014, this does not offer as much clarity as one might hope. Two particular challenges are evident: the first is that, even with a reasonable understanding of flows, we know very little about the processes – what treatment types are being accessed, how treatment and travel is organised, whether travellers are insured, and the risks associated with travel and treatment; and, second, the IPS undoubtedly underestimates these flows, with the error likely to be much larger for particular 'types' of medical tourist.

The first issue is not one that can be explored in much detail here but has been addressed at length elsewhere (see Lunt et al, 2014a). We know the experiences of those travelling from the UK for bariatric care is likely to differ greatly from those travelling from the UK for cosmetic, fertility, dental or orthopaedic procedures (Lunt et al, 2014a). The motivations, demographics and overall processes involved in different types of treatment in different locations vary widely.

The second issue is particularly problematic, relevant for this debate and, unfortunately, not one that can realistically be solved. The IPS, as with any similar attempt to survey medical tourism in such a way will significantly underestimate all those groups that do not consider that, or are unwilling to state that, their primary purpose of travel is to seek medical treatment. Not only is one's health often a rather private issue that a person might not freely disclose, the primary purpose of travel – even if medical treatment is planned for the visit – might not actually be 'medical', with treatment a secondary motivation to travel, or simply something that you organise while you are there. Noree et al (2014), for example, found that the majority of UK residents who had medical treatment in Thailand underwent low-cost elective treatments that were unlikely to have been the primary purpose of travel – for them tourism was their purpose in visiting Thailand. Using patient records from a number of hospitals in 2010, Noree et al (2014) identified 4,000 individual UK residents who had accessed non-emergency treatment in Thailand, while the IPS recorded only 700 UK medical tourists to Thailand.

With regard to the overarching theme of this issue of the *Social Policy Review*, it is clear that those engaged in medical tourism as a form of benefit fraud are not going to appear in records such as the IPS. Indeed, how such people would be recorded is unclear, with no eligibility restrictions placed on the receipt of primary care. Indeed, it is only secondary, often elective, treatments that are possible objects of fraud. Evidence of the extent to which this occurs is mixed (contrast official estimates from the National Audit Office in 2016 with those presented by Migration Watch UK), with a widely and rather vehemently reported (Adams, 2012; Borland, 2012; Miller, 2012) *exposé* by the TV programme *Panorama* estimating a monetary cost of around £40 million per year (BBC, 2012) to the NHS as a consequence of medical tourism fraud. Even if one is to accept such a figure, it is worth noting that it is easily outweighed by the financial benefits 'regular' medical tourism is thought to bring the NHS and the UK economy more widely (Hanefeld et al, 2013). What the *Panorama* investigation demonstrated was the complex nature of the kind of enterprise required to obtain fraudulent NHS numbers and, subsequently, access to secondary care that would otherwise have been charged by the NHS; this involved substantial, organised criminal activity rather than the simple act of travelling to access care. Of course, an additional issue relates to the recovery of costs where an ineligible patient receives care, something the government has invested in heavily since 2012 (DoH, 2014). Matters are undoubtedly complicated by rather ambiguous guidance on who is required to pay, for what, when, and who is responsible for ensuring those who are required to, do pay (Hargreaves et al, 2008). Given that many health care professionals are expected to treat the 'patient in front of them', it may very well be that it is not until after the event that eligibility is even considered. If a health care provider reports that it has provided treatment to someone who is not eligible, it will not be reimbursed. Instead, the provider is expected to retrieve those costs itself, something that is difficult and probably does not incentivise reporting and undoubtedly discourages robust post hoc checks on eligibility.

Such forms of medical tourism fraud undoubtedly exist and enumerating them is impossible. However, given the fact that the undocumented migrant population, many of whom are younger and healthier than the wider population (Audit Commission, 2007; Steventon and Bardsley, 2011; Hawkins and Moses, 2016), was estimated at 533,000 (with an upper-bound of 719,000) in a 2009 study (Gordon et al, 2009), alongside the costs and criminal complexity involved in such an enterprise, it is difficult to imagine this being a substantial issue.

Even if much higher estimates produced by the right-wing think-tank Migration Watch UK (2016) of 1.1 million are accepted, it is most definitely a stretch to believe that it represents a bigger drain on the NHS than the benefit 'regular' medical tourism is believed to bring to the NHS.

In addition to genuine tourism-first medical tourists, such as those highlighted by Noree et al (2014), three other forms of medical tourist are likely to be under- or unreported in mechanisms such as the IPS. One group of medical tourists who are unlikely to be documented through any tool that requires self-disclosure is the aforementioned travellers who travel for treatment that is perhaps illegal in some countries. We do not explore this group here, but work by Cohen (2012a, 2012b, 2015) provides a useful overview. The other two groups of medical tourists that are likely to be under- or even unreported in most medical tourism records are those belonging to diasporas or those with strong cultural or familial ties to a location where they access care, and expatriates. Below we provide an introductory exploration of both types of medical tourists through the examples of Polish residents in the UK who travel to Poland for treatment and UK 'expats' resident in Spain.

Diaspora

The issue of diasporic medical travellers is particularly important; as Connell (2015) notes, much medical tourism is across nearby borders, from diaspora populations, and of limited medical gravity, conflicting with popular assumptions. A substantial component of medical travel consists of migrants travelling to their home countries. Most such returnees probably travel for a multiplicity of reasons, including visiting relatives, and may not be travelling to 'distant' places. Some of the largest flows of cross-border travellers are diasporic, to 'backyard' rather than 'tourist' destinations (Ormond, 2008). One group of medical tourists who are most definitely under-represented owing to the fact that medical treatment is not their primary purpose of travel, is those with cultural or familial ties to a country (Inhorn, 2011; Connell, 2013; Hanefeld et al, 2015). It might even be that diasporas represent the largest proportion of those who travel for treatment, often not travelling far but rather crossing borders. Connell (2013), for example, cites the case of India, often described as one of the biggest medical tourism destinations, where 22% of medical tourists are actually non-resident Indians. This is in addition to large numbers of second-generation overseas Indians. In fact, only 10% were of US or European ancestry (Connell 2013: 4).

Similarly, those in the US with ties to Mexico (Horton and Cole, 2011) and Korea (Lunt et al, 2014b), for example, might travel in large numbers 'back home' to undergo medical treatment. While they might not think of this as their primary reason for travel, it is integral to the journey.

Data from the IPS is particularly interesting with regard to this issue. We see that since 2000 Central and Eastern Europe, in particularly Poland, has seen increased activity. As a source of non-UK residents travelling to the UK primarily to access medical care, Poland was the point of departure for no recorded medical travellers until 2005, since when a steady annual increase saw over 2,000 in both 2012 and 2013 before a decline to just under 1,000 in 2014 (most recent data). Romania and Hungary both demonstrated similar patterns, though with more modest numbers involved, over the 15 years covered by the IPS. What is perhaps more noteworthy is the trend of outward travel from the UK to the region and once again, specifically, Poland. Here we witness a substantial increase in UK residents travelling to Poland primarily for medical treatment, with no recorded departures until 2004 and then an apparent explosion in numbers that has surpassed 10,000 a year from 2009 onwards, standing at just short of 14,000 in 2014. Within the industry this was taken as confirmation that Poland (and other destinations in Central and Eastern Europe) were being successful in their pursuit of what were incredibly 'active' medical tourism strategies. Others even linked this to pressures facing the NHS and the wider financial crisis in Western Europe. The dominant assumption has been that these increases represent the typical medical tourist; a customer in search of value. Given that both Polish (such as the Polish Association of Medical Tourism) and UK sources (such as the industry publication the *Internet Medical Tourism Journal*) report that cosmetic and dental treatment are Poland's services most commonly accessed by medical tourists, and that the UK is a key source of such tourists, IPS data at first glance would seem to support this.

It is important, however, to look beyond the headline figures, something that is not possible through the publicly released IPS data, which might go some way to explaining the assumptions made about this trend of increasing travel to Poland. The ONS makes the full IPS dataset available on request and accessing this provides a rather different picture of this medical tourism activity. Rather than a reflection of commercial success, it would appear medical tourism to Poland is more likely explained by wider processes of migration. As shown in Figure 11.1, when broken down by nationality of passport, just short of 12,000 of the 14,000 UK residents who travelled to Poland in 2014 were indeed

Polish nationals. Similarly, the majority of UK residents travelling to Hungary were not UK nationals and none of the 2,000 UK residents travelling to Lithuania were UK nationals.

Figure 11.1: Outbound medical tourism from the UK to selected Central and Eastern European countries 2000–14

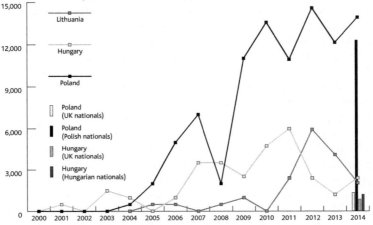

Source: Author's own calculations from: ONS, 2016.

It is unlikely to come as a great surprise that this upsurge in Polish nationals travelling to Poland from the UK for medical treatment is not dissimilar to the trend in migration from Poland over the same time period (see Figure 11.2). While establishing that most medical travellers from the UK are in fact Polish answers some questions, it poses many for both the medical tourism industry and those interested in migration studies and health policy. The obvious question is why are so many Polish nationals travelling back to Poland for care? It is certainly not because they are ineligible for care within the NHS and it is unlikely that it is a consequence of a language barrier – though this is sometimes cited (*The Economist*, 2013; Williams, 2013). Instead, it is thought that dissatisfaction with the NHS plays a significant role, with the experience of a completely different health system in Poland shaping expectations in the UK. In particular, the perceived unwillingness of GPs to refer patients for secondary care, the ubiquitous paracetamol prescription, and the delay between requesting an appointment and being seen appear to motivate Polish nationals to access care outside the NHS (*The Economist*, 2013). Others have even suggested that Polish nationals perceive NHS care to be inferior to that received within the Polish health care system, with the longer qualification period for nurses in Poland being cited as an example of higher standards (Williams, 2013). It must also be acknowledged that, while the notion of paying for health care is largely alien to UK nationals, for many migrants, especially those from Poland, this is not the case and paying for prompt, patient-led (consumer-led?) care is the norm.

Figure 11.2: Polish migrants living in the UK, '000s, 2004–14

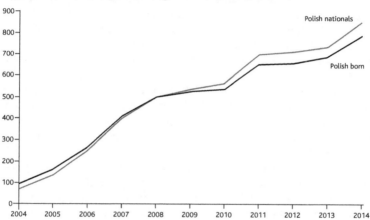

Source: Hawkins and Moses (2016).

The willingness among Polish nationals resident in the UK to travel for treatment outside the NHS, despite being eligible for care merits further study. There is evidence that black minority and ethnic (BME), and migrant communities often encounter difficulties when accessing health care in the UK (DoH, 2008), and studies that have explored the use of health care services among other migrant communities seem to echo, in part, this willingness among Polish nationals to eschew NHS care. In one study (Lunt et al, 2014), members of Somali communities in Manchester and Camden, and a Gujarati community in Leicester, discussed their motivations for travelling outside the UK rather than accessing care from within the NHS.

Most were not travelling for complex or even secondary care; rather, diagnostics was the predominant service sought. The primary motivation to travel was dissatisfaction with the NHS services, usually related to the length of time it took to access services, the process of needing referral from a GP and a perception that, if possible, a GP would simply send you away with a paracetamol (Lunt et al, 2014a).

Expats

If Polish nationals resident in the UK (as well as other migrant groups) represent a group of medical tourists who, for whatever reason, are eschewing their eligibility for NHS care in favour of returning home, UK 'expats' are, quite literally, travelling in the other direction. Despite our contention that many expats who access treatment in the UK are likely to be doing so when visiting 'home' for other primary reasons, of the 54,000 non-UK residents who travelled to the UK primarily for medical reasons in 2014, 21,670 were actually UK nationals (ONS, 2016). The total number of expats who access treatment in the UK, either privately or through the NHS, and whether they are eligible or not, is simply unknown. The eligibility of expats to access treatment (free at the point of use) is actually rather complex, unclear and in a situation of flux, one which is unlikely to be stabilised in the wake of the UK's EU referendum.

Here we focus on Spain for two main reasons: first, the IPS shows that the greatest numbers of patients travelling into the UK for treatment were from Ireland and Spain, and these two countries also show a growing trend of patients coming to the UK; and, second, Spain has become the main European destination for people born in the UK who live in other EU countries. According to the United Nations (2015), the estimated number of British people living abroad in the EU was 1.35 million in 2015, with the key countries of residence being Spain (308,821), Ireland (254,761), France (185,344) and Germany (103,352). Traditionally, one of the most popular regions preferred by the UK expats in Spain has been the Andalusia region, especially the province of Malaga. Although it is quite difficult to estimate the exact number of British people living in Spain in general, and in Andalusia and Malaga in particular (because many of them are not registered as residents), we can use data drawn from the Municipal Register (Spanish National Statistical Institute), which is an administrative register where inhabitants are recorded and updated annually, to quantify the total number of UK expats living in Spain, Andalusia and Malaga during the period 2003–16, respectively.

According to Figure 11.3, first we find that the number of UK expats in Spain has increased from 161,507 to 397,892 people during the period 2003–12 (that is, a mean annual growth rate equals 10.5%). A similar pattern is found for the Andalusia region and Malaga, wherein the mean annual growth rates were 11.5% and 9.4% between 2003 and 2012, respectively.

During this period of growth (2003–12), we have to bear in mind that those UK expats who wanted to use the Spanish public health care system were required to get the social security card, which can be only obtained if they were registered on the Municipal Register (called 'Empadronamiento'). After this, they received a medical card at their local health care centre, which granted them the right to access all services of the nationwide public health network. As such, being included on the Municipal Register was the only requirement to receive medical treatment from the Spanish public health care system. However, this situation changed in 2012 with the public health care reform and the Royal Decree Law (RDL) of April 2012 'Urgent measures to guarantee the sustainability of the National Health System and improve the quality and safety of services' (BOE, 2012). One of the goals of this RDL was to prevent the abuse by foreign visitors of free medical care in Spain (Gallo and Gené-Badia, 2013). In this sense, new access restrictions to the public health care system were included. For example, foreigners who are neither registered nor authorised as residents in the country, lose the right to health care, and it may be granted only in emergency situations (due to serious diseases or accidents, regardless of their causes and during pregnancy, labour and postpartum situations). Only people under 18 years old were granted health care under the same conditions as the Spanish people.

According to the British Parliament, in 2014/15 the UK paid out around £674.4 million to other EU member states to pay for health care treatment for UK pensioners, and received just £49.7 million each year for Europeans living in the UK (Parliament UK, 2016). A recent freedom of information request by the BBC revealed that the number of UK expats registered with health services outside the UK but within the EEA stood at 145,000 in 2016, while only 4,000 expats from EEA countries were registered with the NHS (Greenwood, 2017). According to the Department of Health, this reflects the fact that the UK 'is not the retirement place of choice' (Wormald to the Public Accounts Committee, cited in Greenwood, 2017).

Figure 11.3: UK expat community in Spain, Andalusia and Malaga (2003–16)

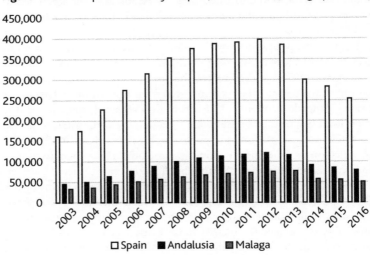

Source: Spanish Government, 2013.

Note: Data for 2016 are provisional.

The Spanish health care system received £223.3 million from the UK for providing health care treatment to British expats (that is, 33.1% of the total amount paid by the UK for British expats). According to the Regional Ministry of Equality, Health and Social Policies in Andalusia report on public expenditure and activity in 2013 (Spanish Government, 2013), 48.3% of the total international patients receiving health treatments from public hospitals in Andalusia in 2013 came from the UK, followed by Germany (11.9%) and France (8.9%). As a result, the total income received in Andalusia alone from the British government for these medical services was around £11.5 million in 2013.

Figure 11.3 also shows that from 2012 onward there has been a significant fall in the number of UK expats living in Spain (from 397,392 in 2012 to 253,928 in 2016). Although this fall in UK expats registered on the Municipal Register may be partly explained due to problems with some unregistered UK expats who are really residents, or the death of older residents, the 2008 financial crisis in Spain is, without doubt, the main reason for this desertion of Spain by EU expats in general and UK expats in particular.

Once again, however, the numbers tell only part of the story. For a start, as alluded to earlier, of the just over 4,000 residents of Spain who travelled to the UK primarily for medical reasons, every single one was a British national. As noted, many of these would have been covered to receive health care in Spain as part of the UK's reciprocal arrangement, yet they chose to return to the UK. Again, we don't know why. We also don't know the status of these individuals; for example, for how long they had been resident in Spain, their age or if they were in receipt of the S1 pension form that grants them the right to access secondary care in the UK. One assumption that has often been made is that, by virtue of having made National Insurance (NI) payments, expats have a life-long right to access NHS services (DoH, 2013), which is not quite right. With NHS eligibility being linked to residence and not other criteria such as place of birth or NI contributions, expats are not automatically entitled to NHS secondary care free of charge. This was further complicated recently when access to the important S1 form was restricted for early retirees (Pallot, 2014; DoH, 2016). We simply do not know what proportion of the 4,000 UK nationals travelling from Spain, or near 22,000 UK nationals travelling to the UK from outside for medical treatment are accessing those services from within the NHS. Nor do we know what proportion are eligible to receive those services free of charge, or what proportion of those who should be paying are doing this or are not.

This is, of course, incredibly important in the wake of the EU referendum; over a quarter of a million UK nationals currently reside in Spain, and while many may choose to return to the UK, others might not. Unless a new reciprocal arrangement is in place at the moment the current EU deal expires, a substantial number of those who have remained in Spain may become liable for the costs of their medical care. It is difficult to imagine a situation in which the number of people returning, either permanently or otherwise, to access medical care doesn't increase.

Concluding thoughts

'Medical tourism' can be thought of as an umbrella term for a number of different processes that see people travelling across national borders and subsequently accessing health care. Recent media and political attention has focused on one particular dimension of this medical tourism, where people travel to the UK with the express motivation of seeking medical care within the NHS. The assertion is that this is a form of fraud or manipulation, one which is placing increasing pressure on the NHS. Of course, this does happen; the Department of Health estimated in 2013 that the cost to the NHS of care for migrants was around £2 billion and, while that is a substantial sum and almost none of it was recovered through fees, four things must be considered. The first is that this £2 billion represents a rather small portion of the overall NHS budget of £113 billion; second, much of the use of NHS services by migrants involves patients who are from countries with which the UK has a reciprocal health care agreement; third, the use of and failure to pay for services by those who are not entitled is estimated to cost the NHS between £60 million and £80 million per year; and, finally, medical tourism, in its broader sense, is believed to directly generate, at the lowest estimate, over £40 million for the 18 hospitals with the highest volume of international patients, and over £200 million for the wider UK economy in associated tourism revenue (Hanefeld et al, 2013).

For certain political organisations and media outlets, even the use of NHS services by migrants from countries with which the UK has a reciprocal agreement is portrayed as some sort of abuse. It is unlikely that drawing a distinction between what they have pejoratively labelled 'health tourism' and wider medical tourism, or highlighting the net benefit of such medical tourism would assuage those making these claims. However, it is important to set this – at worst fraudulent and at best improper – use of the NHS by people who have travelled from outside the UK into some context; not only does this represent a small slice of the medical tourism cake, it misses much. It is clear just by looking at data from the IPS that travel for health care is not unidirectional. Indeed, here and elsewhere it has been demonstrated that migrants from Poland (and other countries) now resident in the UK are travelling to home or other countries in substantial numbers in order to access treatment. Much of this is for routine primary care, to which there is an unambiguous right to access in the UK.

Perhaps more timely is the discussion of expats and how they use the NHS. It is clear that the UK's eventual extrication from the EU and, with it, all existing reciprocal health care arrangements, will present challenges for UK nationals accessing health care abroad. It is difficult to imagine a scenario wherein the NHS doesn't face additional demand from these expats, either through their permanent return or fleeting visits to access NHS care. It is unlikely to be a particularly popular observation for many, but given the principles of access based on residence that underpin the NHS, expats are undoubtedly already the source of much of the illegitimate NHS use and this is likely to increase. As the Department of Health acknowledges: 'It is often difficult to identify those living overseas because they have retained a UK address, GP and NHS number. They may also be unaware that they are chargeable and resentful of the fact if brought to their attention' (DoH, 2013).

Of course the expat who has paid their 'stamp' does not really fit into the narrative of health tourists exerting pressure on an already struggling NHS, but in the wake of the EU referendum the issue is likely to become rather pressing. At a time when NHS finances are incredibly stretched, it is important not only to recognise this and its potential for increased medical tourism, but also to have a much broader understanding of medical tourism, for both its risks and opportunities.

References

Adams, A. (2012) 'Health tourism: GP surgeries selling "black market" access to NHS', *The Telegraph*, 3 October, www.telegraph.co.uk/news/health/news/9582272/Health-tourism-GP-surgeries-selling-black-market-access-to-NHS.html

Audit Commission (2007) *Crossing borders: Responding to the local challenges of migrant workers*, London: Audit Commission.

BBC (2004) 'Facelift holidays', *Inside Out*, 9 February, www.bbc.co.uk/insideout/eastmidlands/series5/cosmetic-surgery.shtml

BBC (2012) 'Britain's secret health tourists', *Panorama*, BBC 1, 3 October, www.bbc.co.uk/programmes/b01nbryp

BBC (2014) 'Cosmetic surgery warning follows Joy Williams' death', BBC, 27 October, www.bbc.co.uk/news/uk-england-london-29791057

BOE (2012) *Boletín Oficial del Estado*, 98 (March–April), www.boe.es/boe/dias/2012/04/24/pdfs/BOE-A-2012-5403.pdf

Borland, S. (2012) 'Health tourists paying £1,000 bribes to get onto GP surgery lists before having thousands of pounds worth of NHS treatment for free', *Daily Mail*, 3 October, www.dailymail.co.uk/health/article-2211994/Health-tourists-paying-1-000-bribes-GP-surgery-lists-having-thousands-pounds-worth-NHS-treatment-free.html

Buckland, D. (2015) 'Exclusive: 200,000 desperate Britons go ABROAD for medical care as NHS waiting lists spiral', *Sunday Express*, 14 April, www.express.co.uk/news/uk/570305/Britons-NHS-waiting-lists-medical-treatment

Burman, J. (2015) 'Failing NHS forced to send British patients ABROAD to Calais hospital in "barking" move', *Daily Express*, 8 Sept., www.express.co.uk/news/uk/603694/NHS-France-South-Kent-Coast-Clinical-Commissioning-Group-Centre-Hospitalier-de-Calais

Chen, Y.Y. and Flood, C.M. (2013) 'Medical tourism's impact on health care equity and access in low- and middle-income countries: making the case for regulation', *Journal of Law, Medicine & Ethics,* 41(1): 286–300.

Cohen, I.G. (2012a) 'How to regulate medical tourism (and why it matters for bioethics)', *Developing World Bioethics,* 12(1): 9–20.

Cohen, I.G. (2012b) 'Medical outlaws or medical refugees? An examination of circumvention tourism', in J. Hodges, L. Turner and A. Kimbal (eds) *Risks and challenges in medical tourism: Understanding the global market for healthcare,* Westport, CT: Praeger.

Cohen, I.G. (2015) 'Medical tourism for services illegal in patients' home country', in N. Lunt, D. Horsfall and J. Hanefeld (2015) *Handbook on medical tourism and patient mobility,* Cheltenham: Edward Elgar.

Connell, J. (2013) 'Contemporary medical tourism: conceptualisation, culture and commodification', *Tourism Management,* 34: 1–13.

Connell, J. (2015) 'Medical tourism – concepts and definitions', in N. Lunt, D. Horsfall and J. Hanefeld (2015) *Handbook on medical tourism and patient mobility,* Cheltenham: Edward Elgar.

Crooks, V.A. and Snyder, J. (2010) 'Regulating medical tourism', *The Lancet,* 376 (9751): 1465–66.

DoH (Department of Health) (2008) *No patient left behind,* London: HMSO.

DoH (2013) *Quantitative assessment of visitor and migrant use of the NHS in England: exploring the data,* London: Department of Health.

DoH (2014) *Visitor and migrant NHS cost recovery programme implementation plan 2014–16,* London: Department of Health.

DoH (2016) *Guidance on implementing the overseas visitor hospital charging regulations 2015: Ways in which people can be lawfully resident in the UK,* London: Department of Health.

Doughty, S. (2011) 'Sickly immigrants add £1bn to NHS bill', *Daily Mail,* 13 May, www.dailymail.co.uk/health/article-185768/Sickly-immigrants-add-1bn-NHS-bill.html

The Economist (2013) 'Polish clinics: another kind of health tourism', 8 June, www.economist.com/news/britain/21579018-health-clinics-immigrant-poles-reveal-nhss-shortcomings-another-kind-health-tourism

European Commission (2016) *Member state data on cross-border healthcare following Directive 2011/24/EU (Year 2015),* Brussels: Jonathan Olsson Consulting.

European Parliament and the Council of Europe (2011) Directive 2011/24/EU of the European Parliament and of the Council of Europe 9 March 2011 on the application of patients' rights in cross-border healthcare, L 88/45, *Official Journal of the European Union*, 4 April.

Francis, N. (2011) 'Pearly flights: the rise of dental tourism', *The Sun*, 9 October, www.thesun.co.uk/archives/news/827844/pearly-flights/

Gallo, P. and Gené-Badia J. (2013) 'Cuts drive health system reforms in Spain', *Health Policy*, 113: 1–7.

Gilmartin, M. and White, A. (2011) 'Interrogating medical tourism: Ireland, abortion, and mobility rights', *Signs (Chic)*, 36(2): 275–79.

Gordon, I., Scanlon, K., Travers, T. and Whitehead, C. (2009) *Economic impact on the London and UK economy of an earned regularisation of irregular migrants to the UK*, London: Greater London Authority.

Greenwood, G. (2017) 'Retired British expats "outstrip European pensioners using NHS"', BBC, 11 January, www.bbc.co.uk/news/38534958

Gregory, A. (2013) 'NHS patients may be sent to INDIA for cheaper treatment at private healthcare firms', *Daily Mirror*, 23 August, www.mirror.co.uk/news/uk-news/nhs-patients-sent-india-cheaper-2208641

Hanefeld, J. and Smith, R. (2015) 'Financing mechanisms', in N. Lunt, D. Horsfall and J. Hanefeld (eds) *Handbook of medical tourism and patient mobility*, Cheltenham: Edward Elgar, pp 104–11.

Hanefeld, J., Horsfall, D., Lunt, N. and Smith, R. (2013) 'Medical tourism: a cost or benefit to the NHS?', *PLoS ONE*, 8(10): e70406.

Hanefeld, J., Lunt, N., Smith, R.D. and Horsfall, D.G. (2015) 'Why do medical tourists travel to where they do? The role of networks in determining medical travel', *Social Science & Medicine*, 124: 356–63, DOI: 10.1016/j.socscimed.2014.05.016

Hargreaves, S., Holmes, A., Saxena, S., Le Feuvre, P., Farah, W., Shafi, G. et al (2008) 'Charging systems for migrants in primary care: the experiences of family doctors in a high-migrant area of London', *Journal of Travel Medicine*, 15(1): 13–18.

Hawkins, O. and Moses, A. (2016) 'Polish population of the United Kingdom', Briefing paper Number CBP7660, 15 July, London: House of Commons Library.

He, A.J. (2015) 'Transplantation tourism in Asia: snapshot, consequences and the imperative for policy changes', in N. Lunt, D. Horsfall and J. Hanefeld (2015) *Handbook on medical tourism and patient mobility*, Cheltenham: Edward Elgar.

Horsfall, D. and Lunt, N. (2015a) 'Medical tourism by numbers', in N. Lunt, D. Horsfall and J. Hanefeld (eds) *Handbook on medical tourism and patient mobility*, Cheltenham: Edward Elgar.

Horsfall, D. and N. Lunt (2015b) 'Medical tourism and the internet', in N. Lunt, D. Horsfall and J. Hanefeld (eds) *Handbook on medical tourism and patient mobility*, Cheltenham: Edward Elgar.

Horton, S. and S. Cole (2011) 'Medical returns: seeking health care in Mexico', *Social Science & Medicine*, 72(11): 1846–52.

The Independent (2008) 'Dental costs and dash: Brits who put less money where their mouth is', 6 Sept., www.independent.co.uk/money/spend-save/dental-costs-ndash-brits-who-put-less-money-where-their-mouth-is-921493.html

Inhorn, M.C. (2011) 'Diasporic dreaming: return reproductive tourism to the Middle East', *Reproductive BioMedicine Online*, 23(5): 582–91.

Inhorn, M. and Patrizio, P. (2009) 'Rethinking "reproductive tourism" as "reproductive exile"', *Fertility and Sterility*, 92(3): 904–6. Kangas, B. (2010) 'Traveling for medical care in a global world', *Medical Anthropology: Cross-Cultural Studies in Health and Illness*, 29(4): 344–62.

Kovacevic, T. (2016) 'Reality check: how much pressure do EU migrants put on NHS?', BBC, 17 June, www.bbc.co.uk/news/uk-politics-eu-referendum-36058513

Krishnan, N., Cockwell, P., Devulapally, P., Gerber, B., Hanvesakul, R., Higgins, R. et al (2010) 'Organ trafficking for live donor kidney transplantation in Indoasians resident in the west Midlands: high activity and poor outcomes', *Transplantation*, 89(12): 1456–61.

Lakhani, N. (2010) 'Kidney patients add to risk by seeking transplants abroad', *Independent on Sunday*, 21 August.

Lunt, N., Exworthy, M., Green, S., Horsfall, D., Mannion, R. and Smith, R. (2011) *Medical tourism: Treatments, markets and health system implications: A scoping review*, Paris: OECD.

Lunt, N., Smith, R., Mannion, R., Green, S., Exworthy, M., Hanefeld, J. et al (2014a) 'Implications for the NHS of inward and outward medical tourism: a policy and economic analysis using literature review and mixed-methods approaches', *Health Service Delivery Research*, 2(2).

Lunt, N., Jin, K., Horsfall, D. and Hanefeld, J. (2014b) 'Insights on medical tourism: markets as networks and the role of strong ties', *Korean Social Science Journal*, 41(1): 19–37.

Lunt, N., Horsfall, D. and Hanefeld, J. (eds) (2015a) *Handbook on medical tourism and patient mobility*, Cheltenham: Edward Elgar.

Lunt, N., Horsfall, D. and Hanefeld, J. (2015b) 'The shaping of contemporary medical tourism and patient mobility', in N. Lunt, D. Horsfall and J. Hanefeld (eds) *Handbook on medical tourism and patient mobility*, Cheltenham: Edward Elgar.

McDermott, N. and Wooller, S. (2016) 'UP THE BLUFF: NHS hospital reveals £5m bill as hundreds of pregnant health tourists deluge Trust', *The Sun*, 12 October, www.thesun.co.uk/news/1958543/nhs-hospital-reveals-5m-bill-as-hundreds-of-pregnant-health-tourists-deluge-trust/

MacReady, N. (2007) 'Developing countries court medical tourists', *The Lancet,* 369(9576): 1849–50.

Migration Watch UK (2016) *Public services and infrastructure | Key Topics: The impact on the NHS*, www.migrationwatchuk.org/key-topics/public-services-infrastructure

Miller, D. (2012) 'Health tourists who come to Britain for free NHS treatment cost the taxpayer £40m', *Daily Mail*, 7 October, www.dailymail.co.uk/health/article-2214173/Health-tourists-come-Britain-free-NHS-treatment-cost-taxpayer-40m.html

NAO (National Audit Office) (2016) *Recovering the cost of NHS treatment for overseas visitors: A report by the Comptroller and Auditor General*, 28 October, London: National Audit Office.

Noree, T., Hanefeld, J. and Smith, R. (2014), 'UK medical tourists in Thailand: they are not who you think they are', *Globalization and Health*, 10(1): 29.

ONS (Office for National Statistics) (2016) *International Passenger Survey*, Newport: ONS.

Ormond, M. (2008) '"First World treatments at Third World prices": the real cost of medical tourism', in R. Anand and S. Gupta (eds) *Medical tourism: A growth industry*, Hyderabad: Icfai University Press, pp 69–77.

Pallot, P. (2014) 'NHS axes free health care for expats', *The Telegraph*, 11 February, www.telegraph.co.uk/news/health/expat-health/10628246/NHS-axes-free-health-care-for-expats.html

Parliament UK (2016) Question by John Mann MP to the Departent of Health and answered by Rt Hon Alistair Burt MP: To ask the Secretary of State for Health, how much was paid to which countries for overseas health treatment of UK nationals in 2015?, www.parliament.uk/business/publications/written-questions-answers-statements/written-question/Commons/2016-02-19/27364/

Pietras, E. (2014) 'The women who went abroad for cheap cosmetic surgery and ended up scarred for life', *Daily Mirror*, 6 January, www. mirror.co.uk/news/real-life-stories/women-who-went-abroad-cheap-2992507

Rhodes, R. and Schiano, T. (2010) 'Transplant tourism in China: a tale of two transplants', *American Journal of Bioethics*, 10(2): 3–11.

Smith, R. (2008) 'NHS surgeons are having to fix botched plastic surgery after patients seek cheap deals abroad', *The Telegraph*, 3 December, www.telegraph.co.uk/news/health/news/3544764/NHS-spending-millions-fixing-botched-plastic-surgery-done-abroad.html

Song, P. (2010) 'Biotech pilgrims and the transnational quest for stem cell cures', *Medical Anthropology: Cross-Cultural Studies in Health and Illness*, 29(4): 384–402.

Spanish Government (2013) *Turismo de salud en España*, Ministerio de Industria, Energía y Turismo/ Escuela de Organización Industrial, www.minetur.gob.es/turismo/es-ES/PNIT/Eje3/Paginas/estudio-turismo-salud.aspx

Steventon, A. and Bardsley, M. (2011) 'Use of secondary care in England by international immigrants', *Journal of Health Services Research & Policy*, 16(2): 90–94.

Syal, R. and Campbell, D. (2016) 'Hospitals may require patients to show passports for NHS treatment', *The Guardian*, 22 November. www.theguardian.com/society/2016/nov/21/hospitals-may-require-patients-to-show-passports-for-nhs-treatment

The Telegraph (2016) 'Crackdown on free access to NHS services for migrants', 8 May, www.telegraph.co.uk/news/2016/05/08/crackdown-on-free-access-to-nhs-services-for-migrants/

Topham, L. (2013) '"They promised luxury – but my cosmetic surgery 'holiday' was a nightmare": Polish practice reduced June's breasts without asking and left a gaping hole in her stomach', *Mail on Sunday*, 20 July, www.dailymail.co.uk/health/article-2371524/They-promised-luxury--cosmetic-surgery-holiday-nightmare-Polish-practice-reduced-Junes-breasts-asking-left-gaping-hole-stomach.html#ixzz4VCw7fHZL

Triggle, N. (2008) 'NHS pays to rectify cosmetic ops', http://news.bbc.co.uk/1/hi/health/7761223.stm

United Nations (2015) *Trends in international migrant stock: Migrants by destination and origin*, www.un.org/en/development/desa/population/migration/data/estimates2/estimates15.shtml

Van Hoof, W. and Pennings, G. (2011) 'Extraterritoriality for cross-border reproductive care: should states act against citizens travelling abroad for illegal infertility treatment?', *Reproductive BioMedicine Online,* 23(5): 546–54.

Williams, Z. (2013) 'NHS: Poles, paracetamol and the myth of health tourism', *The Guardian*, 17 May, www.theguardian.com/commentisfree/2013/may/17/nhs-myth-health-tourism-zoe-williams

Yakupoglu, Y., Ozden, E., Dilek, M., Demirbas, A., Adibelli, Z., Sarikaya, S. et al (2010) 'Transplantation tourism: high risk for the recipients', *Clinical Transplantation,* 24: 835–38.

TWELVE

Controlling migration: the gender implications of work-related conditions in restricting rights to residence and to social benefits[1]

Isabel Shutes

The increasing mobility of people across the world has been accompanied by increasing attempts to control the borders of nation states, with a major expansion of national and supranational systems in the governance of migration since the post-war period (Cornelius et al, 2004; Betts, 2011). Those systems, notwithstanding their limits, have facilitated migration for some, while severely restricting migration for others (Cornelius et al, 2004). At the same time, attempts to control migration have facilitated access to rights within the territory of nation states for some, including rights to work and to welfare, and to permanent legal residence, while restricting access for others. Those restrictions are often framed in policy debates in terms of need for specific types of migrant labour – to select migrants who are seen as contributing to national economies (Ruhs and Anderson, 2010). But they are also framed in terms of resources – to protect welfare states from being 'burdened' by migrants (Bommes and Geddes, 2000). However, controlling the mobility of people is not simply about the inclusion or exclusion of migrants relative to citizens. Citizenship can exclude 'from within' as well as 'from without' (Lister, 2003) in terms of the assumptions underpinning policies in relation to work and welfare, and the conditions for inclusion.

Immigration and welfare reforms in the UK have been underpinned by a market model of citizenship that assumes both citizens and migrants should be increasingly self-sufficient workers. Welfare reforms have reinforced citizens' reliance on the market through both cuts to income-related benefits and increasingly restrictive work-related conditions for claiming those benefits, with the withdrawal of benefits as a penalty for non-compliance (Dwyer and Wright, 2014). At the same time, immigration reforms have restricted migrant workers' access to rights of residence in the UK, and to income-related benefits on the basis of residence, by requiring a certain level of earnings as a condition of access to those rights. Those policies have implications not only for differentiation in access to social rights between citizens and migrants and within those groups. They also have implications for the gendered exclusion of women as citizens and migrants from access to rights and resources. This chapter examines how work-related conditions have been implemented in the UK in restricting European Union (EU) and non-EU migrants' access to rights of residence and entitlement to social benefits, with the aim of controlling migration, and the gender implications. First, it considers the ways in which welfare reforms have, more generally, restricted access to social benefits through cuts and conditionality, and the gender implications of enforcing reliance on the market. Second, it examines how conditionality has played out in restricting migrants' access to rights of residence in the UK – and relatedly entitlement to social benefits – and the gender implications in relation to non-EU and EU migrants. It is argued that these processes of controlling migration reinforce a particular relationship to the labour market as the basis for inclusion – for access to rights of citizenship/ residence. That relationship is one which, by privileging the high-income and continuously employed migrant worker, reinforces women's risk of exclusion from access to rights and resources as migrants.

Work-related conditionality, gender and access to social benefits

With the restructuring of welfare states and the pursuit of labour market activation policies, citizens' access to social benefits has become increasingly conditional upon participation in activities which support entering or re-entering paid work (Dwyer, 2004; Aurich, 2011). While access to social benefits has for long entailed some form of conditionality, the economic crisis of 2008, it is argued, critically undermined the principle that the market could be relied upon to provide adequate incomes for all (Marchal et al, 2014). Income from employment – the main source of household income – fell in real terms in some Organisation for Economic Co-operation and Development (OECD) countries (including Ireland, Italy, Spain, Sweden, the UK, the USA) in the period 2007–9, while income from self-employment fell across most OECD countries (Jenkins et al, 2013). While there were nominal and real increases in levels of minimum income benefits in some European countries in the period 2008–10, notably the conditions attached to claiming those benefits were not relaxed, and in some countries they were intensified (Marchal et al, 2014).

Welfare reforms in the UK have, conversely, sought to increase reliance on the market both through cuts to working-age social benefits (in-work and out-of-work income-related benefits) and conditions attached to claiming those benefits. Cuts to social benefits expenditure and a cap on total household benefits payments, implemented since the 2008 crisis, have restricted the level and coverage of benefits (Hood and Phillips, 2015). With the introduction of the Universal Credit system,[2] work-related conditions attached to claiming benefits are also to be extended further, applying not only to benefits claimants who are out of work but to those in work. In-work claimants will be subject to a 'conditionality threshold' regarding their weekly earnings (Dwyer and Wright, 2014). Those whose earnings fall below the threshold (equivalent to 35 hours at the national minimum wage) will be required to undergo activities to increase their earnings by increasing their hours of work and/or increasing their wages (Department for Work and Pensions, 2011: Universal Credit Policy Briefing No. 12). These reforms have thus not only made paid work a responsibility of the individual citizen but also acquiring an adequate income through work.

Restrictions on access to social benefits, both in terms of cuts and conditionality, are gendered processes with gendered effects. Feminist scholarship has long emphasised the ways in which social rights and access to those rights are shaped by the gender division of paid and unpaid work (Lewis, 1992; Lister, 2003). While policies may assume both women and men's participation in the market as workers, and capacity for self-sufficiency through earnings, gender inequalities in relation to paid and unpaid work shape unequal access to rights and resources that depend on labour market participation. With respect to the gendered impact of austerity, including cuts to social benefits, social benefits make up a higher proportion of women's income as women are more likely to be on a low income in and out of work (Bennett, 2015). Indeed, cuts to expenditure on working-age social benefits have disproportionately reduced the income of groups, such as lone parents (Hills et al, 2016), who are predominantly women, while women within those groups have been worse affected (Bennett, 2015). Gender inequalities in relation to earnings from employment – including gender pay gaps and differences in hours of work – also point to the differentiated relationship of women and men to the market, and thus to the ways in which work-related conditions do not impact 'equally' on women and men.

Work-related conditions and the gendered non-EU migrant worker

Conditions requiring work/self-sufficiency have also been implemented as a means of controlling migration – restricting non-EU migrants' access not only to the welfare state but also to the labour market and to permanent residence in the UK. While being presented as gender-neutral, conditionality in the context of immigration reforms likewise has gender implications in making not simply work but a higher level of income or wealth a condition for the rights attached to permanent residence.

Access to the welfare state for non-EU migrants has for long been highly restrictive: non-EU migrants who are subject to immigration control have 'no recourse to public funds' – no entitlement to social benefits – as a condition of their entry and temporary residence in the UK (unless granted humanitarian protection). However, non-EU migrants are also highly restricted as regards the extent to which they can access the market as a source of income. Non-EU migrants are permitted entry to an EU member state not on the basis of their status as workers per se, but as high-skilled and high-paid workers. Since the late 1990s, immigration policies across OECD countries have increasingly differentiated *between* categories of migrant workers according to their assumed economic value, facilitating the admission of those whose labour is assessed as being of high value, while restricting the entry of low-skilled workers (Ruhs and Anderson, 2010; Ruhs, 2013; OECD, 2015; Beine et al, 2016). The construction of particular types of workers as higher or lower skilled and as of more or less value to national economies has entailed the exclusion of gendered types of paid work, and thus of migrant women from access to rights as workers (Kofman, 2014). The movement of non-EU care workers into the UK – the majority of whom are women – was previously facilitated on the basis of a need for those workers (Shutes, 2012). However, they are now among the type of workers who have been excluded from entry to the UK, following the introduction of the points-based immigration system in 2008, as this work is not paid enough to meet the criteria for inclusion. This has not only resulted in a reduction of entry routes for non-EU migrant workers into low-paid sectors such as care. It has also had gendered effects by shifting entry on the basis of work to the most highly paid. Under Tier 2 of the points-based system (skilled workers), 75% of visas issued were to men (2009–10) (Home Office, 2012a).

For non-EU migrants granted entry to the UK as workers, access to permanent legal residence, which brings with it the same entitlement to social benefits as UK citizens, has also become increasingly restricted according to income and wealth. While eligibility to apply for permanent residence was, in the past, restricted primarily on the basis of length of residence in the UK, there has been a shift towards restricting access on the basis of income and wealth with the aim of 'breaking the link between work and settlement, so that only those who contribute the most economically will be able to stay long-term' (Cameron, 2013). Under the points-based system, only migrants who are categorised as 'high value' (Tier 1) and 'skilled' (Tier 2), the majority of whom are men (see below), are entitled to apply for permanent residence after five years in the UK. Domestic workers, whose work is excluded from the points-based system through a separate visa system, were in the past entitled to apply for permanent residence on the basis of length of residence in the UK. However, domestic workers, the majority of whom are women, are among those who have been excluded from entitlement to apply for permanent residence, with tighter restrictions on their length of stay (Home Office, 2012b).

Access to permanent residence for those categorised as skilled workers has also been further restricted on the basis of income. A minimum salary threshold was introduced in 2016, requiring skilled (Tier 2) migrants to have a minimum salary of £35,000 to be eligible to apply for permanent residence (Home Office, 2013). This is a higher level of pay than the salary required for temporary admission to the UK as a skilled worker (£20,300), and a higher level of pay than the median gross annual earnings of full-time workers in the UK (£28,200 in 2016). It is also an earnings threshold to which women and men do not share an equal relationship, irrespective of their skills, given gender inequalities in earnings (Office for National Statistics, 2016). Data on Tier 2 migrants indicate that men are over-represented among this category, but also within this category women are less likely to meet the earnings threshold to be eligible for permanent residence as a higher proportion are estimated to be working in jobs paid under the £35,000 threshold (Home Office, 2012a). Making access to permanent residence conditional on a higher level of earnings thus has gender implications for the exclusion of women from access to those rights as migrant workers.

By contrast, access to the rights of permanent residence has been facilitated on the basis of wealth. Non-EU migrants categorised as 'high-value' investors (Tier 1) are granted privileged access to permanent residence on the basis of financial investment in the UK. An investment of £2 million confers the high-value investor eligibility to apply for permanent residence after five years, which is reduced to two years for investments of £10 million, with no requirement to demonstrate English language ability for residence (Home Office, 2016). While the buying and selling of citizenship or residency rights (Shachar and Baubock, 2014) has clear implications for extending inequalities of income and wealth more generally, in effect promoting wealth-related tourism, those inequalities are highly gendered. While the proportion of women in the top income groups has risen in some countries over time, the wealthy are still disproportionately men. In the UK, men make up 82% of the top 1% income group (Atkinson et al, 2016: 10) – and the available data suggest the majority of Tier 1 visa applicants (which includes investors) are men (Murray, 2011). The privileged access of the non-EU investor to residence rights thus accords privileged access to rights for wealthy men.

Income-related conditions, as well as regulating the inclusion of non-EU migrant workers as permanent residents – have been applied more stringently as a means of restricting the migration of the non-EU family members of permanent residents, aimed at ensuring 'that they do not become a burden on the state' (Migration Advisory Committee, 2011: 6). UK citizens and permanent residents (including those who have migrated to and settled in the UK) are now required to have a minimum income of £18,600 to apply for their non-EU spouse/partner to join them in the UK, and a higher amount for children (an additional £3,800 for one child and £2,400 for each additional child).[3] Analysis of the impact of those restrictions indicates that 41% of British nationals in full or part time work in 2015 would not have met the minimum income on the basis of their earnings. But given gender inequalities in earnings, British women are less likely to meet the required income threshold: 55% would not meet the criteria for bringing a non-EU partner to the UK, rising to 69% for bringing an additional two children (Sumption and Vargas-Silva, 2016). The income requirements thus, conversely, potentially restrict low-income women from increasing their household income by forming dual-earning households, thereby restricting their capacity for self-provisioning, by excluding them from bringing a non-EU partner to the UK.

Work-related conditions and the gendered EU migrant worker

EU migrants, in principle, are not subject to restrictions on moving to and residing in the UK and other EU countries on the basis of EU citizenship. However, while the intra-EU mobility of workers has been framed as integral to the development of the EU as a market, as well as to the economy of the UK, it has also given rise to debate on the extent to which it may be a 'burden' on national welfare states (Ruhs, 2015). Data on EU nationals coming to the UK indicate that the majority come for work-related purposes, with high levels of employment among those groups (Eurostat, 2016). While there is limited data on access to social benefits, analysis suggests that EU nationals of working age are less likely to claim out-of-work benefits than UK nationals, while they may be more likely to be claiming benefits related to low income while in work (EU migrants from the post-enlargement member states are among the lowest income groups in the UK) (Rienzo, 2016; Sumption and Altorjai, 2016). Indeed, despite the underlying assumptions of political debate that EU mobility has fostered 'benefits tourism', wider evidence suggests that EU migrants are no more likely to be 'welfare dependent', in terms of the extent to which individual income is derived from benefits, irrespective of the 'generosity' of the welfare system in terms of the level and coverage of benefits (Corrigan, 2010).

Notwithstanding EU migrants' relative inclusion within the market, political debate on 'welfare tourism' has given rise to attempts to re-border access to welfare states. The UK, along with Germany, the Netherlands, Austria and Denmark, sought to restrict EU migrants' access to social benefits following the lifting of transitional restrictions on the movement of workers from the post-enlargement member states in 2011 and 2014 (Ruhs, 2015). Negotiations on the terms of the UK's continued membership of the EU, prior to the referendum in 2016, also centred on restricting the access of workers to income-related benefits, with a view to making it conditional on four years of working in the UK. Prior to those negotiations, a more restrictive approach has also been evident in determining EU migrants' access to social benefits on the basis of their status as workers with a right to reside in the UK.

While all EU citizens have the right to move from one member state to another, irrespective of economic status (Article 21(1), TFEU; Article 45, Charter of Fundamental Rights of the EU), conditions apply with respect to which categories of EU citizens have a right to reside in another member state beyond three months of entry (Directive 2004/38/EC). Extended rights of residence are conferred on those who are defined as workers, self-employed, jobseekers, or self-sufficient (including students), and their family members – self-sufficient being defined as those who 'have sufficient resources for themselves not to become a burden on the social assistance system of the host Member State' (Article 7, 1(b), Directive 2004/38/EC). While all EU migrants are entitled to social benefits in the member state in which they reside, only workers/those self-employed and their family members have full entitlement to social assistance on the same basis as nationals of that country, according to the residence requirements (Dougan, 2016). If an EU migrant worker becomes 'involuntarily unemployed', the status of worker can be retained if they register as a jobseeker (Article 7, 3(b), Directive 2004/38/EC). They must, therefore, maintain their attachment to the labour market to maintain their status as a worker. After five years of residence, EU migrants have a right to permanent residence. However, that right is on the basis of continuity of legal residence as a worker/self-sufficient individual, or their family member, for this duration. While leaving the labour market due to childbirth does not affect the conditions of continuity of residence, exiting the market in order to care is time-limited to 12 months without affecting those conditions (Article 16, 3, Directive 2004/38/EC).

While EU migrant workers are, in principle, entitled to social benefits, a more restrictive approach has been adopted in the UK in determining who counts as a worker. The definition of a 'worker', which rests on EU case law, is a broad definition – albeit one which is highly gendered, not least, in excluding unpaid work (Case 66/85 *Lawrie-Blum v Land Baden-Württemberg* [1986] ECR 2121) – including activities which are remunerated and are considered 'genuine and effective' work (Case 53/81 *Levin v Staatssecretaris van Justitie* [1982] ECR 1035). In order to be eligible for income-related benefits, EU nationals have to demonstrate that they have a 'right to reside' in the UK under EU law as a worker/self- employed person or jobseeker (or their family member) (SI 2006/1003; SI 2006/1026). While EU migrants, unlike non-EU migrants, are in principle entitled to social benefits as workers, earnings-related conditions have also been applied in determining their access to the status of worker. A minimum earnings threshold was introduced in assessing if an EU national is a worker/self-employed (HM Revenue and Customs, 2014; Department for Work and Pensions, 2015a), which requires the worker to provide evidence of earnings for the past three months at the level at which national insurance contributions are paid (£153 a week in 2014–15, equivalent to working 24 hours a week at the national minimum wage). Those who do not meet this earnings threshold are subject to an assessment as to whether their work can be considered 'genuine and effective' (HM Revenue and Customs, 2014; Department for Work and Pensions, 2015a). While potentially restricting the access of all workers in low-paid and insecure types of work to the status of worker, given gender differences in hours of work and earnings, women are at greater risk of falling short of the earnings threshold and thus being excluded from the status of worker.

More restrictive conditions have also been imposed on EU migrants' access to social benefits as jobseekers, with gender implications as regards continuity of attachment to the labour market. EU migrants claiming income-related benefits as jobseekers must demonstrate a 'genuine prospect of work' after three months, losing their benefits entitlement unless they can provide 'compelling evidence' that they are continuing to seek employment and have 'a genuine chance of being engaged' (Department for Work and Pensions, 2015b; SI 2013/3032, Regulation 6). Guidance on what constitutes compelling evidence of finding work imposes stricter conditions than those that apply to UK citizens claiming benefits as jobseekers, requiring either an offer of a job that is 'genuine and effective work' and due to start in three months (in which case benefits entitlement can be extended until the job commences), or a change of circumstances, such as relocation, that has resulted in job interviews (in which case entitlement may be extended for up to two months) (Department for Work and Pensions, 2015b). Women who leave the labour market not due to 'involuntary unemployment' but in order to care (and are unable to depend on the status of family member of an EU citizen in work) are thus at risk of losing their entitlement to social benefits by not demonstrating a 'genuine prospect of work' within this timeframe. Moreover, if they fail to maintain an attachment to the labour market by returning to work within a year of childbirth, they may also be denied the status of 'worker' and access to permanent residence on this basis.

The case of *St Prix vs Secretary of State for Work and Pensions* (UK Supreme Court [2012] UKSC 49; Court of Justice of the European Union [2014] C-507/12) illustrates the gender implications of these conditions in restricting EU migrants' access to social benefits. Jessy St Prix, an EU national, made a claim for Income Support following the birth of her child, having stopped work in the latter stages of her pregnancy.[4] Her claim was refused on the basis that she did not have a 'right to reside' in the UK as she was not a 'worker': she was considered to have voluntarily stopped working, and had not registered as a jobseeker, therefore not retaining the status of worker (UK Supreme

Court [2012] UKSC 49). Her gendered relationship to the labour market thus formed the basis for her exclusion from the status of 'worker' and access to social benefits. The refusal of her claim was challenged and the Court of Justice of the EU (CJEU) ruled in favour of St Prix in 2014 regarding the interpretation of the status of worker, ruling that 'a woman who gives up work, or seeking work [...] retains the status of "worker" [...] provided she returns to work or finds another job within a reasonable period after the birth of her child' (CJEU [2014], paragraph 47, C-507/12). While the ruling recognised the rights of EU nationals to retain their status as 'worker' during gendered periods of time not in work, this was on the basis of continuity of attachment to the labour market. Returning to work or taking up another job within a 'reasonable period' was defined in relation to national legislation on the duration of maternity leave (CJEU [2014], paragraph 42, C-507/12), with a maximum of 12 months permitted without affecting the conditions for permanent residence (CJEU [2014], paragraph 45, C-507/12). The EU migrant whose 'right to reside' depends on being a worker is thus obligated to return to the labour market within this period, while the gendered work of care has profound implications for meeting this condition. As a jobseeker, if she fails to demonstrate a 'genuine prospect of work' after three months, she loses her entitlement to social benefits. Moreover, she risks losing an entitlement to permanent residence in the long term by not re-entering work within this period.

Conclusion

Work-related conditions across immigration and welfare reforms in the UK have restricted access to social benefits across citizens and migrants. Those conditions have not simply reinforced paid work as the basis for inclusion – a condition which has for long underpinned the gendered exclusions of citizenship. They have also enforced a particular relationship to the labour market. While work-related conditions vary across policies towards UK citizens and permanent residents, and non-EU and EU citizens without permanent residence, those conditions are gendered, with gendered effects in terms of access to rights and resources across those groups. Earnings-related conditions restrict which types of non-EU and EU migrant workers have access to rights of residence as workers, thereby restricting access to social benefits. The non-EU migrant worker must be a high-income skilled worker to be able to access those rights, conditions which privilege the male skilled worker in terms of inequalities in earnings. The EU migrant worker must have a minimum level of weekly earnings to be recognised as a worker, while they must maintain a continuous attachment to the labour market to retain rights of residence as a worker, conditions which privilege the male worker who is less likely to experience detachment from the labour market on the basis of care. At the same time, entitlements to social benefits for those eligible – irrespective of citizenship status – are subject to increasingly restrictive cuts and conditions that make not simply work but also a minimum income an individual responsibility through earnings.

Debates on so-called 'benefits tourism' are thus not simply misplaced, since access to income-related benefits is highly restricted in relation to work. Justifying restrictions on migrants' access to rights and resources as a means of preventing 'benefits tourism' have gendered effects as regards who is excluded. Gender inequalities in the labour market relating to pay, hours of work, earnings and continuity of work shape the extent to which the gendered EU migrant can claim the status of worker; the extent to which the gendered non-EU migrant can claim the status of high-income worker; and the extent to which they can access rights accorded to workers and their family members, and resources through the market. This highlights the limitations – and gender implications – of attempts to promote the rights of migrants on the basis of work. Justifications for extending rights to the 'hardworking migrant', on the basis of their contribution to the 'national economy' as workers, adopt the same logic as justifications for curbing the entitlements of the 'benefit scrounger' on the basis of being a 'burden on the state'. Framing rights according to the principles of the market reinforces the gender inequalities of paid and unpaid work that extend across citizens and migrants, and women's risk of exclusion from access to rights and resources. Moreover, according value and rights to people on the basis of their income or wealth, irrespective of how 'hardworking' they may be inside and outside the labour market, reinforces wider inequalities that transcend attempts to control migration through the bordering of welfare states.

Notes
[1] Parts of this chapter are adapted from Shutes, I. (2016) 'Work-related conditionality and the access to social benefits of national citizens, EU and non-EU citizens', *Journal of Social Policy*, 45(4): 691–707.
[2] The Universal Credit system replaces various working-age benefits and tax credits with a single benefit and assessment process (Department for Work and Pensions, 2010).

[3] The amount was determined on the basis of the income threshold for a dual-partner household for eligibility for income-related benefits (Sumption and Vargas-Silva, 2016).

[4] Income Support is means-tested and does not require lone parents of children under five to be actively seeking work (www.gov.uk/income-support/eligibility).

References

Atkinson, A.B., Casarico, A. and Voitchovsky, S. (2016) *Top incomes and the gender divide*, London: International Inequalities Institute, London School of Economics.

Aurich, P. (2011) 'Activating the unemployed – directions and divisions in Europe', *European Journal of Social Security*, 13(3): 294–317.

Beine, M., Boucher, A., Burgoon, B. et al (2016) 'Comparing immigration policies: an overview from the IMPALA database', *International Migration Review*, 50(4): 827–63.

Bennett, F. (2015) 'The impact of austerity on women', in L. Foster, A. Brunton, C. Deeming and T. Haux (eds) *In Defence of Welfare 2*, London: Social Policy Association.

Betts, A. (2011) *Global migration governance*, Oxford: Oxford University Press.

Bommes, M. and Geddes, A. (2000) *Immigration and welfare: Challenging the borders of the welfare state*, London: Routledge.

Cameron, D. (2013) 'Speech on immigration and welfare reform', 25 March, Cabinet Office, Prime Minister's Office, www.gov.uk/government/speeches/david-camerons-immigration-speech

Charter of Fundamental Rights of the EU, 2000/C 364/01, www.europarl.europa.eu/charter/pdf/text_en.pdf

Cornelius, W.A., Martin, P.L. and Hollifield, J.F. (2004) *Controlling immigration: A global perspective*, Stanford, CA: Stanford University Press.

Corrigan, O. (2010) 'Migrants, welfare systems and social citizenship in Ireland and Britain: users or abusers?', *Journal of Social Policy*, 39(3): 415–37.

Department for Work and Pensions (2010) *Universal credit: Welfare that works*, London: Department for Work and Pensions.

Department for Work and Pensions (2011) *Universal Credit Policy Briefing No. 12 Conditionality under Universal Credit: the Work Search and Work Availability Requirements*, London: Department for Work and Pensions.

Department for Work and Pensions (2015a) *Decision makers guide*, vol. 2, Amendment 30, February, London: Department for Work and Pensions.

Department for Work and Pensions (2015b) Memo DMG 2/15 Extending GPOW Assessments to Stock EEA Nationals.

Dougan, M. (2016) 'National welfare systems, residency requirements and EU law: some brief comments', *European Journal of Social Security*, 18(2): 101–5.

Dwyer, P. (2004) 'Creeping conditionality in the UK: from welfare rights to conditional entitlements?', *Canadian Journal of Sociology*, 29(2): 265–87.

Dwyer, P. and Wright, S. (2014) 'Universal Credit, ubiquitous conditionality and its implications for social citizenship', *Journal of Poverty and Social Justice*, 22(1): 27–35.

European Parliament and Council of the EU (2004) Directive 2004/38/ EC on the right of citizens of the Union and their family members to move and reside freely within the territory of the Member States, *Official Journal of the EU*, 158: 77–123.

Eurostat (2016) *Migration and migrant population statistics*, http://ec.europa. eu/eurostat/statistics-explained/index.php/Migration_and_migrant_ population_statistics

Hills, J., De Agostini, P. and Sutherland, H. (2016) 'Benefits, pensions, tax credits and direct taxes', in R. Lupton, T. Burchardt, J. Hills, K. Stewart and P. Vizard (eds) *Social policy in a cold climate*, Bristol: Policy Press.

HM Revenue and Customs (2014) *Child benefit and child tax credit right to reside test: Workers and self-employed people*, London: HM Revenue and Customs.

Home Office (2012a) *Policy equality statement. Immigration rules: Changes to settlement rules for skilled workers; changes to Tier 5 and overseas domestic workers rules; and new visitor route for permitted paid engagements*, London: Home Office.

Home Office (2012b) *Statement of intent: Changes to Tier 1, Tier 2 and Tier 5 of the point based system; overseas domestic workers; and visitors*, London: Home Office.

Home Office (2013) *Statement of Changes to the Immigration Rules: HC1039*, 14 March, London: Stationery Office.

Home Office (2016) *Immigration Rules*, Appendix A, www.gov.uk/ guidance/immigration-rules/immigration-rules-appendix-a-attributes

Hood, A. and Phillips, D. (2015) *Benefit spending and reforms: The coalition government's record*, London: Institute for Fiscal Studies.

Jenkins, S., Brandolini, A., Micklewright, J. et al (2013) 'The Great Recession and its consequences for household incomes in 21 countries', in S. Jenkins, A. Brandolini, J. Micklewright and B. Nolan (eds) *The Great Recession and the distribution of household income*, Oxford: Oxford University Press.

Kofman, E. (2014) 'Towards a gendered evaluation of (highly) skilled immigration policies in Europe', *International Migration*, 52(3): 116–28.

Lewis, J. (1992) 'Gender and the development of welfare regimes', *Journal of European Social Policy*, 2(3): 158–73.

Lister, R. (2003) *Citizenship: Feminist perspectives*, Basingstoke: Palgrave Macmillan.

Marchal, S., Marx, I. and Van Mechelen, N. (2014) 'The great wake-up call? Social citizenship and minimum income provisions in Europe in times of crisis', *Journal of Social Policy*, 43(2): 247–67.

Migration Advisory Committee (2011) *Review of the minimum income requirement for sponsorship under the family migration route*, London: Home Office.

Murray, A. (2011) *Britain's points based migration system*, London: Centre Forum.

OECD (2015) *International migration outlook*, Paris: OECD.

Office for National Statistics (2016) *Annual survey of hours and earnings: 2016 provisional results*, London: ONS.

Rienzo, C. (2016) *Characteristics and outcomes of migrants in the UK labour market*, Oxford: Migration Observatory, University of Oxford.

Ruhs, M. (2013) *The price of rights: Regulating international labor migration*, Princeton, NJ: Princeton University Press.

Ruhs, M. (2015) *Is unrestricted immigration compatible with inclusive welfare states? The (un)sustainability of EU exceptionalism*, Oxford: Centre on Migration, Policy and Society, University of Oxford.

Ruhs, M. and Anderson, B. (2010) *Who needs migrant workers? Labour shortages, immigration and public policy*, Oxford: Oxford University Press.

Shachar, A. and Baubock, R. (2014) (eds) *Should Citizenship be for Sale?*, European University Institute Working Paper RSCAS 2014/01, Florence: European University Institute.

Shutes, I. (2012) 'The employment of migrant workers in long-term care: dynamics of choice and control', *Journal of Social Policy*, 41(1): 43–59.

Statutory Instrument 2006/1003 The Immigration (European Economic Area) Regulations 2006.

Statutory Instrument 2006/1026 The Social Security (Persons from Abroad) Amendment Regulations 2006.

Statutory Instrument 2013/3032 The Immigration (European Economic Area) (Amendment) (No. 2) Regulations 2013.

Sumption, M. and Altorjai, S. (2016) *EU migration, welfare benefits and EU membership*, Migration Observatory report, Oxford: Centre on Migration, Policy and Society, University of Oxford.

Sumption, M. and Vargas-Silva, C. (2016) *The minimum income requirement for non-EEA family members in the UK*, Oxford: Migration Observatory, University of Oxford.

TEFU (Treaty on the Functioning of the European Union), Consolidated version of the Treaty on the Functioning of the European Union, *Official Journal of the European Union*, C 326, 26.10.2012: 47–390.

Index